I0875863

Bibliotheca nubica et aethiopica 5
(vormals Bibliotheca nubica)

Bibliotheca nubica et aethiopica

Schriftenreihe zur Kulturgeschichte
des Raumes um das Rote Meer

in Verbindung mit dem Forschungszentrum
für Mittelmeerraumarchäologie
der Polnischen Akademie der Wissenschaften

Herausgegeben
von
Piotr O. Scholz

5

Stuart C. Munro-Hay

Ethiopia and Alexandria

The Metropolitan Episcopacy of Ethiopia

Mit einem Vorwort
von
Manfred Kropp

Warszawa - Wiesbaden
1997

Stuart C. Munro-Hay

Ethiopia and Alexandria

The Metropolitan Episcopacy of Ethiopia

Mit einem Vorwort
von
Manfred Kropp

ZAŚ
PAN

Warszawa 1997

Die Einband-Vignette geht auf die meroitische Terracotta mit der Darstellung des Apedemak aus Meroë zurück (National Museums & Galleries on Merseyside, Liverpool – mit freundlicher Genehmigung der Museen-Verwaltung).

Vorlage für das Bild des Einbandes stellt ein Fragment aus den Wandmalereien in der Kathedrale zu Aksum (Photo P. Scholz)

Schriftführender Herausgeber:
Piotr O. Scholz, Viktoriastr. 12, D-65189 Wiesbaden

Technische Redaktion des Bandes:
Stefan Jakobielski & Maria Zaar

Bibliotheca nubica et aethiopica: Schriftenreihe zur Kulturgeschichte des Raumes um das Rote Meer, Erscheinungsbeginn 1(1987) 1988 als Bibliotheca nubica bei Jürgen Dinter Verlag, Köln (ISBN 3-924794-08-1)

ISBN 83-901809-3-6

Schriftsatz hergestellt bei K. Pluskota & M. Trojan, Warszawa

Druck: Zakład Graficzny Uniwersytetu Warszawskiego. Zam505/97

Vorwort

Ein "obskures Faktum" taucht zuweilen in der neueren Forschung über die äthiopische Kirchengeschichte auf. Gemeint ist die jahrhundertelange Abhängigkeit der äthiopischen Kirche – mit ihrem heutigen Namen *yä-tawahedo ortodoksawi beta krestiyan* "die Vereinigung (der Naturen in Christus) bekennende orthodoxe Kirche" – vom koptischen Patriarchat von Alexandrien. Diese Abhängigkeit fand, gemäß einem Abkommen zwischen Kaiser HAILE SELLASSIE I., seiner äthiopischen Kirche und dem Patriarchen von Alexandrien ihr Ende mit der Amtseinsetzung des ersten äthiopischen Patriarchen Baselyos 1951. Er vereinigte zugleich zum ersten Male das Amt des äthiopischen Kirchenoberhaupts (Abun, bzw. bis dato nur Metropolit, nun aber Patriarch) mit dem des Echage, des Oberhaupts der äthiopischen Mönche und obersten Kirchenadministrators, der in der Vergangenheit als einheimischer Kenner des Landes und seiner Kirche allzuoft Rivale und Gegenspieler des landfremden ägyptischen Metropoliten war. Die Abhängigkeit bestand vielleicht schon seit den Anfängen des Christentums in Äthiopien an, doch das fällt diese Frage schon in den Bereich des noch "Obskuren", zu dessen Aufhellung noch manche Studien wie die hier vorliegenden folgen müssen. Und um den Reflexionen über den allgemeinen Gang der Geschichte gleich eine weitere anzufügen: die die Entwicklung der äthiopischen Kirche oft hemmende Rivalität der beiden genannten Ämter hatte ihr Ende gefunden, die Kirche ihre Autokephalie, wenn auch nicht die Distanz zum Staat, was bis heute nach Einschätzung vieler, auch erklärter Freunde ein Problem bleibt. Mit der Gründung eines zweiten Staates, Eriträa, im historisch-kulturellen Raum "Äthiopien" hat die Konsequenz im kirchlichen Bereich denn auch nicht auf sich warten lassen. Es existiert nun eine eriträische Kirche, die sich bereits eine vorläufige Grundordnung gegeben hat und in einer eigenen Synode über ihre institutionelle Form, ihren Weg in die Zukunft und einen eigenen Patriarchen berät. Doch dies ist die Gegenwart, der Historiker nicht einmal beratend zu begleiten und zu kommentieren das Recht hat. Er kann nur bescheiden, wie Stuart MUNRO-HAY mit seiner hier vorgelegten Geschichte der ersten, rund tausend Jahre Beziehungen zwischen dem Patriarchensitz in Alexandrien und seinem fernen Sprengel in Äthiopien, über den objektiven Erkenntnisgewinn für die wissenschaftliche Öffentlichkeit der Historiker als Sachwalter des kollektiven Gedächtnisses hinaus hoffen, daß die Akteure dieser Gegenwart zuweilen nachdenklich in die Akten der Vergangenheit blicken. Eine noch größere Hoffnung wäre es allerdings, wenn eine Geschichte der Beziehungen zwischen der eriträischen und der äthiopischen Kirche, sollte sie denn einmal geschreiben werden müssen, aufgrund solch nachdenklicher Kenntnisnahme der Vorgänge eine der helleren und freundlichen Seiten in der Geschichte sein könnte.

An einem dünnen Faden hingen in vielen Perioden der äthiopischen Geschichte die Außenbeziehungen des Landes, konkret gesprochen an den Verbindungen zwischen der äthiopischen Kirche und dem koptischen Patriarchen von Alexandrien. Und diese beruhten auf letztlich auf der Fälschung einer Bestimmung in den Kanones von Nicäa betreffend die äthiopische Kirche. Als Souveränitätsdefekt war hier festgeschrieben, daß das Oberhaupt der äthiopischen Kirche nicht von dieser zu wählen sei, ja kein Äthiopier sein durfte, sondern ein vom Patriarchen in Alexandrien auszuwählender (ägyptischer) Mönch sein sollte. Diese Verpflichtung führte notwendigerweise immer nach dem Tode eines äthiopischen Abun (Metropoliten) zu der Reise einer äthiopischen Delegation nach Ägypten, um dort einen neuen Metropoliten zu erbitten, diesen dann auf der Heimreise in seine neue Wirkungsstätte zu geleiten. Allein die konkrete Geschichte dieser Reisen wäre ein gesonderter Untersuchungsgegenstand, besonders für die Zeit, die das vorliegende Werk nicht mehr behandelt – das Mittelalter bis in die Neuzeit – für die aber wesentlich mehr Dokumente vorhanden sind. Manche der erhaltenen Reisebeschreibungen, etwa in den Königschroniken, lesen sich wie Abenteuergeschichten und Kriminalromane. Dies beruht auf den oft abenteuerlichen Umständen und Gefahren einer solchen Reise durch die verschiedensten Länder und auf verschiedensten Wegen unter wechselnden politischen Zeitumständen. Der übliche Weg durch Nubien, den heutigen Sudan, konnte versperrt sein, ein Umweg über das Rote Meer, u. U. sogar über den Jemen mußte gewählt werden. Auf jeder der genannten Etappen war die Delegation der Willkür indifferenter oder feindlich gesinnter muslimischer Obrigkeiten ausgesetzt, mußte sich nur allzuoft den Weg freikaufen. In Ägypten selbst, seit der arabischen Eroberung ein Land, in dem die Christen nur als Bürger minderen Rechts (*dhimmis*) geduldet waren, im Laufe der Jahrhunderte in die Minderheit gerieten, waren Verhandlungen mit dem jeweiligen Machthaber notwendig, um einen neuen Metropoliten wählen und auf die Reise nach Äthiopien schicken zu können. Bei diesem Anlaß wurden diplomatische und politische Differenzen zwischen dem islamischen Ägypten und dem christlichen Reich in Äthiopien ausgetragen, wobei der Hintergrund die Lage und Behandlung der jeweiligen religiösen Minderheit der beiden Partner war: die der Christen in Ägypten, als deren Anwalt sich der äthiopische König empfand, die der Muslime in Äthiopien, deren Wohlergehen, aber auch politisch-militärischer Erfolg, falls die Lage so war, dem Herrscher in Ägypten am Herzen lag.

Ähnlich wie die Pilgerfahrt nach Jerusalem, freilich in der Natur der Sache nicht mit der gleichen Häufigkeit und Intensität, waren die Delegationsreisen Brücken der Information in wechselseitigen Sinn. So erfuhr die Außenwelt von den wichtigsten Vorgängen im äthiopischen Reich; daß diese Informationen in die jeweiligen regionalen historischen Traditionen eingehen, verhilft dem modernen Historiker zu seinen für manche Perioden, etwa die dunklen Jahrhunderte der äthiopischen Geschichte vom 7. bis zum 12. Jhdt., oft einzigen Quellen.

Auf der anderen Seite bedeutet jeder neue Abun für Äthiopien die Chance einer Auffrischung der Verbindung zu den Schwesterkirchen im Orient, der Teilnahme an der Entwicklung der gesamten Christenheit, war somit ein Gegenimpuls gegen die sonst dieser Kultur eigene Selbstgenügsamkeit und Außenvergessenheit. Freilich hing diese Wirkung ganz von der Persönlichkeit des neuen Abun ab, war er doch, einmal im Lande, ganz auf sich und seine Ressourcen, geistiger und materieller Art, gestellt. Die Geschichte der Metropoliten kennt die unterschiedlichsten Charaktere. Man darf nicht vergessen, daß schon die Auswahl des Kandidaten von unterschiedlichsten überlegungen bestimmt sein konnte; bestimmt aber war nicht immer der Gedanke ausschlaggebend, der fernen Kirche das beste und fähigste Oberhaupt zu geben. Für den Ausgewählten bedeutete es darüberhinaus im Grunde eine Verbannung, die er wohl nicht immer aus innerer überzeugung annahm. So kennen wir in ihrer kirchlichen Aufgabe apathische – die Priesterweihe war wohl die einzige als sakramentell-liturgische Handlung wahrgenommene, dafür in ihrem Lebenswandel umso fragwürdigere Metropoliten. Neben ihnen stehen aktive und überzeugte Kirchenreformer, die sich um die Revision der Bibeltexte bemühen, theologische Literatur neu aus dem Arabischen übersetzen lassen, wohl auch selbst an dieser Arbeit kenntnisreich teilnahmen.

Freilich, und auch das ist signifikant für die Geschichte, erreicht keiner von ihnen den Rang und die Bedeutung des Enbaqom im 16. Jhdt. Auch dieser landfremd, ein jemenitischer Qadi, der zum Christentum übertritt und äthiopischer Mönch wird. Er assimiliert die äthiopische Kultur von der Sprache beginnend vollständig und wird zum bedeutendsten Apologeten gegen den Islam, übersetzer aus dem Arabischen, aber auch Verfasser von Originalschriften in Geez, der äthiopischen Kirchen- und Kultursprache. Er wird Echage, Abt des Klosters von Dabra-Libanos in dieser Zeit, und vertritt somit in paradoxerweise den autochthon äthiopischen Kirchenführer (s. o.) in dieser durch Wirren und Gefahren der islamischen Invasion unter Ahmad Grañ – so existenziell bedrohten Kirche.

Stuart MUNRO-HAY legt mit seinem Buch eine zusammenfassende Studie über die ersten knappen 1000 Jahre dieser Geschichte vor. Diese chronologische Beschränkung wird aus verschiedenen Gesichtspunkten heraus plausibel und erklärlich. Es ist, wie gesagt, die Zeit der spärlichen Quellen, die bei aller Spärlichkeit zudem sprachlich und der Gattung nach höchst differenziert sind: von aksumitischen Inschriften und Münzen in Griechisch, Sabäisch und Altäthiopisch über syrische, griechische und arabische Märtyrerakten bis hin zu Berichten christlich-arabischer Kirchenhistoriker in Ägypten, aber auch Passagen aus Werken der klassischen arabisch-islamischen Geographie und Historiographie.

Der Autor ist ein ausgewiesener Numismatiker und Historiker Aksums; auf seine bedeutenden Beiträge in diesen Gebieten verweist die Bibliographie. Nach einer in der Anlage ähnlichen Synthese über Aksum lag es nahe, daß er sich diesem Sonderaspekt der Geschichte widmete. Da auf der anderen Seite der Aksum–Historiker, gezwungen durch die Dürftigkeit und Einseitigkeit seiner Quellen, bei vielen Fragen aus den belegten Verhältnissen im äthiopischen Reich des frühen Mittelalters extrapolieren muß (von Fragen der Königsweihe bis hin zur Thronfolge), ist er *eo ipso* mit den Quellen bis hin zum 13. Jhdt., d. h. mit der Zeit der ersten Herrscher der von den europäischen Historikern sogenannten "salomonischen" Dynastie vertraut.

Das Verdienst des vorliegenden Werk liegt zum einen Teil in der intensiven Aufarbeitung der Fragen des Ursprungs der Kirche in Äthiopien, wo der Autor nicht nur rezipierend und wertend die Forschungsliteratur zusammenstellt und auswertet, sondern auch wichtige Ergebnisse eigener Forschung mit einfließen läßt. Es ist allerdings schade, daß, wohl aus zeitlichen Gründen, die Arbeiten von H. BRAKMANN (etwa: Die Einwurzelung der Kirche im spätantiken Reich vom Aksum, Bonn, 1994) nicht mehr berücksichtigt ist, wie übrigens auch mancher andere Teil der Sekundärliteratur in anderen Sprachen als Englisch und Französisch. Für den folgenden Teil der Studie überwiegt die Aufarbeitung der Forschungsliteratur. Wie in jeder solch umfassenden Synthese, zumal auf einem in vielen Fragen und Problemen noch durchaus unsichere Ergebnisse aufweisenden Gebiet, läßt sich über manches diskutieren, zu vielem Ergänzungen beitragen. Doch das ist nicht ein Mangel des hier präsentierten Buchs, sondern bereits Teil seiner Wirkungsgeschichte.

Manfred KROPP Mainz, Juli 1997

Contents

Preface

Ethiopia saw many changes during the thousand or so years covered by the theme of this book. The advent of Christianity in the first half of the fourth century brought a major new dimension to Ethiopian life at a period when the Aksumite kingdom was at its height. The new faith appears to have advanced steadily, so that by the reign of King Kaleb in the sixth century Aksum was regarded internationally as a Christian power. When eventually Aksum itself ceased to be the capital, the court and government removing elsewhere, Christianity had become so firmly entrenched as to constitute an intrinsic part of the country's fabric.

After the disruption of the Red Sea trade by the Persians from the 570s – confirmed by the later overthrow of the centuries–old Romano–Persian balance of power and the ancient Red Sea trading system by Muslim Arabs in the mid–seventh century – Aksum entered upon its irreversible decline. For Ethiopia as a whole a 'dark age' commenced whose history is illumined by very few sources. The cessation of Aksum's coinage and royal inscriptions removed what are for us the most significant primary documents for modern reconstructions of Aksumite history and chronology. But still, from Arab and other historians, and Ethiopian traditional records, something of the story of post–Aksumite Ethiopia can be pieced together.

From such secondary sources we learn that a still powerful and extensive 'Habash' (Abyssinian) kingdom remained, ruled by a king with the title *najashi* or *negus*, based in the Ethiopian highlands with its capital at a place called Ku'bar. The existence of this kingdom was put in jeopardy, apparently in the late tenth century, by an invasion led by a still–unidentified foreign queen, but it later recovered. Probably in the mid–twelfth century, a dynastic change installed the so–called Zagwé monarchy, based in the province of Lasta, with a new centre of power at Adafa and Roha (Lalibela). By 1270 another dynasty, with a power centre yet further south in Shewa, and claiming descent from the former kings and from King Solomon and the Queen of Sheba, had managed to oust the Zagwé. Amid all these changes, a single thread of contact with the outside world remained; the arrival of the *abun* or metropolitan bishop from the patriarchate of Alexandria.

The unusual position of Ethiopia with relation to its ecclesiastical head, the metropolitan bishop appointed by the patriarch of Alexandria, arose from the consecration by Patriarch Athanasius, in the fourth century, of a Tyrian called Frumentius to the see of Aksum. At some later date, the right to appoint the Ethiopian bishop was 'legalised' by its inclusion in the canons of Nicaea, with the extra proviso that the *abun* must be an Egyptian monk. For this reason, the Ethiopian monarchy and the Coptic patriarchate of Alexandria remained in contact over the centuries. A number of historians, hagiographers, and patriarchal biographers have thus preserved accounts concerning Ethiopia when almost no other sources are available. This study is a survey of the information available about the metropolitan bishops of Ethiopia, and the setting in which they lived, from c. A.D. 330 until just after the 'Solomonic' restoration of around 1270.

In writing this book, the aim has been to make its information available to as wide a circle of readers as possible. Accordingly, the transliteration of names has been kept simple, employing the most easily–recognised forms and avoiding diacritical marks. Conventional latinisations have been used for many Greek names, after the example of the Oxford Dictionary of the Christian Church. The names of patriarchs and metropolitans have often been simplified to their English versions. Most texts in less well–known languages have been translated into English; specialists can easily refer to the originals where necessary.

Acknowledgments

Many people have contributed to the production of this study, and to them I offer my sincere thanks. I am particularly grateful to Glen Kania, for putting the entire typescript of this book onto disk, and thus facilitating the editing work; to Dr. Bent Juel–Jensen for making his superb library available to me, and for his assistance with other matters; to Gianfranco Fiaccadori of Parma and Gillian Clark of Liverpool for translations of Syriac texts, to Dr. Greville Freeman–Grenville who undertook the important task of reading the typescript at an advanced stage and suggesting improvements; and to Pamela Taor for a final check of the print–out. I also thank Dr. Colin Hope for assistance in obtaining documentation, and the staff of the British Library for their usual kindness and unstinting help.

I am very grateful to the Twenty–Seven Foundation and the Spalding Trust for grants to help with travel in Europe and Africa during my research; the Spalding Trust also contibuted to the expenses of publication. Without this timely assistance the book would have been very much more difficult to complete.

S. C. H. Munro–Hay,
Château d'Auzac, Mézin, France;

List of Abbreviations

ASAE	Annales du Service de l'Antiquités de l'Égypte.
AE	Annales d'Éthiopie.
BSOAS	Bulletin of the School of Oriental and African Studies.
BZ	Byzantinische Zeitschrift.
CSCO	Corpus Scriptorum Christianorum Orientalium.
CSHB	Corpus Scriptorum Historiae Byzantinae.
DAE	Deutsche Aksum–Expedition (followed by a number, indicates LITTMANN's Inscriptions in Bd. IV).
DSHCE	Documents pour servir à l'histoire des civilisations éthiopiennes.
ET	Études et Travaux, Travaux du Centre d'Archéologie Méditerranéenne de l'Académie Polonaise des Sciences (Varsovie)
JA	Journal Asiatique.
JARCE	Journal of the American Research Center in Egypt.
JEA	Journal of Egyptian Archaeology.
JES	Journal of Ethiopian Studies.
LAAA	Annals of Archaeology and Anthropology (Liverpool).
PG	P. MIGNE, ed., Patrologiae Curus, series Graeca.
PL	P. MIGNE, ed., Patrologiae Curus, series Latina.
PO	Patrologia Orientalia.
RRAL	Rendiconti della Reale Accademia dei Lincei
RS	Revue Sémitique.
RSE	Rassegna di Studi Etiopici.
RSO	Rivista degli Studi Orientali.
SNR	Sudan Notes and Records.
ZÄS	Zeitschrift für Ägyptische Sprache und Altertumskunde.
ZDMG	Zeitschrift der Deutschen Morgenländischen Gesellschaft.

Certain titles have also been abbreviated in the notes:

ATIYA, History of the Patriarchs,

ATIYA, Aziz., *et al.*, eds., Sawirus ibn al–Mukaffa', History of the Patriarchs of the Egyptian Church, Vol.II;
Part I, Cairo 1943.; Part II, Cairo 1948.; Part III, Cairo, 1959.

AYELE TEKLAHAYMANOT, *Egyptian Metropolitans*
Abba AYELE TEKLAHAYMANOT, *The Egyptian Metropolitans of the Ethiopian Church*, paper presented to the Eighth International Conference of Ethiopian Studies, Addis Ababa, Nov. 1984, pp. 1–62 (subsequently published as AYELE' TAKLAHAYMANOT, *The Egyptian Metropolitans of the Ethiopian Church,* Orientalia Cristiana Periodica, 54, 1988, pp. 175–222).

BURCKHARDT, Travels,
BURCKHARDT J. L., Travels in Nubia, London 1819.

BUDGE, History,
BUDGE, Sir E. A. W., A History of Ethiopia, Nubia and Abyssinia, London 1928, 2 Vols.

BUDGE, Synaxarium,
BUDGE, Sir E. A. W., The Book of the Saints of the Ethiopian Church, The Ethiopic Synaxarium, London 1928, 4 Vols.

CONTI ROSSINI, Storia,
CONTI ROSSINI, C., Storia d'Etiopia, Bergamo 1928.

EVETTS, "History of the Patriarchs",
EVETTS, B., ed., "History of the Patriarchs of the Coptic Church of Alexandria" by Sawirus ibn al–Mukaffa', bishop of al–Ashmunin. Vol. I;
I. St. Mark to Theonas, PO I, fasc. 2, 1904, pp. 99–214.
II. Peter I to Benjamin, PO I, fasc. 4, 1904, pp. 381–518.
III. Agathon to Michael I, PO V, fasc. 1, 1909, pp.1–215.
IV. Menas I to Joseph, PO X, fasc. 5, 1914, pp. 357–551.

ISAAC, *Ethiopian Church*,
ISAAC, E., *An Obscure Component in Ethiopian Church History*, Le Muséon, 85, 1972, pp. 225–258.

JAKOBIELSKI, Faras III,
JAKOBIELSKI, S., Faras III, A History of the Bishopric of Pachoras, Warsaw 1972.

KIRWAN, Firka,
KIRWAN, Sir L. P., The Oxford University Excavations at Firka, Oxford 1939.

MEINARDUS, *Abunate,*
MEINARDUS, O., *A Brief History of the Abunate of Ethiopia*, Wiener Zeitschrift für die Kunde des Morgenlandes, 58, 1962, pp. 39–65.

MONNERET DE VILLARD, Storia,
MONNERET DE VILLARD, U., Storia della Nubia cristiana, Rome 1938.

QUATREMÈRE, Mémoires,
QUATREMÈRE, E., Mémoires géographiques et historiques sur l'Égypte et sur les contrées voisines, Paris 1811.

SERGEW, *Die Aethiopische Kirche,*
SERGEW HABLE SELLASSIE, *Die Aethiopische Kirche im 4 bis 6 Jahrhundert,* Abba Salama II, 1971, pp. 43–75.

SERGEW, AMEH,
SERGEW HABLE SELLASSIE, Ancient and Medieval Ethiopian History to 1270, Addis Ababa 1972.

SHAHID, Martyrs,
Shahid, I., The Martyrs of Najran; New Documents, Subsidia hagiographica 49, Brussels 1971.

TADDESSE TAMRAT, Church and State,
TADDESSE TAMRAT, Church and State in Ethiopia, 1270–1527, Oxford 1972.

TADDESSE TAMRAT, *The Abbots,*
TADDESSE TAMRAT, *The Abbots of Dabra Ilayq 1248–1353,* JES VIII, 1970, pp. 87–117.

TEDESCHI, *Etiopia,*
TEDESCHI, S., *L'Etiopia nella Storia dei Patriarchi Alessandrini,* RSE XXIII, 1967–8, pp. 232–271.

TRIMINGHAM, Sudan,
TRIMINGHAM, J. S., Islam in the Sudan, London 1952.

VANTINI, Faras,
VANTINI, G., The Excavations at Faras, A contribution to the History of Christian Nubia, Bologna 1970.

VANTINI, OS,
VANTINI, G., Oriental Sources Concerning Nubia, Heidelberg and Warsaw 1975.

CHAPTER ONE

Ethiopia : Alexandria and the Ecclesiastical Hierarchy

Introduction

The traditional view of the Ethiopian metropolitanate, which is also the view maintained here, is that it was established in the time of the Emperor Constantine the Great, with the consecration by Patriarch Athanasius of Alexandria of a Tyrian[1] called Frumentius as the first bishop of Aksum.

His successors, though primates of the Ethiopian church, appear to have all been native Egyptian monks drawn from Egyptian monasteries, appointed according to a tradition later embodied into ecclesiastical law by a spurious Nicene canon (see below, I: 2). These bishops were sent by the Alexandrian patriarchate from Frumentius' time, apparently in the third decade of the fourth century, until the mid–twentieth century. The system continued to function in spite of the enormous difficulties posed by the arduous journey from Egypt to Ethiopia and by the various important political and religious changes in neighbouring countries which occurred during this long period. With the separation between the 'melkite' and 'monophysite' churches on doctrinal grounds Ethiopia remained under the influence of the monophysite patriarchate of Alexandria until it finally achieved ecclesiastical independence with its own patriarch on June 29th 1959 during the reign of the late Emperor Haile Sellassie.

The process by which the metropolitanate of Ethiopia was maintained did not always continue unruffled; there were gaps in the succession due to internal political problems, difficulties with surrounding countries, or even disputes with the Alexandrian patriarchs themselves. In spite of all this, the general continuity remained, and provides a remarkable record.

While some of the events which influenced the history of the Ethiopian metropolitans are well known, it is necessary briefly to set the scene of their activities, and to put the contemporary political and religious situation into context.

---

1 S.P. Pétridès, *Essai sur l'évangelisation de l'Éthiopie, sa date et son protagoniste*, Abba Salama III, 1972, pp. 208-232.

The northern Ethiopian highland kingdom of Aksum (II: Introduction), as it expanded its influence from Tigray towards the Nile and the Red Sea, had as its western neighbours first the kingdom of Meroe or Kasu (Kush), then its successor states the Nubian kingdoms of Alodia, Makoria and Nobatia. These three Nubian kingdoms were all in due course converted to Christianity, coming under the ecclesiastical control of Alexandria, as had Aksum itself somewhat earlier. Aksum and the Nubian kingdoms all eventually followed the monophysite definition of the nature of Christ adopted by Alexandria after the Council of Chalcedon in 451. Nubia, including another as yet little-known state called Dotawo which developed in later times, remained Christian at least in part until the fifteenth or even early sixteenth century.

A considerable amount of information has been preserved about the Nubian church. Archaeology in Nubia is much more advanced than in Ethiopia, among other reasons because of the emergency programme of excavations resulting from the flooding of whole tracts of the country by the Aswan dam. Accordingly, the parallel, or partially parallel, situation of the Nubian church in relation to that in Ethiopia has led to some discussion of certain aspects of the Nubian evidence below. To clarify the picture, sections are also devoted below to the nomenclature which ancient historians applied, very uncertainly, to these countries (I: 1), and to the nature of the church in both Nubia and Ethiopia (I: 3).

The power and prestige of the patriarchate of Alexandria, increasing during the great theological controversies of the fourth and fifth centuries, became a force to be reckoned with in political terms as the monophysite belief gained ground. The sixth century was much troubled by struggles between the different parties in the Christological debate; the Romano–Byzantine state, by inclining toward one side or the other as the emperors changed, actually helped to emphasize the divergency. The nationalistic attraction of the anti–Chalcedonian party encouraged disturbances in Egypt, Syria and Palestine, resulting in an atmosphere which may well have actively contributed to the eventual political domination of Islam in the whole region.

Alexandria did not neglect the opportunity for spreading its authority and beliefs. Ethiopia – the kingdom of Aksum – was converted very early, in the second quarter of the fourth century, during the time of Patriarch Athanasius and Emperor Constantine the Great. Nubia, or at least two of the Nubian states, Nobatia in the north and Alodia in the south, adopted Christianity during the reign of Emperor Justinian in the sixth century. Finally the influence of the Alexandrian patriarchate extended to the Pentapolis, the province of Roman Africa, Libya, and the third, central,

Nubian kingdom, Makoria; perhaps even the Himyarite church in the Yemen was in association at times. Ecclesiastical control over these regions, though opposed by the 'orthodox' (or Chalcedonian) Romano–Byzantine state, and later vigilantly watched by the Muslim authorities, was only gradually relinquished as Christianity disappeared from those regions. The official style of the patriarchs still includes Nubia, Abyssinia and the Pentapolis. One of the most striking aspects of the foreign associations of the Alexandrian patriarchate was its retention of authority over Ethiopia until the 1950s (I: 2). This connection between the Ethiopian metropolitanate and the patriarchate of Alexandria, lasting some 1600 years, was one of the twentieth century's most remarkable surviving ancient Christian institutions.

As the Nubian kingdoms, debilitated by wars and Arab infiltration, fell slowly away from Christianity, and the difficulties of intercourse with Egypt multiplied, Ethiopia's ecclesiastical problems grew more acute. The country needed urgently to maintain its religious hierarchy if it wished to preserve its Christian religion; and ultimately this depended on the maintenance of the succession of metropolitans from Alexandria.

Certain details of this varied and protracted Ethiopian association with the Egyptian church have been long available, in the records of Roman and Byzantine historians and later in the works of some Arab writers. These were discussed even by the early historians of Ethiopia. The Ge'ez (Ethiopic) chronicles have become known (outside Ethiopia) more recently, though much is still in unpublished manuscript form. Their value is, naturally, immense. Some useful information has already emerged from the work of Ethiopian scholars quoting from such manuscripts; particularly SERGEW HABLE SELLASSIE and TADDESSE TAMRAT. Accounts of the metropolitanate based on some of these sources have appeared, summarily in certain of the histories of the church or of the Alexandrian patriarchate (see VIII Bibliography), more fully in a few special studies, particularly those of MEINARDUS and TEDESCHI[2]

TEDESCHI was concerned only with the information on Ethiopia contained in the Arabic *History of the Patriarchs of the Alexandrian Church;* MEINARDUS covered a much longer period, but in a very general way. The present study aims to describe the early history of the metropolitanate in Ethiopia as fully as possible, employing all possible sources to illuminate the rather scattered record. Certainly gaps remain, particularly in our information about the metropolitans and their activities in the earlier period;

[2] MEINARDUS, *Abunate*; TEDESCHI, *Etiopia*.

perhaps in the future new discoveries, archaeological or textual, may be able to fill them in, just as the excavations at Faras and Qasr Ibrim have so changed our knowledge of the organisation of the Nubian church and its metropolitanate (I:3a).

The history of the church in Ethiopia, and its Coptic metropolitanate or 'abunate' was summarised by Major HARRIS[3] in that quintessentially Victorian phraseology which characterises his report of the British Mission to Shewa in 1841;

> Converted at the very dawn of Christianity, Aethiopia spread her new religion deep into the recesses of heathen Africa. Extending her wide empire on every side, the praise of the Redeemer soon arose from the wildest valleys, and the most secluded mountains. From the great river Gochob to the frontiers of Nubia, the crutch and the cowl pervaded the land. Churches were erected in every convenient spot, and the blue badge of nominal Christianity encircled the necks of an ignorant multitude. The usual wars and rebellions arose, and schism and sects fill up the archives of ten centuries with all the uninteresting precision of more civilized countries. But still the church flourished; the patriarch was regularly received from Alexandria and a long list of ninety–five Aboons flows quietly through the dull pages of Abyssinian record, from the time of Frumentius the First, until the days of the venerable Simon, who, whilst gallantly defending the faith of his fathers, was barbarously murdered by the European partisans of the Italian Jesuit.

The last sentence refers to the death of Metropolitan Simon at the battle of Tsadda, May 13th 1617, during the wars which resulted from Emperor Susenyos' conversion to Catholicism.

While it is true that some of the Ge'ez lists of metropolitans (I: 4) may offer ninety–five names from Frumentius to Simon, very few of these are extant in any other record. Though the Coptic monophysite or Jacobite church long preserved its control over the non–autocephalus church of Ethiopia, this association has been relatively ill–documented. Only a few tantalising references survive.

The different aspects of the patriarchal function, both at home and abroad, were categorised by the historian–bishop, Sawirus (Severus) ibn al–Muqaffa', secretary to the Patriarch Philotheus (979–1003) and later bishop of Ashmunein[4] ;

> Now who will not marvel when he hears these wonders, namely that every patriarch who sits upon this holy throne directs his care towards three depart-

[3] W.C. HARRIS, The Highlands of Ethiopia, London 1844, Vol III, p. 66.

[4] PO X, fasc. V, p. 507.

> ments of business; the care for the synodical letter to the patriarch of Antioch; secondly our relations with the Abyssinians and the Nubians; and thirdly the carrying out of decrees issued by the governor of Egypt to the patriarchs and bishops, that the affairs of the Orthodox churches may be kept in good order.

The records pertaining to the second of these departments of patriarchal care, though scanty and often confusing, present a clear picture of the Ethiopians' place in the ecclesiastical structure. Patriarch Athanasius' (328–373) consecration of Frumentius to the new see of Aksum founded the vital principle of the Ethiopian church's dependence on Alexandria; it was a logical step since, the church being united throughout the empire, Alexandria was the nearest patriarchal seat. But in Athanasius' and Frumentius' own lifetimes a rival patriarch of Alexandria professing the Arian heresy, George of Cappadocia, was installed. Later there were both monophysite and melkite (imperially–supported Chalcedonian) patriarchs in office simultaneously in Alexandria. But Ethiopia seems to have followed Athanasius and his orthodox successors in defiance of Arianism, then to have adhered to the monophysite patriarchs ever afterwards. The Arian and melkite patriarchs had apparently little or no influence in Ethiopia.

1. Ethiopia (Abyssinia), Nubia, and India; Historical Nomenclature

There is considerable confusion in the terminology employed by various authors, ancient and modern, for the Aksumite kingdom, present–day Ethiopia (Abyssinia), Nubia, Meroitic Ethiopia in the modern republic of the Sudan, and India. Some eastern writers, in Hebrew and Syriac for example, used the name Kush, originally an ancient Egyptian designation for Nubia, for Nubia/Meroe or Aksum. Ancient Greek and Latin writers generally referred to the Meroitic and Nubian kingdoms as Ethiopia, and to present–day Ethiopia as India. In such texts India may be referred to as simply India, or with a set of definitions to distinguish the various Indias, themselves by no means consistent; India major, minor, interior, exterior, ulterior etc. Sometimes Ethiopia is meant, sometimes South Arabia, sometimes the subcontinent of India itself; once apparently even Caucasian Iberia, the modern Georgia.

Occasionally the example of the Aksumite kings on their own coins and inscriptions is followed, using the name of their capital city. They referred to themselves in Greek on the coins as *basileus Aksomiton,* 'king of the Aksumites', or in Ge'ez as *negusa Aksum,* 'king of Aksum'. Some ancient authors accordingly adopted the terms 'the Auxumitae' or, 'the Aksumite Indians', as distinguished from 'the Homerite Indians', the Himyarites of southern Arabia.

Similarly the Nubian 'Ethiopians' were at times designated by their kingdoms, as the Nobatae (Nobatia), the Makoritae (Makoria), and the Alodaei (Alodia). In this case, though, the similarities with other tribal names sometimes have caused further problems of interpretation. The Coptic author of the *Life of Isaac*[5] inserted the names MAKOYPIA and MAYPωTANIA in reference to a dispute between countries named by the Arab text of the *History of the Patriarchs*[6] as *al–Habasha* and *al–Nuba,* or Abyssinia and Nubia. The historian John of Nikiu [7] referred to the "barbarians of the provinces of Nubia and Africa, called Mauritani and other barbarians called Marikos", while John, abbot of Biclarum[8] wrote of the Maccuritai, and the geographer Claudius Ptolemy[9] of the Makkourai. Both ancient and modern writers have at times hesitated whether to assign these names to the Nubians of Nobatia, which was later often called *al–Maris,* and Makoria (Muqurra), or to Saharan tribes bordering the Roman province of Africa.

The Arab writers, though not necessarily always reliable in their narration of events, do at least sometimes follow a regular system of nomenclature. Nubia, *al–Nuba,* refers to the united kingdom of Nobatia and Makoria. The king is entitled 'the king of Nubia and Makoria' *(al–Nuba w–'l Muqurra),* and later the 'king of Dongola' (Dunjala, Dunqala, Dungala etc.). The province of Nobatia is called *al–Maris*. The other, southern, Nubian kingdom is called *Alwa* (Alodia). These are distinguished from *al–Habasha* (Abyssinia), and *al–Hind,* the sub–continent of India.

However there is still occasionally a repetition of the confusion; John the Deacon[10] in writings preserved in Severus of Ashmunein's work, referred to King Kyriakos of Nubia as *al–malik al–maqurra al–habashi al–urthuduksi,* 'the orthodox Abyssinian king of Maqurra', probably due to the translation of the Coptic word *egoosh,* which could be applied gen-

---

[5] E. PORCHER, ed. and trans., "Vie d'Isaac, Patriarche d'Alexandrie de 686 à 689", PO IX, p. 377.

[6] PO V, fasc. I, p. 24.

[7] H. ZOTENBERG, ed., Chronique de Jean, évêque de Nikiu, Paris 1883, p. 404.

[8] TH. MOMMSEN, ed., *Chronica Joannis abbatis monasterii Biclarensis*, Monumenta Germaniae Historica, Leipzig 1894, xi, pp. 212-3.

[9] Ptolemy, *Geography*, iv.2.19.

[10] PO V, fasc. I, p. 145.

erally to all the black nations south of Egypt. The Armenian writer Abu Salih[11] uses the same designation; he seems to have taken this passage bodily from the work of John the Deacon. There is also confusion about the use of the term *al–Hind* in interpreting information from the biography of Patriarch Simon[12] (III: 22).

The works of some other writers in Arabic show that the term *habasha* was applied to all the black races south of Egypt. In some cases there is only the vaguest understanding of the real situation in those distant regions. To illustrate the differences in Arab descriptions of the Nubian–Ethiopian area and its inhabitants, a few may be quoted.

Al–Fazari[13], c. 800, refers to the "territory of the Nuba under the rule of the Najashi"; al–Farghani[14], writing before 861, calls Jarmi, Dungala and the town of the Nuba "towns of the Kingdom of Habasha". Al–Jahiz[15] (776–869) observes that the Habasha and the Nuba dwell on the banks of the Nile in al–Habasha, and al–Ya'qubi[16] writing c. 872–891, mentions, in relation to one of the Beja kingdoms, "a king of Habash called Naqis". Al–Tabari (d. 923) also employs "habash" as a blanket term: "the Beja are Habash, a branch of the race of the Habash of the Maghrib".[17] Al–Mas'udi (d. 956) refers to both Dongola and Alwa as capitals of the Nuba; he mentions "the country of those Nuba, whose king is called Najashi" and also "the Habasha who are descendants of Habash (Hubsh) b. Kush b. Ham. The largest of their kingdoms is the kingdom of the Najashi...".[18] Al–Marwazi (d. after 1120), refers to the Habasha as "a race which includes several kinds such as the Nuba, the Zanj, and others", while al–Zuhri, writing around 1137–50[19] refers to the Habasha capital as Dunjala[20], but also mentions that Abreha (Aksumite ruler of the Yemen during Kaleb of Aksum's reign in the sixth century) was of the Habasha.

---

11 B.T.A. Evetts and A.J. Butler, eds., The Churches and Monasteries of Egypt and some Neighbouring Countries, attributed to Abû Sâlih, the Armenian, Oxford 1895, fol. 105a, p. 286.

12 PO V, fasc.I, pp. 36-42.

13 Vantini, OS, p. 49.

14 *Ibid.*, p. 53.

15 *Ibid.*, p. 54.

16 *Ibid.*, p. 71.

17 *Ibid.*, p. 99.

18 *Ibid.* pp. 136, 138-9, 143.

19 *Ibid.*, p. 263.

20 *Ibid.*, p. 250.

Certain Aksumite inscriptions[21], in their Greek versions, use "Ethiopians" (written ΑΙΘΙΟΠΩΝ) in parallel to the term "Habashat" found in their Ge'ez and epigraphic South Arabian versions. In this work the terms Ethiopia and Abyssinia are used for present day Ethiopia alone; that is, those northern and central parts of the country which were ruled by the Aksumite, Zagwé, and Solomonic dynasties.

It may be incidentally noted that the Nubians, too, sometimes called themselves Ethiopians. This is illustrated by the protocol of King Silko, who could not conceivably have ruled anywhere further afield than the Nile valley. In his Greek inscription from Kalabsha he calls himself "basiliskos of the Nobadae and all the Ethiopians".[22] There is also a Coptic document belonging to a certain King Johannes, from Aswan[23], which declares that "all the Ethiopians are subject to him, from Tilimaura to the castrum of Philae".

The Ge'ez inscriptions refer to the peoples of modern Sudan or north–west Ethiopia by their tribal designations, such as Mangurto and Barya for smaller groups, and Kasu (from Kush or Meroe), Noba (Nuba) and Beja for more important peoples. In the present work the different peoples of Nubia and other modern Sudanese regions are referred to either as Nubians, or by the specific names of their kingdoms.

The Ravenna geographer, after Castorius[24], settled the problem of Ethiopian nomenclature by referring to the two Ethiopias, of Aksum and of Candace, a sensible but retrospective reference to a situation prevailing centuries before. MEINARDUS adopted a similar system by referring to Ethiopia Meroitica and Ethiopia Axumita[25], comprehensible but cumbersome designations not employed here, being inappropriate both for post Meroitic Nubia and Ethiopia after the decline of Aksum.

2. Alexandrian Ecclesiastical Control in Ethiopia

The supremacy of the Alexandrian patriarchs over the Ethiopian church is generally regarded as having followed as a natural concomitant of the consecration of Frumentius, though this is not undisputed (see below).

[21] E. LITTMANN, DAE, Bd. IV. 4,6 & 7.

[22] R. LEPSIUS, Denkmäler, Abth. VI, Bl. 95.

[23] F. LL. GRIFFITH, *Christian Documents from Nubia*, Proceedings of the British Academy, XIV, London 1928, nos. 4 & 5, p. 16.

[24] M. PARTHEY and G. PINDER, Ravennatis Anonymi Geographia et Guidenis Geographica, (reprint of 1860 ed.,) Aalem 1962, p. 166.

[25] MEINARDUS, *Abunate*, p. 39.

Recognition of the position was, probably in the seventh century[26], given the sanction of the apocryphal 42nd (or sometimes numbered 36th or 47th) canon of the Council of Nicaea. The Council sat in 325, when Frumentius must indeed have been in Ethiopia in the process of encouraging the foundation of the church, but had almost certainly not yet been consecrated bishop of Aksum. This canon (quoted below), which passed from Arabic into Ge'ez, concerned the autonomy of the church, rendering it subject to the authority of the occupant of the patriarchal throne of Alexandria; he alone could consecrate the metropolitan of Ethiopia, who, further, must not be a native Ethiopian, but a Copt or Egyptian Christian. This meant, in effect, a Coptic monk, since translation of bishops was not a feature of the Egyptian church, though exceptions like that of Michael, bishop of Fuwa, are attested (VI: 54-5); and even Michael was only selected after a considerable search, when the impatience of the Abyssinian messengers had become pressing.

It was this system of the government of the church of Ethiopia which kept alive the link between the patriarchate and its most remote dependent church; a link at times made tenuous by reason of the immense difficulties of the route, and the frequent presence of enemies along one part or another of it, but always revived. Scarcely "forgetful of the world, by whom they were forgotten", as GIBBON's famous phrase put it[27], the Ethiopians did their best through the centuries, with more or less success, to maintain the succession of their metropolitans, and thereby preserve their Christian faith. Their dependence on the distant Egyptian church for metropolitans meant that on the death of the incumbent the kings of Aksum and their successors in Ethiopia had to write to the patriarchs in Alexandria or Cairo – where they moved (V: 37) after 1045[28] – to request them to appoint, consecrate, and despatch a new one. It is the arrival and fate of these messages which forms the backbone of the information which has survived on the condition of the Ethiopian church and state during its most obscure period.

The Coptic church historians, who naturally wished to emphasise the influence of Alexandria, hark back frequently to the supremacy of their patriarchate in Ethiopia. Bishop Severus of Ashmunein even quotes it anachronistically[29] in reference to Patriarch Demetrius (189–231) claiming

---

[26] MEINARDUS, *Abunate*, p. 41, n. 8: AYELE TEKLAHAYMANOT, *Egyptian Metropolitans*, p. 17, n. 17.

[27] E. GIBBON, The History of the Decline and Fall of the Roman Empire, London, 1788, Vol. IV, p. 617.

[28] See note 451.

[29] PO I, fasc. II, p. 155.

that he had jurisdiction over "Nubia, Abyssinia (al–Habasha), all Egypt, and Pentapolis". To Patriarch Maximus (264–282) the Ethiopian *senkessar* or *Synaxarium*[30], a collection of saints' lives arranged according to their name–days, attributes letters to Egypt, Ethiopia and Nubia exhorting the people to entreat God to "remove from the world the opinion and error of Paul of Samosata, the infidel".

Similarly al–Maqrizi (1364–1442), knowing Abyssinia to be under the authority of the successors of St. Mark, attributes[31] their conversion to the evangelist himself;

> He converted, by preaching, men in Rome, in Egypt, in Habash (Abyssinia) and in Nubia; and ordained Hananiah bishop of Alexandria.

Several Arab writers through the centuries commented upon the Ethiopian subordination to the Egyptian Coptic patriarchate. Abu Salih al–Armani[32], writing around 1200, described the current practice;

> A metropolitan is sent from the see of Mark the Evangelist to Abyssinia, from the patriarch of Alexandria in Egypt; and this metropolitan of the Abyssinians ordains priests and deacons for them.

Ibn Khaldun (1332–1405/6), in the *Muqaddima*[33], wrote

> the patriarch of the (Christian) subjects in Egypt is of the Jacobite persuasion. He resides among them. The Abyssinians follow the religion of (the Egyptian Christians). The patriarch of Egypt delegates bishops to the Abyssinians, and these bishops arrange religious affairs in Abyssinia.

The Portuguese Jesuit father, Balthasar TELLES[34], using information taken from the work of a predecessor working in Ethiopia, Emmanuel d'ALMEIDA, remarked in the seventeenth century that

> ...as that Saint (Frumentius) was sent from Alexandria by Saint Athanasius, so, from that time onwards, all the other bishops or Abunas have been sent from the same patriarchal see, down to our own times, in which Rome despatched certain patriarchs.

---

30 S.C. MALAN, trans., "A Short History of the Copts and of their Churches," trans. from the Arabic of Taqi ed-Din El-Maqrizi, London 1873, p. 23.

31 EVETTS and BUTLER, *op. cit.*, pp. 285-6, fol. 105a.

32 Ibn Khaldun, "The Muqaddimah, An Introduction to History", trans. F. ROSENTHAL, New York 1965, Vol. I, p. 481.

34 "Historia geral de Ethiopia a alta", composta... pelo Padre M. d'Almeyda... abreviada pelo Padre B. Tellez, Coimbra 1660, p. 93.

Alexandrian authority, then, rested on the Nicene pseudo–canon, quoted here in full;

> The Ethiopians have no power to create or choose a Patriarch, whose prelate must rather be under the authority of the Patriarch of Alexandria; or in case they should come at any time to have one among them in the place of the Patriarch and who should be styled Catholicos, he shall not, notwithstanding that, have a right to ordain Archbishops as other Patriarchs have, having neither the honour nor the authority of a Patriarch; and if it should so happen that a council should be assembled in Greece, and this prelate should be present at it, he shall have the seventh place therein, next after the bishop of Seleucia; and in case he should at any time have power given to him to ordain Archbishops in his province, it shall not be lawful for him to advance any of the natives to that dignity; whosoever does not yield obedience to this, is excommunicated by the Synod. [35]

The insertion of this canon was accepted in Ethiopia as the legal statement of the position of their church, and passed into the Ge'ez *Synodos,* and into the *Fetha Nagast,* the Ethiopian legal code. Only in 1959 did Alexandria, at the Cairo Council for reform of the church, relinquish its direct jurisdiction over the Ethiopians, this being reduced to an honorary attachment; from 1948, it had been agreed that the metropolitan or *abun* should not be an Egyptian, an enactment finally implemented on January 14th 1951 with the consecration of the Ethiopian metropolitan Basilios in Cairo.

Fr. VANTINI[36] considered that the Nicene canon, which he attributed to the eighth and ninth centuries, applied to Nubia, as part of the propaganda of a shift there from the melkite to the monophysite persuasion. Here the familiar problem of nomenclature, noted above, is the issue. But evidently the canon did in fact apply to Ethiopia, since the Ethiopians continued to obey its provisos until modern times. It was reiterated on several occasions through the centuries even after the end of the last Nubian Christian kingdoms, Dotawo and Alodia/Alwa. A further point in favour of Ethiopia is that the bishops were not to be selected from the native population, whereas

---

[35] For the canons quoted from Mansi (II, Bd 964 and Bd 994) see; VANTINI, Faras, pp. 62-63; ID., OS, pp. 45ff. Most of the early books on Ethiopia quote them in part or in full, as for example M. GEDDES, *The Church-History of Ethiopia*, London, 1646, p. 20; and the Dissertation on the Conversion of the Abyssins which is included in Dr. Samuel JOHNSON'S translation: A Voyage to Abyssinia, by Father Jerome LOBO, London, 1789, p. 297ff. LUDOLF (Ludolphus), Iob, History of Ethiopia, London 1684, (trans. anon.) Book III, ch. VII, p. 306.

[36] VANTINI, Faras, pp. 61ff.

frescoes at Faras[37] of bishops designated as 'metropolitan' depict Kyros and Petros I as black, as is also the 'orthodox' bishop Georgios. A black bishop, possibly of Upper Egyptian origin, could conceivably have been sent from Egypt, but not only are there several of them shown in the Faras frescoes, but also Nubian kings, George I and II, the queen mother, Martha, various queens and princesses, and an eparch, are similarly painted dark brown or black. It seems probable, then, that these metropolitans were natives of the country, who would not have been eligible for the office if the proviso set out in the canons of Nicaea had been applied. The last known bishop, Timotheos of Pachoras (Faras) and Ibrim, is specifically stated in his consecration documents to have been a Nubian by birth.[38]

3. Monophysites and Melkites in Ethiopia and Nubia

The second governing principle of the Ethiopian church, and one which was continually renewed by the association with Alexandria, was its subscription to the monophysite creed, denying the validity of the decisions of the Council of Chalcedon which met in 451. At its inception, of course, the Ethiopian church was orthodox in that it followed the 'orthodoxy' of the Greek patriarch Athanasius of Alexandria instead of the then imperially–supported Arian heresy. But after 451, when Chalcedon confirmed the split in the church over the nature of Christ, Ethiopia seems from the scanty evidence available to have remained under the spiritual control of the monophysite patriarchs of Alexandria rather than the melkites. The country seems to have largely avoided the terrible schisms which at intervals caused such problems in the Roman Empire. The firm hand of the kings in the absence of a metropolitan doubtless helped to ensure the continued peace of the church. With only the metropolitan and perhaps a very few other bishops (IIA: 9–10) in the country, and a long tradition of sacred kingship – pre–Christian Aksumite kings were designated 'Son of Mahrem', a deity associated with Mars, God of War – there was much less chance of disruption. Though John of Ephesus does report that there were Aksumites who supported the heresy of Julian of Halicarnassus

---

[37] Some of the surviving frescoes are preserved in the museum at Khartoum. Excellent photographs and descriptions are available in the many works of the Polish team which worked at Faras, particularly those of MICHAŁOWSKI and JAKOBIELSKI. Illustrations and descriptions may also be found in VANTINI, Faras.

[38] J.M. PLUMLEY, The Scrolls of Bishop Timotheos: Two Documents from Medieval Nubia, London 1975.

in Alodia[39], these were persuaded to recant and we hear no more of them (see I:3a below). Michael the Syrian, the Jacobite patriarch of Antioch from 1166–99, affirmed that Julian's heresy

> perverted the minds of the simple in some places, in the countries of Rum, the Persians, the Indians, the Kushites, the Himyarites, and the Armenians.[40]

But in general, the Ethiopian Orthodox (monophysite) church was apparently left to develop peacefully into one of the characteristic features of Ethiopian life. Schisms and concomitant persecutions only appeared, as far as we know, at a much later stage of the church's development.

However, not all authorities have agreed on the nature of the church in Ethiopia and Nubia. It has been suggested that the melkite ('orthodox') belief was pre–eminent at different times; the problem is discussed below.

a. Ethiopia.

In Ethiopia there is no doubt that the foundation of the church, through the missionary zeal of Frumentius, was orthodox (Nicene), since Frumentius was appointed by Patriarch Athanasius, the great upholder of orthodoxy. However, the Arian heresy being supported by the Emperor Constantius II, Athanasius' tenure of the patriarchal throne was to be a much–interrupted one. He was exiled several times; during one of these periods of exile he was replaced by the Arian patriarch George of Cappadocia. The emperor, in about 356, wrote[41] to the Aksumite rulers trying to persuade them to send Frumentius to Alexandria for examination by George and others; but, in spite of this and the mission of Theophilus the Indian (IIA: 7b), there is nothing to show that Arianism influenced the Ethiopian church. The Ethiopic *Synaxarium*, though not a primary source,

---

39 R. PAYNE-SMITH, trans., The Third Part of the Ecclesiastical History of John, Bishop of Ephesus, Oxford 1860, p. 323; E.W. BROOKS, ed., Iohannis Ephesini Historiae Ecclesiasticae Pars Tertia, versio, CSCO 106, Scriptores Syri 55, Louvain 1952, p. 180. J.S. ASSEMANI (Assemain), Bibliotheca Orientalis, Rome 1725, Vol. I, p. 386.

40 "Chronique de Michel le Syrien, Patriarche Jacobite d'Antioche (1166-1199)", ed. and trans. J.B. CHABOT, Paris 1905, Vol. III, p. 226.

41 Athanasius, "Apologia ad Constantium Imperatorem", PG XXV, col. 636-7. *ditto*, trans. J.M. SZYMUSIAK, Paris 1958, pp. 125ff. The letter was translated into English by GEDDES, *op. cit.*, p. 11. The remarks of F. ALTHEIM, and R. STIEHL, *Die Datierung des Königs 'Ezana von Aksum*, Klio XXXIX, 1961, pp. 234-248, whilst stimulating, are not at all convincing in their attempt to put Ezana at a later date. See also S.C.H. MUNRO-HAY, *The Dating of Ezana and Frumentius*, RSE XXXII, 1988, pp. 111-27

relates the Ethiopian tradition that Frumentius died "in peace".[42] The attempt to have the Aksumite church subjected to Arianism as represented by George of Cappadocia at Alexandria was, it seems, unsuccessful.

The heresy of Julian of Halicarnassus was a monophysite heresy which caused a schism in Alexandria at the death of Patriarch Timothy III in 536. Official support from Emperor Justinian in 565 came late, as he died in that year, but the heresy is known, from John of Ephesus' report, to have spread from Abyssinia to Alodia.[43] It is not known whether those who professed the heresy were Aksumites working with official sanction, or whether they were at odds with the Aksumite church itself. In any event, Longinus, first bishop of the Nobadae, appointed around 580, had these Aksumites prepare written renunciations of the heresy. Perhaps his watchfulness had a similar effect of stopping its currency among the Aksumites.

Some writers on the subject have been reluctant to accept that Ethiopia followed the monophysite belief. Fr. Balthasar TELLES[44] considered that the Ethiopians belonged to the 'catholic' party as long as they were in strength in Alexandria;

> But notwithstanding that in the Days of the wicked Dioscorus, who liv'd about the Year 444, there were presently Errors introduc'd into Ethiopia, which came from Alexandria, yet, as long as the Catholick Party prevail'd in Alexandria, which we find was till the Year 610 or 620, when the Holy Men S. Elogius and S. John the Almsgiver, were Patriarchs of Alexandria, we suppose that the greatest part of Ethiopia was subject to the See of Rome, and always followed the Doctrine of the Teachers sent into it.

He cites as proof that the Ethiopians honoured non–monophysite prelates as saints, and that the Aksumite King Kaleb was obedient to the catholic patriarch set up by Justin in Alexandria; (for this latter point, see the discussion of the affairs of Ethiopia and the church during and after the Himyarite war of Kaleb, IIB: 13–14).

---

42 BUDGE, Synaxarium, III, pp. 1164-5. This is, of course, to acccept that Frumentius was consecrated bishop of the see of Aksum in Ethiopia; others have suggested different interpretations (see II: 7a).

43 Both in his account of the conversion of Nubia and that concerning the troubles of the Ethiopian and Himyarite churches, which are discussed at length below.

44 B. TELLEZ (Telles), The Travels of the Jesuits in Ethiopia, trans. into English, London 1710, p. 102.

Abba AYELE TEKLAHAYMANOT[45], who regards the sending of the Egyptian metropolitans as "terrible conditions of blind dependence... made incredibly heavy and harsh by the patriarchs of Alexandria", writes of the "domination" of the Egyptians, but suggests that at an earlier period the church "was still in communion with the Catholic Church, being ruled probably by a bishop sent by the Pope of Rome". This is based on the listing of Adulis among the "ancient episcopal seats of the Catholic Church" (see I: 5 below); Ethiopia apparently only would have "of necessity" adopted monophysitism ("taking sides with Dioscorus") after the establishment of the Muslim empire had cut off the melkite succession. Abba AYELE supports the theory that Patriarch Benjamin's appointee, Qerlos (Cyril), was the first of the monophysite bishops, the 24th in the succession (III: 20), stating that from his time on monophysitism penetrated into Ethiopia "because the metropolitans did not admit to Sacred Orders those who did not profess their doctrines".

In fact, as will emerge later in the discussion, there is no reliable indication that the Ethiopians adhered to the catholic or melkite belief after Chalcedon. Indeed, it seems from Ethiopian traditional and other sources that they probably followed Dioscorus' monophysitism, and that this belief, once established in the country, was always retained by the connection with the monophysite patriarchate of Alexandria. Certainly this is how a number of ancient writers regarded the matter. Al–Qalqashandi[46] quoting the Coptic Christian writer Girgis ibn al–'Amid al–Makin, d. 1272, asserts that Dioscorus, on his retirement from Chalcedon, went to Jerusalem, and remained there, collecting followers from Palestine and Egypt; "He was followed also by the Nuba and the Habasha, who have remained in the same way until today".

A rather vague account of the position of the Ethiopian church by ISAAC,[47] proposes that

> Monophysitism is attributed to the Ethiopian Church primarily on the basis of its relationship with the Coptic Church... Ethiopian contact with the (Monophysite) Coptic Church remained minimal until 1270... the status of monastic Coptic Abunas presiding over the Ethiopian Church was never fully regularized before the time of... Täkle–Haymanot in 1270.

---

45 AYELE TEKLAHAYMANOT, *Egyptian Metropolitans, loc. var.*

46 VANTINI, OS, p. 502.

47 ISAAC, *Ethiopian Church*, pp. 245-252.

ISAAC quotes the forged Nicene canon as the basis for this dependency, and summarises the known history of the abunate (concentrating on the unfavourable aspects – but at the same time illustrating a contact which was hardly "minimal") from the time of Metropolitan Peter (III: 29) until 1270. He asserts that the Copts were given "encouragement by the Fatimid Sultans of Egypt to make friendly overtures to Christian Ethiopia, ironically with the hope of encouraging the overthrow of the Christian establishment".

But as far as the Coptic metropolitans are concerned, whatever their quality as men may have been when put to the proof, the very fact that all of them were sent from monophysite Alexandria to be accepted in Ethiopia as heads of the Ethiopian church, is a sure indication that Alexandria had, and retained, the right, duly "regularized", to appoint them. ISAAC does not suggest any other foreign source from whence these bishops came. If the Coptic church did not have the right to appoint metropolitans, some other church must have maintained this succession without which there could be no priests and bishops. There were long gaps in the melkite succession after the 640s (III: 18); only the monophysites retained a permanent functioning ecclesiastical system in Egypt and the Nubian kingdoms.

It seems that ISAAC envisages an independent Ethiopian church, since he continues;

> Täkle–Haymanot may be said to be the first Ethiopian to be "converted" to Coptic Monophysitism and ...thus became the main mediator for the Coptic alliance with the Ethiopian Church. Ironically, in his time Täkle–Haymanot functioned as an Abuna, the last such indigenous prelate we hear of: which fact gives still more support to the belief that preceding (him) there indeed must have been native Ethiopian Abunas.

But if so, why did Ethiopia accept the long line of foreign *abuns* that ISAAC details, who arrived long before the time of Tekla–Haymanot, and who kept on coming even in spite of their bad behaviour? There seems to be no actual evidence for this suggestion that there were Ethiopian native *abuns*, in contrast to the plentiful indications concerning the Alexandrian–appointed Egyptian ones.

GETATCHEW HAILE[48] also suggests that the faith of Kaleb, and Pantelewon, as well as the rest of the Nine Saints (see II: 12 below), was Chalcedonian. He merely notes that "an anti–Chalcedonian Church would not

[48] GETATCHEW HAILE, *A New Ethiopic Version of the Acts of St. Mark*, Analecta Bollandiana, 1981, pp. 121-3.

have admired the religion of the "Romans" or Constantinopolitans during the reign of Kaleb of Ethiopia and Patriarch Timothy III of Alexandria, all of whom lived after the Council of Chalcedon", without commenting on the particularities of the period (see IIB below), or the historicity of the manuscripts involved.

b. Nubia.

For Nubia, the literary and archaeological record is fuller, and accordingly more complicated. The following discussion, though not strictly relevant to the theme of Ethiopian ecclesiastical history, is of value in that it illustrates the parallel developments in Ethiopia's nearest, and, thanks to archaeology, much better known, Christian neighbours. However little evidence we have for mutual contact, it is certain that there must have been some communication between Ethiopia and the Nubian kingdoms, which may have affected the development of the church. As yet, we know of such contacts in only two instances; the story of the Julianist heresy in Alodia already noted, at a time just after the last known (mid–sixth century) Aksumite royal inscriptions claiming control over the Noba people and, much later, from the account of the letter sent to King Girgis II of Nubia by an unnamed Ethiopian king (IV: 30).

As with such texts as the letter of Constantius II (IIA:7a), or Ezana's 'monotheist' inscription, subjective interpretation of the evidence is difficult to avoid in discussing the Nubian church and its origins. Some modern attitudes[49] towards the biases of ancient church historians of Nubia themselves make interesting historiographical reading. The interpretation of events in the country rests, to a greater or lesser degree, on impressions and inferences from the work of writers whose personal religious involvement imbued their records with a strong emotional savour.

[49] See for example KIRWAN, Firka; ID., *Studies in the later History of Nubia*, LAAA XXIV, pp. 69-105; Id., *Some Thoughts on the Conversion of Nubia to Christianity*, Nubian Studies, ed. J.M. PLUMLEY, Warminster 1982, pp. 142-5. M. KRAUSE, *Zur Kirchengeschichte Nubiens*, Nubian Culture Past and Present, ed. T. HÄGG, Stockholm 1987, pp. 293-308, provides an excellent summary of the present state of studies. MONNERET DE VILLARD, Storia, p. 61; F.F. GADALLAH, *The Egyptian Contribution to Nubian Christianity*, SNR XL, 1959, p. 41 and comments p. 34.

The events narrated by John of Ephesus[50] have been discussed at length by MONNERET DE VILLARD[51], KIRWAN[52], VANTINI[53], and others; and, similarly, the contribution of John of Biclarum[54], Eutychius and Maqrizi (see below) on the melkite side. Most authorities assume that John of Biclarum referred to the Nubian kingdom of Makoria when he mentioned the Maccuritae (I: 1). Their presents to Justin II in 573, elephant tusks and a giraffe, are not unlikely gifts from a king of one of the Nubian states; the Nubian king Shakenda, for example, later agreed to send elephants and giraffes among his tribute to Egypt[55]. The 'orthodox' Emperor Justin II's reception of the Maccuritae's embassy is cited by MONNERET DE VILLARD[56] as a point towards indicating Makoria's melkite leanings. But, bearing in mind the apposite remark of a seventeenth century historian of the Ethiopian church, Michael GEDDES[57], that "The Popes are civiller to remote Hereticks, than domestick ones", and the apparent illustration of this kind of diplomatic double–standard in the relations of Justin and Justinian with King Kaleb of Aksum at the time of the Himyarite war (IIB: 13–15), Justin II's polite reception of the embassy furnishes no positive proof that it came from a melkite land (see below).

John of Biclarum records the Garamantes, a people of modern Libya, as having adopted Christianity in the third year of Justin II, 568–9. But Kosmas Indikopleustes[58], writing around 549, already mentions the flourishing state of Christianity in various lands, including those of the Nobadae and the Garamantes.[59] VANTINI[60] regards these remarks as "somewhat exaggerated" from the Nubian point–of–view, but Kosmas seems to have selected those particular peoples for specific mention. He had perhaps heard enthusiastic accounts of the work of Julian and Theodore of Philae from 543 onwards in

50 John of Ephesus, *op. cit.*, trans. PAYNE-SMITH, p. 250f and 314f; BROOKS, *op. cit.* (n.39), CSCO 106, p. 136f, p. 175f

51 MONNERET DE VILLARD, Storia, p. 63f.

52 L.P KIRWAN, *A Contemporary Account of the Conversion of the Sudan to Christianity*, SNR XX, 1937, pp. 289ff; GADALLAH, *op. cit.*, pp. 38ff.

53 VANTINI, Faras, pp. 53ff and *loc. var.*

54 MOMMSEN, ed., *op. cit.*, pp. 212-13.

55 Maqrizi, in VANTINI, OS, p. 649; QUATREMÈRE, Mémoires , II, p. 98.

56 MONNERET DE VILLARD, Storia, p. 66.

57 M. GEDDES, The Church-History of Ethiopia, London 1646, p. 289.

58 "Cosmae Indicopleustae Topographiae Christianae", Lib. III, PG LXXXVIII, col. 169.

59 L.P. KIRWAN, *Christianity and the Kura'an*, JEA XX, 1934, pp. 201-3.

60 VANTINI, Faras, p. 57.

Nobatia, and, we may guess, similar accounts from missions to the Garamantes. Though John of Biclarum stated that the Garamantes and Maccuritae received the Christian faith, this does not necessarily imply that he was aware of the exact circumstances. He may have merely assumed that they had been converted by melkite missionaries. However, MONNERET DE VILLARD and VANTINI both take him to mean the melkite faith, and if the Garamantes applied to the Roman/Byzantine authorities for their teachers in the Christian religion, it is likely that this interpretation is correct. The Garamantes and the Maccuritae are mentioned in such close apposition that it may be valid to assume that what is true for the one is also true for the other.

From the point–of–view of the Nobatae (Nobadae), John of Ephesus[61] commented;

> Longinus prevailed upon the king of that people (Nobadae) to send an ambassador to the king of the Romans with presents and gifts of honour, and on his arrival, he had an audience, and was honourably received in the presence of myself (John of Ephesus) and the rest of the court.

Emperor Justin II, then, received the Nobadae, in spite of his personal dislike of Longinus, with as equable a face as he received the apparently melkite Maccuritae. He was evidently not blind to the advantages of peace in the regions to the south of Egypt, regardless of the violence he showed towards monophysitism in his own dominions after the failure of his attempt to regulate matters in the church by his Edict of Union.

Eutychius – whose information was repeated later by al–Maqrizi[62] – was as likely to be biased as the monophysite John of Ephesus, since he served as melkite patriarch of Alexandria from 933–939. His testimony is also some centuries later than that of John of Ephesus and John of Biclarum. Nevertheless Eutychius' argument that the lack of melkite patriarchs in Egypt gave the monophysites there the chance to gain the right to appoint to the Nubian bishoprics is plausible. In the difficult state of dependence on a foreign patriarch as the source for their ecclesiastical nominations, the Nubians could have had some considerable trouble in obtaining bishops, and been driven to seek where they could. An instance of this for Nubia is related in the *Life of Isaac*.[63] A much later instance is

---

61 PAYNE-SMITH, *op. cit.*, pp. 256-7.

62 "Eutychii Patriarchae Alexandrini Annales", PG CXI, 1122-3; H.F. WÜSTENFELD, Macrizi's Geschichte der Kopten, Gottingen 1845, p. 57; both of these are quoted in full, in Latin, in KIRWAN, Firka, p. 49.

63 E. PORCHER, *Vie d'Isaac, Patriarche d'Alexandrie de 686-689*, PO XI, fasc. 3, pp. 377ff.

recorded by Francisco ALVARES[64], concerning a plea submitted to the then king of Ethiopia, Lebna Dengel, for priests and bishops; "While we were in the country of the Prester John there came six men from that country [of the Nobiis] as Ambassadors to the Prester, begging him to send them priests and monks to teach them. He did not choose to send them; and it was said that he said to them that he had his Abima [*abun*] from the country of the Moors, that is to say from the Patriarch of Alexandria, who is under the rule of the Moors; how then could he give priests and monks since another gave them to him". In the opinion of Fr. Giacomo RZIMARZ[65] in 1742, it was the final inability to find any priests that destroyed the Nubian church; "For why did Nubia depart from the faith of Christ? Solely through lack of pastors". It is this same argument of lack of melkites in Alexandria that TELLES (see above) adduced for the rise of the monophysite supremacy in Ethiopia. Patriarch Joseph's phrase[66] "If the shepherds be not many to guard the flock, the sheep will perish" shows that the Coptic patriarchate of Alexandria also fully understood this problem.

As well as al–Mas'udi and the patriarchal biographers, several other writers in Arabic testify to the later presence of the Jacobite faith in Nubia. Ibn al–Faqih al–Hamadhani, c. 902 AD, declared that "the Nuba are Jacobites"[67], "they are Jacobite Christians who read the gospel without understanding". Al–Mas'udi himself also confirms that "The Copts of Egypt, with the exception of some who are Melkites, the Nubians, and the Armenians too, are Jacobites".[68] He was writing at just about the time of the death of Eutychius, which seems to imply that the melkite claim of this patriarch, as mentioned later by Yusuf the Egyptian (I:5), to the control of metropolitanates in Ethiopia and Nubia, was largely speculative. That the claim for Nubia and al–Maris was revived after a long gap, Eutychius admits; but when the claim for al–Habasha was first instituted cannot be said. However, it may be that Eutychius had hopes of bringing Ethiopia into his communion, since the affair of the Metropolitan Peter (III: 29) had left the metropolitanate in the hands of Peter's uncanonical successor by royal appointment; current relations with the Alexandrian monophysite patriarchate were cold, indeed, apparently completely frozen. Nevertheless, about

64 F. ALVARES, The Prester John of the Indies, the translation of Lord STANLEY of Alderley (1881) revised and ed. by C.F. BECKINGHAM, and C.W.B. HUNTINGFORD, ch. CXXXVIII, p. 461 VANTINI, Faras, pp. 137-8.

65 VANTINI, Faras, p.14.

66 PO X, p. 512

67 VANTINI, OS, p. 91

68 *Ibid.*, p. 126.

forty years later, probably in the 980s, when the king of Ethiopia eventually decided to send for a metropolitan (IV: 30), it was through the Nubian king Girgis (George) II that he did so. His letter, as copied in Patriarch Philotheus' biography, seems to indicate quite clearly that both Girgis II and the Ethiopian king recognised Philotheus as their spiritual father.

The patriarchal biographies mention Nubia and its monophysite connexions during the same 11th–12th century period when VANTINI[69] asserts that there was a restoration of the melkite communion at Pachoras (Faras), capital of Nobatia/al–Maris in later times. Early in the episcopate of Patriarch Christodoulos (1047–1077), we learn that "the first (trial) which came upon the father, the patriarch, (was) that a calumnious report was written about him to the wazir al–Yazuri (1047–58), that he (Christodoulos) had forbidden the king of Nubia to send the offering"[70]. This was during the incumbency of Bishop Merkurios of Pachoras (1036–56), the third of those bishops whom VANTINI asserted were melkites (see below). It is however evident that the contemporary Egyptian government still believed that the monophysite patriarchs were in control of the Nubian church; a control which continued, since Bishop George of Batu (Natu) later consecrated a church in Nubia, having been sent there by Christodoulos around 1070[71]. The correspondence between Egypt and Nubia over Metropolitan Victor in the time of Patriarch Cyril II (1078–1092) is also well known (V: 38).

Arab writers, though often merely copyists of earlier information, continue to refer to the Nubians as monophysites. Al–Dimishqi, d. 1327, commented[72] that "the Nubians are Jacobite Christians", adding that they "read the Gospel in Greek, according to the Melkite rite *(al–Malkaniyya)*. They have ancient Greek churches". Even al–Bakuwi, d. 1413, calls the inhabitants of Dunqala Jacobite Christians, but he is quoting from al–Qazwini, d. 1274.[73]

Al–Mas'udi further adds;

> The Jacobites have only two seats *(kursiyani)*, not more; one is that of Antioch, and the other that of Misr. The doctrine which predominates among the Christians in Misr is that of the Copts *(aqbat)*; more are found in Fustat and in its other districts and in the adjoining land of Nubia; and in the (country of the) Ahbash; it is the doctrine *(ra'i)* of the Jacobites *(al–ya'qubiyya)*.[74]

---

69 VANTINI, Faras, pp. 225-6.
70 "History of the Patriarchs", II, III, p. 263.
71 *Ibid.*, p. 281.
72 VANTINI, OS, p. 457.
73 *Ibid.*, pp. 566 and 385.
74 *Ibid.*, p. 139.

Finally, there is the brief comment by Yaqut, d. 1229, that "The Nuba are Jacobite Christians (*nasara ya'aqiba*)."[75]

Clearly the literary sources for the period of the actual conversion of Nubia are equivocal. The inscriptional evidence has some importance here. Study by JUNKER[76] and others of the funerary formulae used on Nubian tombstones, a category of object sadly almost unknown for Christian Ethiopians, has shown that use of the Byzantine–style 'Euchologion Mega' formula occurred both early, at the end of the eighth century, and later at the beginning of the eleventh century, in Christian Nubia. Some scholars hold that this usage represents an early influence of the Byzantine belief, with a later revival of the same. The lack of the 'Euchologion Mega' formula on Coptic tombstones, the relative rarity of Coptic, together with the translation of Old Nubian books from Greek rather than Coptic are supposed to mark a primarily Greek, and therefore Byzantine, influence in Nubian ecclesiastical affairs. But archaeology is providing more and more instances of the importance of Coptic in Nubia (the foundation stones of Bishop Paulos at Faras, and a number of Coptic letters from Ibrim, are examples). The international position of Greek somewhat earlier may have favoured its adoption quite apart from the religious corollary of melkite influence. The Nubian court used Byzantine–style titles from at least the eighth century, and Nubian royal and other inscriptions were sometimes written in Greek – as were Aksumite inscriptions rather earlier, and the legends on Aksumite coinage until the seventh century.

Architecturally, the Nubian churches were apparently not of the Egyptian style, but rather after Byzantine originals in Syria and Palestine, according to VANTINI.[77] The same has often been stated about Ethiopian churches, but attributed rather to the importation of the style by monophysite exiles like the Nine Saints (see II: 12 below) fleeing the persecutions of the 'orthodox' party in the church, than to melkite influence. Certain churches at Adulis may even have been built, or at least partly furnished, under Byzantine auspices, but still without any assumption that

---

75 *Ibid.*, p. 346.

76 H. JUNKER, *Die Christliche Grabsteine Nubiens*, ZÄS, 60, 1925, pp. 11-148. J. OATES, *A Christian Inscription in Greek from Arminna in Nubia*, JEA, 49, 1963, pp. 161-71. See also S. JAKOBIELSKI, Faras III, pp. 71-2 and *loc. var.*; VANTINI, Faras, *loc. var*; J.W.B. BARNES, *Christian Monuments from Nubia*, Kush II, 1954, pp. 26-32.

77 VANTINI, Faras, p. 178; W.Y. ADAMS, *Architectural Evolution of the Nubian Church*, JARCE IV, 1965.

they were for melkite congregations.[78] Political advantage was also involved in the conversion of new lands to different aspects of the Christian faith in the period in question. Makoria, at enmity with its northern and southern neighbours, may have considered it advisable when it saw those neighbours allying with the party of Emrpess Theodora and Egyptian monophysitism, to seek association with the melkites and Justinian. For their part, the emperors may have hoped that the newly–Christianised nations would fall to some degree into the Romano–Byzantine sphere of influence, promoting peaceful relations on the fringes of the empire instead of the raiding which, in spite of the Roman subsidies, was still perpetrated by the Nobatae and Blemmyes in Justinian's day, as Procopius relates[79]. For the local kings, anxious perhaps to gain the advantages offered by a conversion which meant the favour of the empire, the thornier problems of which aspect of the faith to select to fit with imperial policy may only have became obvious later; for Ethiopia this happened as early as the Arianism of Constantius II in the mid–fourth century, and for the Nubian kingdoms with the increasingly anti–monophysite policy of the emperors in the later sixth century. Nubia, or at least the two kingdoms of Nobatia and Alodia, even began its monophysite adherence irregularly, under Theodore, a monophysite anti–patriarch elected by Longinus and others around 575.

That in due course the Nubians obeyed the monophysite patriarch of Alexandria is, as we have noted, well established. It is clearly indicated by various accounts of the relations between the patriarchate and the kings, for example the story of Patriarch Isaac and the letters from Makoria (III: 21), John the Deacon's record of Nubia in the time of Patriarch Michael I (III: 23a), the letter to Patriarch Mark III[80] from the rulers of Nubia (VI: 52), and al–Mas'udi's mention of Jacobite influence in the time of a Nubian ruler he calls Kabil (Kubri) ibn Surur[81].

Evidence for a melkite claim to a metropolitanate in Nubia in 1316, with a bishopric in Maris, comes from Yusuf the Egyptian[82], apparently based on Eutychius (I: 5). Discussion of the various points in favour of a

---

[78] D. BUXTON, The Abyssinians, 1970, p. 97; S.C.H. MUNRO-HAY, *The British Museum Excavations at Adulis, 1868*, The Antiquaries Journal LXIX, 1989, pp. 43-52.
[79] H.B. DEWING, trans., "De Bello Persico", Loeb ed., 1914, p. 187.
[80] J.M. PLUMLEY, *Qasr Ibrim 1974*, JEA 61, 1975, p. 7.
[81] VANTINI, OS, p. 130.
[82] *Ibid.*, pp. 450-1.

melkite supremacy in Nubia in the 11th–12th century has become rather complicated, and has had uncertain results. The arguments are summarised here, since it is of some importance to establish the position of Nubia, Ethiopia's nearest Christian neighbour, at this period.

VANTINI[83] identifies five bishops as melkites, Johannes III (997–1005), Marianos (1005–1036), Merkurios (1036–1056), Petros II (1058–1062), and Georgios (1062–1097); he does not specify the particular belief of Chael II (c.1097 - 1125/30) and Jesu II (c.1125/30 - 1170/75). JAKOBIELSKI[84] however, believes that whilst the bishops from Johannes III to Merkurios were melkite, there was a restoration of the monophysites under Petros II and Georgios, but that Chael II and Jesu were also melkites. These attributions are based on comparison of paintings – both portraits and other themes – the stelae, and the literary and textual evidence. The presence of (apparently) rather un–monophysite iconography in the paintings (the virgin 'galaktotrophousa' and 'eleousa'), as well as the lack of a sort of head–covering called the *shamla* on certain of the portraits, has been adduced as evidence for the presence of the melkite rite. The use of the title 'orthodox', which VANTINI mentions for the bishops Marianos, Merkurios and Petros II – this last is not in fact certain, but likely[85] – from 1005–1062 is taken to be a sign of melkite influence, the title "metropolitan" being, he notes, "a purely Coptic title".[86] Marianos and Merkurios are linked with Johannes because they are both called "(spiritual) son of Abba Johannes, bishop of Pachoras". The phrase occurs in a note by the portrait inscription of Marianos, and on the list of bishops for Merkurios.[87]

However, apart from doubt as to whether the title of metropolitan may be regarded as a purely Coptic one – considering the list of Yusuf (I: 5), and a report that four bishoprics were raised to the rank of metropolitanates in Egypt by the melkites about the time of Patriarch Joseph[88] – there is other evidence which seems to make the contrasting of monophysite 'metropolitan' and melkite 'orthodox' unlikely. First, Aaron (952–972), who is called on his funerary stela 'bishop of the Metropolis of Pachoras'[89] also appears as an 'orthodox' bishop.[90] Second, the study of

---

83 VANTINI, Faras, p. 222.
84 Discussed at length in the appropriate chapters of Faras III, pp. 140ff.
85 See the portrait of Petros, and its legend; JAKOBIELSKI, Faras III, p. 153.
86 VANTINI, Faras, p. 189.
87 JAKOBIELSKI, Faras III, p. 145.
88 BUTCHER, op. cit., vol. I, p. 445, note.
89 JAKOBIELSKI, *Faras III*, p. 121, line 8 of stela.
90 *Ibid.*, p. 125.

the tombstones for the presence of the 'Euchologion Mega' formula, which is JAKOBIELSKI's key to identification of the owners as melkite or monophysite, does indeed show that those bishops of Pachoras called metropolitans (that is, possibly Kolluthos (903–923)[91], and certainly Stephanos (923–926), Aaron (952–972), and Petros I, (972–999) all have funerary stelae with primarily monophysite formulae, in Greek for Kolluthos and Stephanos, Coptic for the other two. But the two 'orthodox' bishops Petros II (1056–1062), and Georgios (1062–1092), also have monophysite texts in Coptic on their stelae. Bishops Kyros (866–902) – whose stela has not been found – Petros I, and Georgios wear the *shamla,* whereas Marianos does not. Marianos, like Johannes III, uses the 'Euchologion Mega' in Greek. Clearly the evidence is equivocal, and the use of certain formulae or iconographic details in Nubia is not yet well–enough documented to employ as proof for a melkite presence.

Although JAKOBIELSKI brought a stronger case for melkite incumbents at Faras than that of VANTINI, it is still far from convincing. VANTINI did add the interesting observation that the reigns of the Nubian rulers Zacharias III and George II, both praised by the monophysites for their faith, would coincide with his 'monophysite' metropolitans at Faras, whilst the melkites' rise to favour in Egypt under the Fatimid caliph al–Hakim (996–1021) would be paralleled by the change from a metropolitanate there. The overlap between the episcopates of Petros I, who died in 999 and Johannes III, bishop in 997, could indicate simultaneous occupancy by bishops of both persuasions. However, this may only mean that Petros resigned his functions to Johannes, since he was over ninety years old at the time. The discrepancy which appears at this point between the list and the stela was probably caused by inaccuracy in the records, the list being compiled by someone who knew Petros' enthronement and death dates, but did not know that he had retired two years or so before his death, hence the figure of (probably) 25 years in the list.[92]

That 'orthodox' need not mean 'melkite', is shown by the frequent use of the word by Severus ibn al–Muqaffa in reference to persons certainly or probably monophysite. It is hardly necessary to point out that both sides in the dispute held that their own party represented 'orthodoxy', and the word was used tendentiously. For example, the arrival of the Armenian patriarch in the time of Patriarch Cyril II is recorded by Severus' continuator Mawhub ibn Muffarij al–Iskandarani, who notes the:

---

91 *Ibid.*, p. 104.
92 *Ibid.*, p. 138.

> Orthodox upright Faith which is our Faith, (we) the company of the Jacobites *(Ya'akibah).*

He adds;

> and was made known that day the genuineness of the agreement of the Copts *(al-Kibt)* and the Armenians *(al-Arman)* and the Syrians *(al-Suryan)* and the Abyssinians *(al-Habashah)* and the Nubians (*al-Nubah*) on the Orthodox upright Faith on which the saintly, virtuous, fathers agreed, and with which Nestorius *(Nastur)* and Leo *(Lawun)* and the Council of Chalcedon *(Khalkuduniah)* disagreed.[93]

It would seem that this is a direct quote as the first person is employed, and the copyist of the manuscript, Yuhanna ibn Sa'id ibn Yahya ibn Mina, called Ibn al-Kulzumi, notes his own interpolations diligently.[94] Cyril II was patriarch from 1078–1092, that is, during the 'orthodox' Bishop Georgios' time (1062–97), last of those so entitled; this if anything supports JAKOBIELSKI's view rather than VANTINI's.

Under the patriarchate of Christodoulos, Cyril II's predecessor, Nubian monophysite interest is also confirmed. A certain Victor (see V: 39) was sent as metropolitan to Nubia by Christodoulos[95] We thus have evidence for a monophysite metropolitan in Nubia during the vizirate of Badr al-Jamali (1073–94) and the patriarchate of Christodoulos (1047–1077). Victor was therefore metropolitan bishop in Nubia after 1073, a contemporary of the 'orthodox' bishop Georgios (1062–1097), who has no special title beyond bishop of Pachoras.

Another incident illustrating the close ecclesiastical connexions between Nubia and the monophysite patriarchate of Alexandria during the time of Cyril II and the 'orthodox' Georgios, was the arrival of messengers from King Basil of Nubia. This king was the nephew of his predecessor, probably to be identified as King George, nephew of King Solomon. The son of the late king was to be made a bishop since the matriarchal system of inheritance prevented his succession to the throne, which customarily went to the late king's nephew. QUATREMÈRE[96] translated the term *usquf* here as 'metropolitan', though in general Severus of Ashmunein seems to use *mutran* if he means that. A further suggestion[97] that the cousin of

---

93 "History of the Patriarchs", II, III, pp. 345-6.
94 *ibid.*, pp. 365, 369.
95 *ibid.*, p. 316.
96 QUATREMÈRE, Mémoires, II, p. 89.
97 AL-HAJJ HAMAD MUHAMMAD KHEIR, unpubl. M.A. Thesis, Univ. of Khartoum.

Basil took the chief ecclesiastical place in the hierarchy of Nubia, is based on a study of the succession system. To avoid friction, the religious and secular authority would be shared; the metropolitans would be appointed from among the sons of the preceding king. The arrival of the Nubian prince in Egypt may indicate, in spite of the word *usquf*, that he was to be the next metropolitan, since otherwise the metropolitan currently in office, who had the right to consecrate bishops, could have consecrated him. However, it may be that for royal bishops an exception was made.

GRIFFITH[98] records a document from Nauri, of c. 1080, mentioning a King Basil, and Simeon, *papas* (metropolitan?) of Sai. If Severus of Ashmunein and this document both refer, as seems certain, to the same King Basil, it may well be that Simeon was George's son, and the royal bishop. The metropolitan seat, if there was only one in Nubia, would have shifted from Faras, perhaps on Petros I's death in 999.

The metropolitans in Nubia may not necessarily have been incumbents of a particular see. It seems that at times the metropolitanate was held by the successive bishops of one see, after which it was shifted to another. The Aksum–Adafa shift in Ethiopia was another example of this (VI: 56). As noted above, it is not clear whether the monophysites appointed metropolitans to Nobatia (Maris) as a separate kingdom after the unification of Nobatia and Makoria, or whether they merely sent one metropolitan for the entire kingdom. The latter seems implied by the records, in particular the report of Severus of Ashmunein in the biography of Patriarch Michael I,[99] concerning Bishop Cyriacus and his successor John. It is uncertain to which see they were appointed, as the text simply states "the city of the king". Dongola comes immediately to mind from the context, though one might recall that Ibn Salim al-Aswani,[100] writing as late as 975–996, refers to Bedjrash (Pachoras/Faras) as the "city of their king"

But these prelates may not have been the primates of Nubia, since they are not accorded the title of metropolitan. The trouble over the old Bishop Cyriacus, and the consecration in Egypt of John, selected by King Abraham of Nubia, may not imply, as MONNERET DE VILLARD[101] assumed, that they were metropolitans needing patriarchal consecration, but that the special requirement for the excommunication of Cyriacus needed the patri-

98 GRIFFITH, *op. cit.*, pp. 13, 17.
99 PO V, fasc. I, pp. 141-3.
100 Ibn Salim (Sulaym) al-Aswani preserved in Maqrizi's "Khitat"; VANTINI, OS, p. 609; See also BURCKHARDT, Travels, App. III, p. 452.
101 MONNERET DE VILLARD, Storia, p. 97.

arch's intervention. In King Kyriakos' reign soon after, a certain Kyri–Nosk (?) is called 'episkopos', which GRIFFITH[102] translated as "metropolitan bishop". MONNERET DE VILLARD assumed that Kyri–Nosk was bishop of Dongola[103], and it seems that Faras at this time was not a metropolitan seat.

The later history of the Nubian metropolitanate and the bishopric of Faras is shadowy. Though we may assume that the *papas* of Sai was the Nubian metropolitan in the time of Basil and Bishop Georgios of Pachoras (1062–97), even so the bishopric of Pachoras continued until the death of Jesu II in 1170's, according to the list, and on to at least 1372. By this date, a consecration document indicates that the office was combined with Ibrim (in the Arabic text, Ibrim is always written in above Bakhiras or Pachoras), Timothy being consecrated by Gabriel IV of Alexandria on 15th February 1372 to succeed Athanasios as bishop of both places.[104] The consecration documents found in Bishop Timothy's tomb are interesting; they state that Timotheos was a Nubian by birth. They also include references to the jurisdiction of the patriarch. The Coptic text calls him "archbishop of the great city of Rakoti (Alexandria) and Babylon and its territories and Nubia and the Ethiopians (*niethaush* – "probably here a reference to the inhabitants of modern Ethiopia", according to PLUMLEY) and those which are theirs". The witnesses signatures are even more interesting, in that both Mark, bishop of Kebto, and Athanasios of Kosberbir refer to the Ethiopian part of the titulary as ΞΟΜΙΤΗϹ ΚΕΘΕΟΠΙΑϹ, using the ancient name of the capital Aksum. The Arabic text, as expected, uses al–Habasha. KRALL[105], after BONJOUR, notes part of the Coptic version of the patriarchal title as *nieksomides nem nouthosh terou,* "the Aksumites with all the Ethiopians".

[102] GRIFFITH, *op. cit.*, p. 14.

[103] MONNERET DE VILLARD, Storia, p. 163.

[104] The actual deeds of consecration, buried with the deceased bishop, have been preserved; J. M. PLUMLEY, *The Scrolls of Bishop Timotheos: Two Documents from Medieval Nubia*, London 1975, pp. 15, 18, 21-2 & *loc. var.*; ID., *Qasr Ibrim 1966*, JEA 52, 1966, pp. 3ff.

[105] J. KRALL, *Beiträge zur Geschichte der Blemyer und Nubier*, Denkschriften der Kaiserlichen Akademie der Wissenschaften, (Phil-Hist. Classe), Band 46, Vienna 1900, IV, pp. 1-26; p. 16, n. 3; quoting BONJOUR's Monumenta coptica seu aegyptiaca bibliothecae vaticanae brevis exercitatio, Rome 1699, S.11.

During the period of the decline of the Dongola kingdom, other references to bishops appear. A document of Moses George (c.1144–1199), ruler of the apparently newly–formed northern Nubian state of Dotawo, calls him 'nephew of David who was king', perhaps the same David referred to in an undated document mentioning Bishop Khael (Chael) of Phrim (Ibrim), and *papas* Shenoute.[106] From 1097 to c .1125/30 Khael II was bishop of Pachoras. Perhaps he, and his successors at Pachoras were, like Timothy, also bishops of Ibrim? In any event, Shenoute's see must have been elsewhere, perhaps at Sai like Simeon? Another bishopric, Silim, which occurs in Old Nubian documents from Qasr Ibrim, must also have been of some importance at this time.[107]

In 1287, under King George Simon, Kosmas was *papas,* with no seat specified. Much later in 1464, under Joel, 'king of kings of Dotawo', mention is made of Merkos, *papas* of Ibrim, and again in 1484, of Merki, bishop of Ibrim. To conclude, as far as we can distinguish, political exigencies seem to have wrested the primacy from Pachoras, possibly after the last attested metropolitan, Petros I, transferring it to Sai, perhaps under Victor, elevated around 1073–1077. Here it remained (assuming after PLUMLEY that *papas* indicates metropolitan) during the episcopate of Simeon, perhaps Shenoute, and doubtless others like Kosmas. During this period the bishopric of Ibrim absorbed the ancient metropolitan seat of Pachoras to eventually became the seat of the *papas,* as testified by the documents of Joel of Dotawo.[108]

---

[106] J.M. PLUMLEY, *The Christian Period at Qasr Ibrim; Some Notes on MSS Finds*, in: Nubia: Récentes recherches, K. MICHAŁOWSKI, ed., Warsaw 1975. pp. 101-7 see esp. p. 106.

[107] I am indebted for this information to Ustaz ALI OSMAN, of the Dept. of Archaeology, Univ. of Khartoum.

[108] S.C. MUNRO-HAY, *Kings and Kingdoms of Ancient Nubia*, RSE XXIX, 1982-3, pp. 87-137, attempts to chart the chronology of the Nubian monarchy from the end of the Meroitic period to the eclipse of Christianity.

4. The Metropolitans of Ethiopia

The metropolitan bishops occupied a uniquely difficult post in the Ethiopian church, a strange combination of problems and privilege. The rules formulated by the pseudo–canon of Nicaea (I: 2) for the appointment of this prelate, under the influence of the Alexandrian patriarchate, emphasised that he must be an Egyptian, or at least not an Ethiopian. Thus, upon selection and consecration, a new metropolitan had to undertake a long journey, very dangerous at times, before he even reached his future diocese. The reports of the lives of these metropolitans from the *History of the Patriarchs* is naturally biased towards Alexandria; a less sympathetic view, indeed a view with an emphatic bias in the opposite direction, can be obtained from some modern critics of the system such as Ayele Teklahaymanot and Isaac.[109]

Once arrived in Ethiopia, though according to some accounts his reception seems to have been distinguished by great honours, the newly–elevated monk had to tread extremely carefully. Court intrigues or the over–zealous practice of admonitions to the king caused the fall from favour of some of the metropolitans. Others appear to have ill–understood that the Egyptian sultans were no longer their masters, and that neither the king nor the people of Ethiopia would tolerate interference on behalf of the Muslims; though of course the Ethiopian kings themselves had to bear in mind that the future episcopal succession depended in some considerable measure on the Muslim rulers' good will. The Ethiopian sovereign remained master in his own country; the metropolitans had not the rank to overawe the king as a patriarch claiming apostolic succession might.

It seems from the later accounts of the Portuguese Catholic priests, that the metropolitans were not much distinguished for their learning either. Only with Salama III 'the interpreter', 1348–88, do we find a scholar recorded as metropolitan. Though of course we know very little of the attainments of earlier metropolitans, almost no details about them having survived, few seem to have gone down in Ge'ez records for anything remarkable. Only a few homilies survive, attributed to certain among them, preserved in the Ge'ez religious literature.

The newly–arrived metropolitan probably had only the vaguest idea – if any at all – about the customs of the country which was to be in his spiritual care in the future. The communication of the head of the church with his officers must frequently have been only through such channels as

---

[109] Ayele Teklahaymanot, *Egyptian Metropolitans*; Isaac, *Ethiopian Church*.

the *qala–pappas,* the metropolitan's spokesman or interpreter, as any acquaintance with the local languages of Ethiopia, at least in the early stages of each episcopate, is improbable. From later Portuguese writings, we learn that even after years in the country – fifty years according to the Metropolitan Mark – a metropolitan could, during an ordination ceremony, make a speech in Arabic from his mule, which had to be translated to the crowds by his *qala–pappas*[110].

Often the political situation in the country must have been highly disorienting for the newly–arrived prelate. Though the metropolitan found himself in a Christian country, where his position ranked as the highest in a venerated and influential church, the royal power remained supreme. Very likely from Aksumite times onwards there was some sort of local ecclesiastical organisation. Probably it was led by the equivalent of the high officials mentioned in later documents, such as the *abun* 's immediate next in rank, the *echage,* the monastic head of the country, or his deputy the *liqa–kahenat,* controller of the secular priests, or the *'aqabe sa'at,* literally 'Guardian of the Hours', the chief ecclesiastic at court and third in rank after the *abun*. Such ecclesiastical officials, natives of the country, would have dealt with the day to day administration of the church. They, with the king, must have controlled church affairs after the death of the incumbent metropolitan until the arrival of the next, and even then the day to day administration must have continued chiefly in their hands and those of any assistant bishops who might have been in the country at the time.

Possibly resentment towards new metropolitans from such native ecclesiastics made the position of the former even more uncertain. Some metropolitans may have become rather unpopular with the people in general, with whom communication must have been difficult. Not one Egyptian–appointed metropolitan – excluding the Syrian Greek Frumentius – is included in the hagiographies among the local or foreign sanctified kings, martyrs and monks whose stories fill their pages. On the contrary, some of the Ethiopian holy men are recorded as having had to admonish contemporary metropolitans for simony; the Ethiopic hagiographies assert that both Libanos and Basalota–Mika'el were exiled for their temerity in such matters (IIB: 16; VII: 67). While some of the metropolitans may have been good men, and acted to the best of their ability in the difficult circumstances, others evidently regarded the sudden elevation to the primacy of a national church as the opportunity to amass wealth.

---

110 ALVARES, *op. cit.*, II, p. 350.

David MATHEW commented that the Egyptian metropolitans, "consecrated to what would prove a life–long exile...always remained in thought and speech a foreigner...at the period of his greatest influence the *abuna* was an object of reverence, anxiety and an unfatigued suspicion".[111] MATHEW also noted a remark made by King Tekla Haymanot II in 1770 through his *qala–atse,* or spokesman, and recorded by James BRUCE. It is revealing in a number of aspects. During the trial of the *'aqabe sa'at* Abba Salama, King Tekla Haymanot conveyed the message that "The king requires of you to answer directly, why you persuaded the Abuna to excommunicate him? The Abuna is a slave of the Turks, and has no king; you are born under a monarchy; why did you, who are his inferior in office, take upon you to advise him at all? or why, after having presumed to advise him, did you advise him wrong, and abuse his ignorance in these matters?" MATHEW interpreted this as a "glimpse of the age–old feeling against the metropolitans come out of Egypt", and indeed, much earlier the hagiographers' records of the simonical practices of certain metropolitans in the days of Abba Libanos and Basalota–Mika'el does seem to confirm that there was unfavourable feeling towards some of them. It was almost inevitable under the circumstances. The incident in Tekla Haymanot II's reign, when the metropolitan had favoured or been made to favour another pretender, in some ways recalls the quandary of the Metropolitan Peter, (III: 29) who similarly had to choose between two claimants, suffering deposition and exile as a result.

REY[112] and others had a rather different view of the situation with regard to the Egyptian church and the bishops of Ethiopia. REY considered that

> the practice of importing a Copt as Abuna is stated to have been introduced by the great Abyssinian ecclesiastic Tekla Haymanot as part of the arrangements made on the restoration of the Solomonean dynasty. The reason for this was twofold, partly in order to maintain a link with the outside world, and partly in order to avoid the discords that would undoubtedly have been caused by the election to the headship of the church of a native of the country – the intrigue and rivalry would have been immense. It may also be surmised that Tekla Haymanot was shrewd enough to see that a foreign Abuna would be far more likely to be able to maintain an independent position than a native, who would most probably have been a creature of the king.

[111] D. MATHEW, Ethiopia. The Study of a Polity, London 1947, pp. 12, 94.
[112] C.F. REY, The Romance of the Portuguese in Abyssinia, London 1929, pp. 114-5.

Aside from the question of Tekla–Haymanot's role in instituting the system (VII: 66), there is certainly some truth in the idea that the metropolitan could, in some situations, maintain an independent position when ecclesiastical problems arose. Thus the Metropolitan Michael Habib al–Atfihi refused to consecrate bishops on the demand of the Ethiopian king without permission from his patriarch in Alexandria (V: 44). But it seems that Egyptian metropolitans, although they could in theory protest to their distant chief if pressed, were in real terms in such a remote and unprotected position that they were as much 'creatures of the king' as any native Ethiopian would have been under the same circumstances. In the early fifteenth century the *abuna* Mark, according to ALVARES, felt isolated and unable to even fulfil his spiritual duties towards the King Lebna Dengel; ..."if he had an associate or two, who would help him in speaking the truth, he would free the Prester [Lebna Dengel] from many things and errors, in which he and his people were". He had formerly made an attempt to change some of the Ethiopians erroneous practices, but complaints from the priests had made the king cancel his efforts.[113]

According to Abu Salih[114] the kings were themselves priests, celebrating the liturgy within the sanctuary. But his account is so confused that one cannot be certain where he refers to Abyssinia, or where to Nubia. It appears that he considered that the 'great kings' of Abyssinia (Ethiopia) and Nubia and all the lesser kings were priests. Much later, TELLES[115] describes the kings of Ethiopia as deacons. TADDESSE TAMRAT[116] considered that the only priest–king who could safely be so designated was the Zagwé dynasty ruler Yimreha Kristos, who continued to celebrate mass after his coronation.

LUDOLF[117] comments on the royal influence in ecclesiastical affairs, adding that the secular power was paramount; secular judges were superior to ecclesiastics. Royal authority and governance of the church is clearly illustrated in many instances; conversely, ecclesiastical writers lay emphasis on the royal repentance for anti–ecclesiastical acts wherever possible, as for example in the story of the letter sent by a king of Ethiopia to Girgis II of Nubia (IV: 30). Despite the royal supremacy, it is perhaps not surpris-

---

113 ALVARES, *op. cit.*, II, pp. 349, 357-8.

114 ABU SALIH, *op. cit.*, Fol. 105b, p. 286.

115 B. TELLES, The Travels of the Jesuits in Ethiopia, London, 1710, p. 52.

116 TADDESSE TAMRAT, Church and State, p. 58 n. 1.

117 LUDOLF, Job, History of Ethiopia, London, 1684, p. 305 for the king as supreme power in ecclesiastical affairs; also pp. 198ff, where the comment is made that the Patriarch of Alexandria is not consulted either, not true of earlier times.

ing that, coming from a land where the church was suppressed or at best subordinate, some metropolitans presumed on their authority as Christian leaders in a Christian country, overreached themselves, and were punished accordingly.

The process of acquiring a new metropolitan, according to al–'Umari (VII: 65) was humiliating for the king, as far as his correspondence with the Egyptian sultans was concerned. It was also, probably, expensive, as both the Egyptian ruler and the patriarch were traditionally in receipt of gifts from the Ethiopian sovereigns when a new metropolitan was required. But it had its advantages from these monarchs' point–of–view, in that the Egyptian monks whom custom decreed for Ethiopia would need to be exceptionally strong and energetic characters to interfere in the politics of the country. When they possessed authority for political acts, as in the case of Metropolitan Peter (III: 29), it was deliberately bestowed by the king, and was not by right.

Glimpses of the functions of the *abun's* come from a number of sources, but inevitably the more detailed ones are the later ones. Though we might very well expect that their activities as recorded by ALVARES and others from the early sixteenth century onwards reflect the activities of earlier metropolitans, there may have been some changes from time to time, the result of reforms or of altering customs or even simply of the level of respect or reverence accorded to individual metropolitans.

An important ceremony performed by the metropolitan was the coronation of the Ethiopian kings. The first mention of this is in Zagwé times, in the account of Abu Salih (VI: 50), but it may be supposed that the Lasta monarchy continued the customs of Aksum in this respect. At Aksum there are a number of ancient stone thrones and pedestals, one of which was reserved for the metropolitan at the coronation ceremonies there in later times, when rulers such as Zara Ya'qob and Sartsa Dengel revived the custom – though to what extent it was authentically 'Aksumite' is not known. Coronation ceremoniess are recorded in certain Ethiopian royal chronicles and in the various Portuguese accounts about the country. The metropolitan's presence is sometimes mentioned. He was present at the place called *mebtaka fatl*, 'cutting of the cord', where the king was received into Aksum as 'king of Zion', and later in the ceremony, though it is never specifically stated, it was presumably he who anointed the king and performed the tonsuring ceremony. It is mentioned that the *abun* participated in the final blessing of the king. In the account in the chronicle of Sarsa Dengel, however, the metropolitan is never singled out for mention during the ceremony.

Another, and absolutely essential, part of the metropolitans' functions was the conferring of orders. An occasion which ALVARES[118] described involved, he thought, some five to six thousand people to be ordained to the priesthood and to the lesser orders; he was told that this was normal. The 'Abima', as ALVARES always calls Metropolitan Mark, explained that this was necessary as he was old and they did not know when the next metropolitan would come. The country had been twenty–three years without one before him.

Other metropolitans in later times kept some sort of watch over the kings' behaviour. In certain circumstances they even excommunicated or threatened to excommunicate kings, or dissolved the oaths of allegiance – this even happened as late as the reign of Lijj Iyasu early in the twentieth century. But there is no evidence that the earlier metropolitans dared go so far. Metropolitan Severus drew the line at insisting that the king of his time send away his extra wife (V: 40). From the later evidence, excommunication was a dangerous step for the *abun* or any other ecclesiastic who had the temerity to act in such a way. When Anorewos (or Basalota–Mika'el) excommunicated King 'Amda Tseyon for taking his father's concubine, the result was a severe flogging. When the *abuna* Peter excommunicated King Za Dengel (1603–4), and then Susenyos, supporting their rival Jacob, he was killed in the battle that gave Susenyos the victory in 1607. *Abuna* Simon, his successor – and the classic example of an immoral and disloyal Egyptian *abun* – is said to have rebelled against Susenyos and been killed in the very act of excommunicating him by a loyal soldier.

We are fortunate in knowing where many of the metropolitans originally came from; and inevitably, given the system, they were predominantly selected from the great Coptic monasteries such as those of St. Anthony near the Red Sea, and of St. Mercurius (Dayr Anba Makarios) and the Romans (Dayr al–Baramus) in the Wadi al–Natrun (formerly called Scetis or the Wadi Habib). Such an origin (though Dayr Anba Makarios, for example, gave Alexandria numerous patriarchs) may not have been the best to have prepared the chosen monks for the quite different challenges of the metropolitanate of a vast and distant country. Perhaps it is little wonder that some failed to succeed in their new resposibility.

We have one personal description of a metropolitan, the Coptic bishop, Michael of Fuwa, who was, exceptionally, transferred to Ethiopia

[118] ALVARES, *op. cit.*, II, pp. 349-51.

when no suitable monk could be found (VI: 54–5). He was

> a virgin, learned in the Old and New (Testaments), of cheerful countenance, tall of stature, with black eyes, brown in colour with redness, very handsome in appearance, with a lisp in his speech (literally, a bite in his mouth), perfect in his members and his knowledge.

With all these advantages, however, his sojourn in Ethiopia was terminated by his flight to Egypt, where he was deposed for "misuse of his stewardship".[119]

The arrival of an illegally usurping metropolitan appears to have been a perennial threat, hard to prevent if the usurper could forge good enough credentials (eg. III: 29). On occasion, the Egyptian sultans, too, interfered in the appointment of a metropolitan, as in the affair of Severus (V: 39–40), with disastrous results. At other times the sultans favoured the uncanonical demands of the kings against the patriarchs (V: 44).

The metropolitan of Ethiopia was an exile for life. Only those returned who had offended the king, or the queen in the case of Metropolitan John (III: 24), or were unfit for their office, like George (V: 42), or Michael of Fuwa (VI: 55); the latter was formally deposed in Cairo by the patriarch. On the other hand, in an instance like that of the aged Michael, Habib al–Atfihi, the king's wishes were not respected, even under pressure, in the matter of replacement, since the patriarch considered that the right stood on the side of the metropolitan (V: 44). If the metropolitan remained in Ethiopia, it is evident, at least from the time of Metropolitan Michael in the days of King Lalibela, that he led a life by no means bereft of luxuries; a well–appointed residence, slaves, horses and mules, and a high place amongst the great men of the land.

The metropolitan, as a monk, would have been celibate; but although patriarchs, archbishops and bishops were also celibate, unlike the secular priesthood, this state was apparently not always observed by the Egyptian metropolitan after his arrival in Ethiopia. Again, we only have specific information from later times,[120] but some metropolitans, like Simon in the reign of Susenyos, were notorious for their behaviour in this respect. Simon is said to "have lived in open adultery with the wife of an Egyptian domiciled in the country and kept a large harim of native girls. When one of these gave birth to a child the Abuna had it exposed for the

---

119 "History of the Patriarchs", III, III, pp. 185, 192.

120 BRUCE, *op. cit.*, in the summary of the annals of Susenyos; BUDGE, History, II, p. 389; P. CARAMAN, The Lost Empire, London, 1985, pp. 88, 139-40; P. PAIS, História da Etiópia, III, Porto 1946, p. 128.

hyenas to devour". Naturally, this was written by his opponents, but it seems to have been true enough. PAIS lists Metropolitan Simon's "m.tos peccados publicos e cousas que não conuem aos Prelados da Igreja ne aos fieis de Christo", with "having many women, dishonouring maids" and the Egyptian's wife, as the first out of ten heads of criticism including drinking wine, rich clothing and high living. In the extraordinary manifesto issued by King Susenyos at Aksum in 1624, when he gives his reasons for his conversion to Catholicism, he castigates the morals of four successive metropolitans; Mark, Christodoulus, Peter and Simon. "They turned their back on righteousness to pursue paths unworthy of the lesser clergy, let alone bishops and patriarchs, by shamelessly marrying and siring children, whose own children and grandchildren bear witness in Ethiopia to the lust of their fathers. And worse, they were in the habit of deflowering young marriageable girls as well as indulging in other unspeakable iniquities. They would offer to confer Holy Orders and consecrate altars in exchange for gold and salt bars, imposing their rapacious demands on ordinands, forcing them for six months or a whole year to carry water, wood or stone for the construction of their houses and enclosures... The Abuna Peter was convicted of the foulest possible crimes, unmentionable in polite society, for he put himself on a level with those who, lusting after other men's bodies, called down from heaven fire and sulphur... The Abuna Christodoulus was surrounded by troops of concubines, an affair notorious both to his contemporaries and to persons still alive". This state of affairs, though, it seems, the norm in the seventeenth century, may not have been so prevalent a feature during the earlier metropolitanate. We hear of no specific accusations of this sort against the metropolitans of earlier times, though some of those deposed (George, for example; V: 42) may have been guilty of such misbehaviour.

Not much is known about the Ethiopian metropolitans' place of residence. It was probably very much subordinate to the current chosen residence of the king. However, DE CONTENSON noted that "Nazare (ou Nazret) a servi de résidence aux métropolites d'Axoum sous les derniers rois et jusqu'au XI siècle". This information is based on MORDINI's researches at Nazret.[121] MORDINI found, in a small trench which he dug near the church, coins of the Aksumite kings Hataz and Gersem, indicating occupation in late Aksumite times (probably the late sixth to early seventh centuries

121 H. DE CONTENSON, *Principales étapes de l'Ethiopie antique*, Cahiers d'Études Africaines 2, 1961, p. 2; A. MORDINI, *Informazioni preliminari sui resultati delle mie recherche.*, RSE IV, 1944, pp. 145-150. See also FIACCADORI, *op. cit.*, p. 364, n. 38.

according to the latest coin–chronologies). This is one of the most southerly of all Aksumite sites. MORDINI adds that Nazret seems to have been the seat of the metropolitans in the time of Lalibela; he collected a legend that King ʻAmda Tseyon had built the church for an *abuna* Sinoda (Shenoute) who was buried there with three other metropolitans; Luqas, Yohannes and Matyas. He noted that according to the account of the *soi–disant* patriarch Bermudes in the sixteenth century the district was called ʻAddi Abunaʼ. One list of metropolitans (Paris ms. Ethiop. 160) notes Nazret as the burial place of six metropolitans before the Zagwé period. A luxurious residence of the metropolitan, called ʻthe Castleʼ, is mentioned in the story of Michael of Fuwa (VI: 55); this seems to have been at the royal city of Adafa, Lalibela's capital. Other earlier metropolitans doubtless lived at Aksum, and some are recorded as having been buried there.[122] After the Zagwé period some may have again resided occasionally at Aksum (see VII: 58).

At least in the period after the Solomonic restoration, another burden seems to have been added to the already strange life style of these prelates, inasmuch as they had to follow the kings in their ʻtented capitalsʼ. We have virtually no information from the earlier period, but it may be that they were sometimes expected to follow the kings on their military expeditions, like Metropolitan Qerlos when he accompanied King Kaleb to "Tanbalat" (IIB: 16). Later, the metropolitans are frequently mentioned as included in the peripatetic court of the kings, with a special area reserved for their tents in the inner circle of tents surrounding the royal pavilion. One gets the impression that this was partly to keep an eye on them; an extreme case was Metropolitan Salama in the later part of Emperor Tewodros' reign (1855–68) when he was kept imprisoned on Amba Maqdala. In some cases, as ALVARES[123] noted, the metropolitan's part of the camp formed a considerable ʻsuburbʼ of the royal camp. Metropolitan Mark had numerous tents, forming a district in the camp, as there were many people who came to him to be ordained from all over the country, or foreigners seeking his favour and protection.

122 I. GUIDI, *Le liste dei Metropoliti d'Abissinia*, Bessarione, 37-38, 1899, p. 8, mentions Frumentius, Minas, Abreham and Yohannes "e con loro trentasette metropoliti, i cui nomi non si conoscono; sono sepelliti in Aksum". After them Bartalomewos was buried in Hagaray, and another metropolitan in Nazret. Further metropolitans, including a Gabra Kristos (Christodoulos) and three others, are mentioned as being buried at Beguena (GUIDI's list I, no. XIII) and a number of other places, in later times.

123 ALVARES, *op. cit.*, II, pp. 443-4.

5. The Lists of Metropolitans, and the *Notitiae Episcopatuum*

The Ge'ez lists[124] of metropolitans are of relatively little use for either historical or chronological purposes. They disagree radically amongst themselves and do not include metropolitans known from such other records as the patriarchal biographies and the Ethiopic hagiographies *(gadlat/gadlan)*. These latter, too, are difficult to reconcile amongst themselves, particularly since they employ several dating systems; the Incarnation, calculated to begin on 29/30 August AD.7; the Era of Martyrs (from the accession of Diocletian 284 AD, beginning 29/30 August); both of these could be counted in cycles of 532 years – called Amata Mehrat, Era of Mercy – so that new cycles of the Era of Martyrs began in 817 and 1349 AD, and those of the Incarnation differed by 67 years; the Era of Alexander, (beginning from October 1st BC 311, counting from the year when Seleucus I proclaimed himself king of Syria); or even from the date of the creation of the world, calculated from 5500 BC.

CHAÎNE noted those metropolitans whose dates could be fixed from documentary evidence. He also identified two types of lists of metropolitans among those published by ZOTENBERG, GUIDI, and WRIGHT. CHAÎNE's account can now be supplemented. The surviving Ge'ez lists are at variance between themselves, and both types are at variance with the historical evidence. Beyond the name (or rather the respectful epithet) Abba Salama, bestowed on Frumentius and at least one other, there is no reason to assume that new names were bestowed on the metropolitans at their consecration — except in the case of Metropolitan Michael (see V: 44), of whom the patriarchal biogapher records that "his name before his consecration (as) Metropolitan (mutran) of Ethiopia (al–Habasha) (was) Habib". The lists appear to be almost totally incorrect for the earlier period, but rather more accurate later in the version of WRIGHT. Where there is reason to respect the evidence of the lists, or where they unexpectedly agree, this will be noted.

[124] Lists have been published by: H. ZOTENBERG, Catalogue des manuscrits ethiopiens de la Bibliothèque Nationale, Paris 1877, p. 263; I. GUIDI, Catalogue of the Ethiopian Manuscripts in the British Museum, London 1871, pp. 291, 320; M. CHAÎNE, La chronologie des temps chrétiens de l'Égypte et de l'Éthiopie, Paris 1925, App. IV, p. 265. The lists, with another published in Amharic by AKLILABERHAN WALDAQIRQOS, were also discussed by AYELE TEKLAHAYMANOT, *The Egyptian Metropolitans of the Ethiopian Church*, a paper read to the Eighth International Conference of Ethiopian Studies, Addis Ababa University, Nov. 1984 and since published in: Orientalia Cristiana Periodica 54, 1988, pp. 175-222.

A list of metropolitan sees was copied by Yusuf the Egyptian in about 1316, apparently from a document written by Sa'id ibn Batriq, or Eutychius, the melkite patriarch of Alexandria in the 930s; the list was published by BEVERIDGE[125], LE QUIEN, and GELZER. VANTINI[126] and MONNERET DE VILLARD[127] also used this list, the latter comparing it with the melkite list of POCOCKE[128], which includes Nubian and Libyan bishoprics, but does not mention Ethiopia. He also compares Yusuf's list, which names a metropolitanate of al–Habasha, a bishopric of al–Maris, and a metropolitanate of Nubia, with the Jacobite list of WANSLEBEN, which includes Maracu (Makoria/Muqurra), Albadia (Alodia/Alwa) and Niexamites (the Aksumites).

VANTINI[129] supplied an English translation of Yusuf the Egyptian's list;

In the name of God, the Father, the Son and the Holy Ghost. Notice of the metropolitan seats under the Patriarch of the City of Alexandria, and their order of precedence, which were found in a document written by the Father and Patriarch Eutychius, who is Sa'id Ibn Batriq..

I. The first is the Archbishop (arshiabiskubos) of Mareotis and its region.
II. The second is the Metropolitan (matran) of Barqa and the Western Five Cities.
III. The third is the archbishop of Misr and its districts, villages and ham lets until the southern border of the Thebaid.
IV. The fourth is the Metropolitan of al–Sind and al–Hind and their dependencies.
V. The fifth is the Metropolitan of al–Habasha and all its depen dencies.
VI. The sixth is the Bishop of al–Maris and its other dependencies.
VII. The seventh is the Metropolitan of Nubia, and all its dependencies..."

---

125 W. BEVERIDGE, II, Oxford 1672; "Annotationes", p. 148, for the list of bishoprics subordinate to Alexandria. For GELZER and LE QUIEN, see note 128.

126 VANTINI, Faras, p. 100.

127 MONNERET DE VILLARD, Storia, pp. 158-9, n. 1.

128 R. POCOCKE, Description of the East, I, 1743, pp. 279ff. The melkite list is republished by H. GELZER, *Ungedruckte und wenig bekannte Bistümerverzeichnisse der orientalischen Kirche*, BZ II, 1893, pp. 36-7; See also U. MONNERET DE VILLARD, *Note Nubiane*, Aegyptus XII, fasc. IV, p. 309; M. LE QUIEN, Oriens Christianus II, Paris 1740, p. 375.

129 VANTINI, OS, p. 450ff, from Prince YOUSSEF KAMAL, ed., Monumenta Cartographica Africae et Aegypti, Le Caire 1928-39, 1150, v (after BEVERIDGE and GELZER).

BEVERIDGE added some comments to the list. He had never come across a word like al–Maris indicating any region or town, but noted that the bishop of al–Maris was clearly "a metropolitan, since dependencies are there attributed to him". As far as the metropolitanate of Nubia was concerned, BEVERIDGE noted

> This province was Jacobite and its bishops were ordained by the Jacobite patriarch, according to Eutychius' statement; "Then the Patriarch of the Jacobites ordained bishops for them so that Nubia became Jacobite since that time".....Eutychius' statement is also quoted by George Elmacinus (al–Makin)..... From all this one can gather that Nubia was restored to the Orthodox Patriarch of Alexandria some 200 years before Patriarch Eutychius...

Theodore PAPADOPOULLOS[130] commented on these lists or *Notitiae* from the Nubian point of view, noting that GELZER mentioned the "Metropolitan sees and Bishoprics under the jurisdiction of the Patriarch of Alexandria, indicative of the penetration of the Byzantine Church into the Nubian geographical sector". But he qualifies; first, that the data vary in date from the Council of Nicaea to that of Chalcedon, thus incorporating different stages of Byzantine jurisdiction, and second, that it represents the geographical extension of the Byzantine church at the time when the Nubian church was a dependent of the Constantinopolitan–controlled patriarchate of Alexandria. He adds that after the Arab conquest, the Nubian church proceeded along independent lines (Eutychius and, after him, al–Maqrizi mention the Jacobite ascendancy of this period), and he suggests that there must have been considerable alteration in the shape of the *Notitiae episcopatuum* of the Nubian church.

[130] T.C. PAPADOPOULLOS, Africanobyzantina; Byzantine influence on Negro-Sudanese Cultures, tomos 27, Pragmateiai tes Akademias Athenon, Athens 1966, p. 36. In Appendix II, p. 119 et seq., he quotes lists, gathered from many sources of different dates including the relatively modern African jurisdiction of the Alexandrian patriarchate, of G. SKALIERES, in: To Patriakheion Alexandreias: To klima kai i dikaiodosia autou, Athens 1927. This quotes 11 bishops under the metropolitan see of Aksum (in the province of Middle Eastern Ethiopia) and four under that of Adulis, which is subsumed with the sees of maritime Ethiopia up to Azania. See also J.M. WANSLEBEN, Nouvelle relation d'un voyage fait en Egypte, 1677, pp. 384-413.

WANSLEBEN preserves some details about the Jacobite list[131] as follows.

Dans la Nubie, il y avoit autrefois, selon le même manuscrit cy–dessus cité, trois provinces divisées en dix–sept évêchés.

Dans la province de Maracu il y avoit sept, qui étoient;
1. Celui de Korta.
2. Ibrim.
3. Bucoras.
4. Dunkala qu'on prononce Dungala.
5. Sai.
6. Termus.
7. Scienkur.

Dans la province d'Albadia, il y en avoit six, qui étoient;
1. Celuy de Borra.
2. Gagara.
3. Martin.
4. Arodias.
5. Banazi.
6. Menkesa.

Dans la province de Niexamitis, il y en avoit quatre, que étoient;
1. Celuy de Soper, qui est la ville royale.
2. Coucharin.
3. Takchi.
4. Amankul.

CONTI ROSSINI[132] published a very similar list to that quoted by WANSLEBEN taken from a Coptic manuscript in the Bibliothèque Nationale, Paris; the names are written both in Greek and Arabic, and there are some brief notes exactly as in WANSLEBEN's list.

Nieksametes (in which there are four sees);
Soper (which is the city of the king),
Takkhi,
Khoukharin,
Amankoul.

---

[131] J.M. WANSLEBEN, Historie de l'église d'Alexandrie, Paris 1677, pp. 29-30. The ms. he refers to in the quotation is noted on p. 17, "un vieux ms. Copte, que l'Évêque de Siut, nommé Amba Jean, me communiqua, lorsque j'étois chez luy, en 1673". QUATREMÈRE also quotes this list, in Mémoires, II, p. 36.

[132] C. CONTI ROSSINI, *Studi su popolazione dell'Etiopia. IV, Antichi popolazioni Nuba-Etiopiche*, RSO VI, 1913, p. 394, n. 1, from ms. Copt. n. 53, Bibliothèque Nationale, Paris.

Conti Rossini hinted at a possible original source for the manuscript dating to the eighth or ninth century. He wondered at the absence of Aksum and Adulis. The first he tried to form from COΠEΠ = Ku'bar in Arabic = Aksum in Arabic through faulty copying; the second "verosimilmente gia era tramontata dal principio del secolo VII". There may be some truth in the transfer, by copyists errors, of Ku'bar into Soper, but there is no evidence that Aksum and Ku'bar were one and the same town. Most likely neither Aksum nor Adulis appeared because the one was no longer the capital and the seat of the metropolitan bishopric, and the other had already been abandoned.

De Mas Latrie's arrangement[133] of the territorial divisions of the church during the seventh century may be summarised as follows;

The Patriarchate of Alexandria, with seven provinces in Egypt, and two in Libya.

The church of Ethiopia or Abyssinia and of Nubia, including Axoum (with reference to Le Quien, p. 643), Nubia (Le Quien 659), Homerita (Le Quien 661) and Adoula or Zeila (Le Quien 665).

Le Quien includes forty brief sketches of the lives of the bishops of Aksum or metropolitans of Abyssinia, from Frumentius to Christodoulos in the eighteenth century. For Nubia he mentions only three, for the Himyarite church five, including the "Indian priest" mentioned below (III: 22), and for Adulis only Bishop Moses (IIA: 9).

6. Ecclesiastical Offices and Titles in Ethiopia

A variety of titles are used more or less indiscriminately for different church officials by many modern authors, and some clarification is necessary.

The patriarch of Alexandria was the head of the church hierarchy. Wansleben[134] commented that the Egyptian church

> acknowledges only seven patriarchs, of whom four, according to them, are Oecumenic, and three honorary. The Oecumenic ones are... Rome.., Alexandria.., Ephesus..., (now transferred to Constantinople).., and Antioch. The honorary ones are Jerusalem, Selk (or Seleucia or Baghdad).., and Abyssinia; who, although he is only a Metropolitan, since on consecrating

133 L. de Mas Latrie, Trésor de Chronologie et de Geographie pour l'étude et l'emploi des documents du Moyen Age, Paris 1889; Prince Youssouf Kamal, ed., Monumenta Cartographica Africae et Aegypti, III, I, fol. 497. Vantini, OS, p. 28.

134 Wansleben, *op. cit.*, Histoire... pp. 8-10. See also S.C. Malan, op. cit., p. 24, note.

> him the prayers for a patriarch are not read over him, but only those of a Metropolitan, he yet is called 'patriarch' on account of his extensive diocese.

Evidently, the title 'patriarch' belongs really to the first six prelates mentioned. The Alexandrian patriarch is often called by his title of archbishop – ΑΡΧΙΕΠΙCΚΟΠΟC – (of Alexandria), for example by the Coptic bishop Menas[135] in his *Life of Isaac*. It is probably the Patriarch John IX (1320–27) to whom the Kudanbes inscription[136] at Aswan refers as

Λ X Κ ΟΞ
...ΘC . ΜΟΝΟΝ . ΑΡ ΕΠΙC . ΟΡΘΔ ΟΝ... "the pious, single–minded archbishop of the orthodox".

The Arab texts refer to the patriarch of Alexandria as *al–batrik (batrak* etc). Only in one manuscript of the church history (see VI: 55) is the Abyssinian metropolitan thus referred to (presumably by mistake, other versions using *mutran*.) The Abyssinian prelate is only rarely called 'catholicos', the title being generally reserved for the Nestorian primate of Persia and the Armenian monophysite primate. In practice he is usually designated 'metropolitan' – in Arabic *mutran (mitran, matran;* the vocalisation varies) – or *pappas* or *abun(a)* in Ethiopia itself. The latter word means something like "His Paternity", and might also be employed when referring to high ecclesiastics or holy men. The *abun* was of course a bishop. The earliest ones, if we can extrapolate from Athanasius' references to Frumentius, were called bishop of Aksum, or of the Aksumites, but later, for example, the monk Isaac was consecrated bishop of the royal city of Arafa, and "over all Ethiopia" (VI: 55). Possibly his predecessor Michael of Fuwa still used the title bishop of Aksum, since he in turn consecrated Hirun as bishop of the capital, Arafa, but this is uncertain. He may even, although there is no evidence whatsoever, have been bishop of the successor capital, Ku'bar.

The metropolitan, consecrated for whatever Ethiopian episcopal see currently held the primacy in the country, may have been regarded as *primus inter pares* in that respect amongst the bishops of Ethiopia; but his presence was indispensible as the consecrator of other bishops. The bishops of Egypt regarded the situation there as similar, judging from their representations to Patriarch Michael IV. They declared[137] that "the patriarch is but the bishop of Alexandria, and has the presidency over the bishops of Egypt, but is not a sharer with them in their Sees". Inasmuch as

---

135 PORCHER, ed., op. cit., p. 378 for example.
136 GRIFFITH, *op. cit.*, pp. 18-29.
137 "History of the Patriarchs", II, III, p. 383.

the metropolitan of Ethiopia held a similar presidency, he may be regarded as an archbishop; hence perhaps the occasional reference to him in Ethiopic as *liqa–pappasat,* a title generally reserved for the patriarch, instead of the usual *pappas*. A land–grant dated to 1431, in a King Dawit's time (though no King Dawit was actually reigning then)[138] refers to the *liqa–pappasat* Abba Yuhannes, Patriarch John IX of Alexandria, and the *pappas* Abba Bartolomewos, the metropolitan. The *Synaxarium* notes that the *liqa–pappasat* Athanasius designated Frumentius as *pappas* (see below).

Ibn Khaldun explained the meaning of the titles pope, patriarch and others, as he understood them, before providing his description of the ecclesiastical arrangements in Ethiopia quoted above.[139] LUDOLF[140] also noted something about the ecclesiastical titles in Ethiopia;

> Their Chief Head is called Papas, or Metropolitan, Tho the Title or Sir–name of Abuna, that is to say, Our Father, be more frequently given him..... This Abuna is by some, tho improperly, call'd Patriarch, his truer Title being that of Bik Papas, or Bik Papaste, Prince or Master of the Metropolitans....

However, as we have seen, this title of master of the metropolitans is better accorded to the patriarchs of Alexandria than to the Ethiopian metropolitans. LUDOLF also mentions that

> In none of their Kingdoms or Provinces have they any Bishops or Arch–bishops. So that unless the Icegue, with the assistance of his Monks, had taken some care of the Church, all thought of Religion had fallen to the ground long e're this.

But in fact there is some evidence for bishops in Ethiopia other than the metropolitan at various periods (I: 9–10; VI: 62). These dignitaries, *usquf* in Arabic, *episqopos* in Ethiopic, when present presumably ranked next after the patriarch and metropolitan. WANSLEBEN (see above, I: 5) noted four bishoprics in Ethiopia, and there is occasional evidence for their existence. Quite how they were appointed is not clear; some may have been designated to come with the metropolitan from Egypt, others may have been consecrated by the metropolitan himself, as Michael of Fuwa conse-

---

138 TADDESSE TAMRAT, *The Abbots of Däbrä Hayq 1248-1535*, JES VIII, 1970, pp. 104-5.

139 Ibn Khaldun, "The Muqaddimah, an Introduction to History", trans., F. ROSENTHAL, New York 1956, I, p. 481.

140 LUDOLF, *op. cit.*, p. 306ff.

crated Hirun (VI: 55). Michael's reluctance to perform the consecration might have been due to his knowledge that for one reason or another it was uncanonical. In the time of one of his predecessors, another Michael, called Habib al–Atfihi (V: 44), there were apparently seven bishops in Ethiopia, and an attempt was made to force him to create more. This, he said, required the patriarch's permission, which was withheld. The point at issue was the ability of ten bishops to elect their own patriarch; that the metropolitan of Ethiopia could himself consecrate up to seven bishops seems implied.

Only the metropolitan is recorded as coming from Egypt in most cases, though, as the records grow fuller, assistant bishops are mentioned (VI: 61). These are probably the churchmen we have already noted, referred to in the Ethiopian records as *episqopos*, contrasting with the metropolitan, *pappas*; though sometimes *episqopos* is used to designate the metropolitan himself.

It is just possible that bishops who accompanied the metropolitan to Ethiopia could succeed him, since they were consecrated by a patriarch claiming apostolic succession direct from St. Mark, whereas the bishop or *episqopos* consecrated by the metropolitan could not make such a claim, not having received the patriarchal prayers read over him or the laying on of hands. ALVARES[141] wrote of a case rather later in the history of the Ethiopian metropolitanate when two metropolitans were apparently created. In the reign of King Eskender (1478–94) the king "sent to Cairo to seek for an Abima from the Patriarch of Alexandria who was there, and he sent him two, so that one should succeed the other, and both were alive in our time. Whilst we were here the Abima Jacob died, to whom this one who is now living succeeded". The second of these metropolitans, *abuna* Mark, was supposed by then to be between one hundred and ten and one hundred and twenty years old, but was still exercising his functions.

The odd position of 'Patriarch' Joâo Bermudes is worth briefly noting here, though also outside the chronological limits of this study. There are different interpretations of the story[142] JONES related that when the aged Metropolitan Mark was dying King Lebna Dengel ordered him to make Bermudes his successor, which he did after ordaining him in the

---

[141] ALVARES, *op. cit.*, II, p. 357.

[142] See R.S. WHITEWAY, The Portuguese Expedition to Abyssinia, 1541-3, London, Hakluyt Soc., 1902, for Bermudes' own story. See also A.H.M. JONES, and E. MONROE, A History of Abyssinia, Oxford, 1935, p. 86; REY, *op. cit.*, p. 128 (and opp. p. 200 for a sketch of his tomb inscription, which does entitle him "patriarch of Alexandria"); P. CARAMAN, The Lost Empire, London, 1985, pp. 7-8.

lesser orders. Bermudes then went to the Pope, who not only confirmed him in his office but made him patriarch of Alexandria (REY writes, patriarch of Abyssinia). Such a nomination to succession by a metropolitan at the king's command does not seem to have been possible, and JONES regarded Bermudes' story as "a tissue of lies". In an earlier situation, a royal command had made Metropolitan Peter's successor 'acting metropolitan' (III: 29), but it was evidently not regarded as an acceptable expedient. CARAMAN appears to believe that in 1538 Mark "consecrated Bermudes bishop, handed over to him all his rights and prerogatives, and acknowledged his leadership of the Ethiopian Church", but adds that "his acts, however, were not ratified by Pope Paul II, who was hesitant to accept Bermudes's consecration by a schismatic bishop", though he was accepted as patriarch of Ethiopia in Lisbon.

Clarification of some ecclesiastical titles comes from Nubia, where a similar, but not entirely parallel, situation to that of Ethiopia was in force. As already noted, the bishops of certain cities held, it seems successively, the title metropolitan (I: 3b). Thus some of the bishops of Pachoras, in the Pachoras (Faras) list, are called 'metropolitan', and some bear the title 'orthodoxos', of uncertain significance. But the majority are simply 'episkopos'. When this is the case, it seems that the primacy has shifted elsewhere, to Sai, or perhaps to Dongola. The title of the prelate called in Arabic *mutran* seems, as in Ethiopia, to have been *papas*. John the Deacon[143] in his *Life of Michael*, wrote

> and he (King Kyriakos of Nubia) has in his country an orthodox bishop *(usquf urthuduksi)*, whom the patriarch ordains as metropolitan *(mutran)*, and who ordains for him (the king) the bishops and priests in that land.

This would seem to be the situation for Ethiopia also; Ethiopia, as we have seen, was limited to seven bishops, and the same applied to Nubia (V:44).

The title 'patriarch' refers here only to such prelates as the patriarchs of Alexandria, Antioch and Jerusalem. The title 'Pope', nowadays usually reserved only for the Roman pontiff – Ibn Khaldun also noted that "the name of 'Pope' is specially reserved for the patriarch of Rome at this time" – is not employed here for any other prelate. It is, however, in the form *pappas,* legitimate for the other ecumenical patriarchs, and was used, it seems specifically, in Nubia and Ethiopia for the prelate in whom was vested the primacy of their lands, the metropolitan.[144]

---

[143] PO V, fasc. I, p. 146.

[144] Though MONNERET DE VILLARD, Storia, p. 162, suggested that it was perhaps adopted in Nubia for "episkopos".

The Alexandrian patriarchs presumably bestowed the title 'bishop of Aksum' or 'of the Aksumites' upon the earliest incumbents of the see of Aksum, since that is how Patriarch Athanasius designates the first bishop, Frumentius, in his *Apologia ad Constantium Imperatorem.* It is probable that it was only later, as the Ethiopian church developed, that the title 'metropolitan' came to be employed. The first use of it for Ethiopia – it appears earlier for Nubia – in the *History of the Patriarchs* is in the biography of Patriarch Kosmas III, 923–934 (III: 29). In the present work this title is used – whether anachronistically or not – for all those prelates appointed to head the church in Ethiopia, except when directly quoting from documentary sources which use *pappas, abun* etc.

As far as the lesser ecclesiastical orders are concerned, Abu Salih[145] comments that the metropolitan of the Abyssinians ordains the priests and deacons of the church. The Cairo Council of Patriarch Cyril III Ibn Laklak's time (1235–1243) decided that ex–slaves could be priests in Ethiopia and Nubia only.[146] It is apparent that priests' families in Ethiopia inherited a certain prestige, since it is often quoted to a person's credit in the *gadlan* that he was of a priestly family. An unusual aspect of the Ethiopian church was the ordination of children as deacons. The custom may perhaps have helped to safeguard the existence of some of the functions of the church when there was a delay caused by the long process of selection and despatch of a new metropolitan, or even a gap in the succession. TELLES comments that this degree was bestowed especially on the sons of great men, so that they could have the privilege of receiving the sacrament inside the church with the clergy.[147]

---

[145] EVETTS and BUTLER, *op. cit.*, fol. 105a, p. 286.

[146] "History of the Patriarchs", III,III; BUTCHER, *op. cit.*, p. 143; NEALE, *op. cit.*, II, p. 303.

[147] TELLES, *op. cit.*, p. 109.

CHAPTER TWO

The Kingdom of Aksum

Introduction

The Ethiopian episcopate came into existence during the heyday of the Aksumite kingdom. Since even today relatively little is known about Aksum, an introductory sketch of the kingdom's development and secular history may serve as a useful prelude to its ecclesiastical history.[148]

The Aksumite period – that during which kings of Aksum ruled from their eponymous capital in Northern Ethiopia – lasted for over six centuries from the beginning of our era. The kingdom was the successor of an earlier Ethiopian civilisation in whose excavated material, dating from about the fifth century BC or possibly even earlier, a strong South Arabian influence in architecture, religion, writing, the monarchy, technology and the arts can be detected. An Ethiopian kingdom called D'MT (perhaps pronounced something like Di'amat) is attested in inscriptions at this early date; it seems to have been centred around Yeha, not far from Aksum. Though the period between this and the development of Aksum around the beginning of the Christian era is virtually a blank for us at present, it may be surmised that the D'MT monarchy's successors, and perhaps other Ethiopian chiefdoms, continued something of the same Ethio–Sabaean civilisation until these smaller entities were eventually subordinated by the rise of Aksum. At Yeha the largest of all the pre–Aksumite structures, a stone built temple, still survives, a magnificent testimony to the capabilities of these earlier peoples. Elsewhere, other temples and religious and votive objects attest to the pre–Aksumite religion of the country. In Aksumite times, several cultural features, including particularly religion and the script, show connexions with the earlier period, though the evidence for direct links is still missing.

Aksum, the capital city of the new polity, was situated in the Ethiopian highlands, in the western part of the province of Tigray. From there Aksumite rulers came to control both Tigray and Eritrea to the north,

---

148 The following is based on S.C.H. MUNRO-HAY, Excavations at Aksum 1972-4, London 1989; ID., Aksum. An African Civilisation of Late Antiquity, Edinburgh UP 1991.

with access to the Red Sea coast and a port at Adulis in Eritrea. The Aksumites were able to exploit a series of favourable situations, some of which we can only guess at this stage, to become the dominant power group in the region, and to develop their very characteristic civilisation. The country around Aksum had been prosperous in pre–Aksumite times; the favourable climate, the rich agricultural potential, and the strategic situation which had allowed the earlier development, were probably also vital factors in Aksum's own rise. Aksumite inscriptions mention a number of subordinate kings or chiefs. It seems that the developing state gradually absorbed its weaker neighbours, but frequently retained traditional rulers under a tribute system. The title *negusa nagast,* or king of kings, used by Aksumite and successive Ethiopian rulers until the reign of the late Emperor Haile Sellassie, is a reflection of the sort of loose federation under their own lead which the Aksumites achieved throughout a large part of Ethiopia and neighbouring lands.

The Aksumite rulers became sufficiently hellenized to employ the Greek language, the *lingua franca* of the Red Sea trade. This is noted by the author of the *Periplus of the Erythraean Sea,* an anonymous trade and shipping guide, now generally accepted as dating to the mid–1st century AD; it is later evident from the Aksumites' own inscriptions and coins. The *Periplus* mentions a king of these regions who may well be the first historically identified Aksumite ruler, King Zoskales. By the late second or early third century Aksumite rulers like GDRT (conventionally vocalised Gadarat) and 'A<u>D</u>BH ('Adhebah/Azbah) had expanded their interests into South Arabia, where their control over a considerable area is attested by their Arabian enemies' own inscriptions. Later in the same century two other Aksumite leaders, DTWNS (Datawnas) and ZQRNS (Zaqarnas), appear in South Arabian inscriptions, indicating that Aksumite concerns in the region, a direct reversal of the earlier process of South Arabian influence in Ethiopia already mentioned, were of sufficient importance to occupy the attention of the kings themselves.

The consolidated Aksumite kingdom grew prosperous. Monuments and finds at Aksum and other sites attest to the development of an original and monumental architectural style in a number of urban centres, the use of Greek and the local language, Ge'ez, on inscriptions and the very unusual coinage, many indigenous arts and crafts, a vigorous internal and international trade, and a rising position in the African and overseas politics of the period. In the towns, the lack of walls, even at Aksum itself, might hint at relatively peaceful internal conditions, though inscriptions do mention occasional revolts among the subordinate tribes. Exploitation of the agricultural potential of the region, in places probably much higher than today, allowed these urban communities to develop to a considerable size. Perhaps the best–known symbols of the Aksumites' particular ideas and style are the great carved monoliths or stelae, some of which still stand at Aksum, erected to commemorate their dead rulers; they also record the considerable skill of the Aksumite quarrymen, engineers, and stone–carvers.

The prosperity which such works bespeak came from Aksum's key position in the exploitation of certain costly luxuries, mostly destined for the Roman world. We have accounts of the export of such precious items as gold, turtle–shell, obsidian, ivory, rhino–horn, and emeralds (or beryl). Other commodities including civet, incense, exotic animal skins, and hides seem also to have been among Aksum's exports. Inscriptions attest to Aksum's claim to control parts of neighbouring regions such as the old Kushite or Meroitic kingdom, the Noba people, the Beja, certain areas of South Arabia, together with other unidentifiable regions. Part of such claims may be wishful thinking, but the general prosperity and reputation of the country led the Persian religious leader Mani to name Aksum as third, after the 'super–powers' Persia and Rome, among the kingdoms of the world in the later third century AD. Something of this reputation is substantiated by the production of an independent coinage at about this time, paralleling the country with the few other contemporary issuers of gold coinage, Rome, Persia and a little earlier the Kushana kingdom in northern India. The coinage seems to have started around 270 AD or just afterwards with King Endubis, who, with his immediate successors Aphilas, Wazeba, Ousanas and Ezana all issued coins bearing the religious symbol of the disc and crescent.

As noted below (IIA: 7a), it was in the second quarter of the fourth century that the Aksumite King Ezana was converted to Christianity. Previously he had worshipped a pantheon including Astar, Meder, Beher and Mahrem (identified in parallel Ge'ez, South Arabian and Greek language inscriptions with Greek deities like Zeus, Poseidon, and Ares). From his reign the coins and inscriptions emphatically indicate, by their symbolism and phraseology, the royal support for the new religion. Even so, it may have taken a considerable time to spread among the people of the remoter regions under Aksumite control.

Little is known about fifth century Aksum, though Ethiopian literature preserves tales about a number of Christian missionaries active in the country at the time (IIA: 12). At Aksum some of the buildings uncovered by recent excavations contained fifth–century coins; gold examples of these have also been found in large numbers in South Arabia. Whether the presence of gold Aksumite coins in South Arabia points to any sort of political control there is impossible to say. It might imply that trading ties with the regions across the Red Sea remained close, but it is also possible that the coins entered the Yemen at a slightly later period, during the famous expedition of King Kaleb of Aksum (IIB: 13).

Whatever effect Kaleb's expedition might have had on ecclesiastical historians, it was Aksum's swan–song as a significant power. As the sixth and seventh centuries progressed, Aksum's position grew more difficult. The virtual independence of the Yemen under the Abyssinian usurper Abraha was followed by its conquest around 570 by the Sassanian king, Khusrau I (531–579). Further Persian disruption of the Roman east followed with the conquest of Syria and Egypt under Khusrau II. This seems to have dried up much of Aksum's flow of trade, and the kingdom's expansionist days were over. Arab conquests in the former Roman east, permanent this time, followed in the mid–seventh century, confirming the destruction of the whole commercial system in the Red Sea that had maintained Aksum's prosperity. Aksum itself seems to have been abandoned as the capital of the Ethiopian kingdom by about 630 AD.

IIA The Earliest Christian Period

7a. Frumentius

The Aksumite kingdom in Ethiopia at the time of Patriarch Athanasius of Alexandria (328–373) was ruled by King Ezana Bisi Halen, son of Ella 'Amida. Ella 'Amida has been tentatively identified with the pagan king Ousanas known from the coinage, in the sequence of which his coins seem directly to preceed those of Ezana.

Whilst there were undoubtedly Christians in Ethiopia at this period[149], probably foreign merchants dwelling particularly at the port of Adulis or at the capital, the conversion of the country is generally attributed to a Tyrian called Frumentius, honoured even today by the Ethiopians as their first *pappas* or metropolitan under the title 'Abba Salama'. The story of his arrival, as a prisoner who rose to be a trusted

[149] Rufinus, "Historia Ecclesiastica", PL XXI, col. 179, "Deo mentem ejus et animos instigante requirere sollicitius coepit, si qui inter negociatores Romanus Christiani essent"... ;SERGEW HABLE SELLASSIE, *Die Aethiopische Kirche im 4. bis 6. Jahrhundert*, Abba Salama, II, 1971, pp. 43-75, esp. pp. 56-7.

royal servant and eventually bishop of Aksum, was recorded by Rufinus of Tyre (c. 345–410) and his near–contemporary, the lawyer or *skholastikos* Socrates (c. 380–450). It was then repeated in more or less the same terms in several other sources; Theodoret of Cyrrhus (c. 393–466), Pseudo–Dionysios of Tell Mahre, John of Nikiu, the early fifth century writer Sozomen, Gelasius of Kyzicos, writing shortly after 475, Theophanes, Nicephorus Callistus (c. 1256–1335), and the Ethiopian *Synaxarium*.[150] Some of these sources, which report a slightly different version of events, may have used a lost account from the history written by Gelasius of Caesarea, who died in 395[151], while others may have added embroideries to the basic tale as interest in church history grew.

Since Rufinus' account is so important for the history of Christianity in Ethiopia, it is cited here in full in translation;

> One Metrodorus, a philosopher, is said to have penetrated to further India in order to view places and see the world. Inspired by his example, one Meropius, a philosopher of Tyre, wished to visit India with a similar object, taking with him two small boys who were related to him and whom he was educating in humane studies. The younger of these was called Aedesius, the other Frumentius. When, having seen and taken note of what his soul fed upon, the philosopher had begun to return, the ship on which he travelled put in for water or some other necessary at a certain port. It is the custom of the barbarians of these parts that, if ever the neighbouring tribes should report that their treaty with the Romans is broken, all Romans found among them should be massacred. The philosopher's ship was boarded; all with himself were put to the sword. The boys were found studying under a tree and preparing their lessons, and, preserved by the mercy of the barbarians, were taken to the king. He made one of them, Aedesius, his cupbearer.

[150] Rufinus, op.cit., col 479. Nicephorus Callistus, "Historia Ecclesiastica", PG CXLVI, col. 132; J. CHABOT, CSCO 121, Scriptores Syri Ser. III, T.1, versio; Incerti auctores, "Chronicon Pseudo-Dionysionum vulgo dictum", I, Paris 1933, p. 122; Socrates, "Historia Ecclesiastica", PG LXVII, col. 125ff; Sozomen, "Historia Ecclesiastica", PG LXVII, col. 996ff; Theodoret, "Historia Ecclesiastica", PG LXXXII, col. 969ff; Gelasius, "Kirchengeschichte", Die Griechischen Christlichen Schriftsteller der ersten drei Jahrhunderte, Bd 28, Leipzig 1918, pp. 148-50; John of Nikiu, *The Chronicle of John of Nikiu*, trans. R.H. CHARLES, London, 1916, pp. 69-70; BUDGE, Synaxarium, IV, pp. 1164-5; DILLMAN, *op. cit.*, (reprinted Berlin 1950) p. 33; R. HENNIG, *Frumentius und Aedesius im Reiche Axum*, Terrae Incognitae I, 1944, pp. 5-17.

[151] An exhaustive and very useful analysis of the Frumentius story is that of B.W. DOMBROWSKI and F.A. DOMBROWSKI, *Frumentius/Abba Salama*, Oriens Christianus 68, 1984, pp. 114-69. See also F. THELAMON, Païens et Chrétiens au IVe siècle, (ch. premier, *L'introduction du christianisme dans le royaume d'Axoum*), Paris 1981.

Frumentius, whom he had perceived to be sagacious and prudent, he made his treasurer and secretary. Therefore they were held in great honour and affection by the king.

The king died, leaving his wife with an infant son as heir of the bereaved kingdom. He gave the young men liberty to do what they pleased but the queen besought them with tears, since she had no more faithful subjects in the whole kingdom, to share with her the cares of governing the kingdom until her son should grow up, especially Frumentius, whose ability was equal to guiding the kingdom – for the other, though loyal and honest of heart, was simple.

While they lived there and Frumentius held the reins of government in his hands, God stirred up his heart and he began to search out with care those of the Roman merchants who were Christians and to give them great influence and to urge them to establish in various places conventicles to which they might resort for prayer in the Roman manner. He himself, moreover, did the same and so encouraged the others, attracting them with his favour and his benefits, providing them with whatever was needed, supplying sites for buildings and other necessaries, and in every way promoting the seed of Christianity in the country.

When the prince for whom they exercised the regency had grown up, they completed and faithfully delivered over their trust, and, though the queen and her son sought greatly to detain them and begged them to remain, returned to the Roman Empire. Aedesius hastened to Tyre to revisit his parents and relatives. Frumentius went to Alexandria, saying that it was not right to hide the work of God. He laid the whole affair before the bishop and urged him to look for some worthy man to send as bishop over the many Christians already congregated and the churches built on barbarian soil. Then Athanasius (for he had recently assumed the episcopate) having carefully weighed and considered Frumentius' words and deeds, declared in a council of the priests: "What other man shall we find in whom the Spirit of God is as in thee, who can accomplish these things?" And he consecrated him, and bade him return in the grace of God whence he had come. And when he arrived in India as bishop, such grace is said to have been given to him by God that apostolic miracles were wrought by him and a countless number of barbarians were converted by him to the faith. From which time Christian peoples and churches have been created in the parts of India, and the priesthood has begun. These facts I know not from vulgar report but from the mouth of Aedesius himself, who had been Frumentius' companion and was later made a priest in Tyre".[152]

[152] English translation from A.H.M. JONES, and E. MONROE, A History of Ethiopia, Oxford 1935, pp. 26-7.

PÉTRIDÈS[153] has analysed the chronology of the evangelisation of Ethiopia, suggesting that Frumentius was consecrated in 329–330, and that the Ethiopian court formally accepted the Christian faith in 333 AD. This is the date accepted by many Ethiopian traditional accounts, and certainly from the coinage point–of–view seems the most likely. There have been other suggestions within an acceptable range for the coinage, varying from around 340–50 for the introduction of Christianity[154], 340 or "after 346" for the consecration of Frumentius[155], and 320 for the conversion of the royal family.[156] In addition, there is a further series of dates possibly reflecting a second evangelisation in the fifth century (see below).

The king of Ethiopia at the time of Frumentius' arrival was, according to the *Synaxarium*, a certain Alada, or, after BUDGE's version, Alameda. This ruler having died, leaving a little son, Frumentius with his companion Aedesius helped the queen–regent in the administration of the country. Frumentius took the opportunity to spread Christianity as much as he could. A name, Ella Azguagua, apparently that of another ruler, is also mentioned in the text, with no further information. Rufinus' earlier account (which he states was related to him by Aedesius himself), from which the main lines of the *Synaxarium* version of the story probably ultimately derive, does not mention either the king's name, or this other ruler (?), but otherwise accords with the *Synaxarium* 's account. Later, when

---

[153] S.P. PÉTRIDÈS, *Essai sur l'évangelisation de l'Éthiopie, sa date et son protagoniste,* Abba Salama III, 1972, pp. 208-232.

[154] I. GUIDI, *La Chiesa Abissina*, Oriente Moderno II, 1922, p. 124. W.R.O. HAHN, in a review of MUNRO-HAY, Aksum. An African Civilisation of Late Antiquity, in: Numismatic Chronicle, 1993, pp. 316-9, basing himself on the very late (eleventh or early twelfth century) historian Cedrenus, takes 326 as the date of Metrodorus' return, which would in turn have inspired Meropius to visit India. Ezana would have succeeded c. 330 under Frumentius' mentorship. This scarcely seems to leave time for the events outlined by Rufinus. Even if the "small boys" had left with Meropius in c. 327, it is surely impossible for them to have visited India, returned, been captured, lived as treasurer and cupbearer, and in Frumentius' case been elevated to virtual regency by about three years later. Cedrenus' date for the c. 519 war of Kaleb is 542. In any case, the attribution to Metrodorus is vague; it may be an addition of Rufinus' own, or possibly came from Aedesius; who may have merely hazarded it, unless perhaps he was repeating something he remembered hearing from Meropius.

[155] MEINARDUS, *Abunate*, p. 40; BAIRU TAFLA, *The Establishment of the Ethiopian Church*, Tarikh, Vol. 2, no. 1, p. 30; A. DIHLE, Umstrittene Daten, Köln und Opladen 1965, p. 54, also suggests the third period of Athanasius' patriarchate (346-355) for the ordination of Frumentius.

[156] ISAAC, *Ethiopian Church*, p. 242.

the young king had grown up, Frumentius travelled to Alexandria, whence he returned after his consecration as first bishop of Aksum in the reign of the joint–kings Abreha and Asbeha, as they are named in the *Synaxarium* and Ethiopian tradition.

CONTI ROSSINI[157] discussed the Ethiopian traditional account of the arrival of Christianity in the country, and its origins, concluding that the sixth century rulers Atsbeha (Kaleb Ella Atsbeha) and Abraha (king of the Yemen) were those who, in the popular imagination, became confused with rulers contemporary with Abba Salama. Both these monarchs were conspicuously Christian, Kaleb being celebrated for his invasion to counter Jewish persecution of Christians in the Yemen, Abraha for his construction of al–Qulays, a great church apparently at San'a, in an attempt to divert Arab pilgrimage to his own country. CONTI ROSSINI adds that the Ethiopic *senkessar (Synaxarium)* probably derived directly from Rufinus but with certain peculiarities, such as the inclusion of the names Ella Alada and Ella Azguagua, or Abreha and Atsbeha. The first names occur in CONTI ROSSINI's[158] king–list C, but not in the earlier versions A and D; he therefore suggested that they derived from Ella Amida and Ella Aizana, by way of a Coptic copy of Rufinus' work which became later the origin of the Ge'ez version.

The identification of Abreha and Atsbeha with Ezana, king of Aksum, and perhaps also his brother Sazana, the historical personages in control of Aksum at the time of the conversion, is suggested by a large and varied accumulation of evidence, outside the province of the present work.[159] It may be noted, however, that a letter written by the Emperor

---

[157] C. CONTI ROSSINI, *A propos des textes éthiopiens concernant Salama (Frumentius)*, Aethiops I, 1922, pp. 2-4, 17-18.

[158] C. CONTI ROSSINI, *Les listes des rois d'Aksum*, JA, 1909, pp. 265-320

[159] BUDGE, History, I, p. 258; E. ULLENDORFF, *Note on the Introduction of Christianity into Ethiopia*, Africa 19, 1949, pp. 61-62; S.C. MUNRO-HAY, *The Chronology of Aksum*, unpublished doctoral thesis, SOAS, Univ. of London, 1978; ID., *Ezana (Ezana/Ezanas): Some Numismatic Comments*, Azania XV, pp. 109-120; ID., *The Dating of Ezana and Frumentius*, RSE XXXII, 1988, pp. 111-27; J. PIRENNE, *L'imbroglio de trois siècles de chronologie aksumite, IVe á VIe s.*, Documents pour servir à l'histoire des civilisations éthiopiennes, fasc. 6, 1975, pp. 49-58; R. SCHNEIDER, *A propos de l'imbroglio de trois siècles de chronologie aksumite*, DSHCE, fasc. 7, 1976, pp. 41ff; ISAAC, *Ethiopian Church*, dates (p. 242) Ezana to c. 320-350, the last date being some six years earlier than the letter of Constantius II; in addition, the inscription published by ANFRAY, CAQUOT and NAUTIN mentions Christ and the Holy Spirit, and so does not support ISAAC's contention that there was a Jewish emphasis in the conversion (which he regards as being mainly the work of "Jewish Christians".)

Constantius II, of which a copy has been preserved among Patriarch Athanasius' writings, was addressed to two Aksumite princes called Aizanas and Sazanas, and that the inscriptions[160] of Ezana from Aksum render his name as 'Ezana, Azanas, or Aeizanas, also mentioning his brother Saizana, Sazanan, or Se'azana. Further, the phraseology of Ezana's inscriptions, and the imagery of his coinage (where his name is written Ezana or Ezanas) became unequivocally Christian[161] after an earlier pagan sequence. There is one inscription (no. 11 in the 1913 publication of the Deutsche Aksum–Expedition led by LITTMANN in 1906) which has a dedication to the 'Lord of Heaven' which has been held to represent a transitory 'monotheistic' stage in Aksumite religion; but its apparent parallels in other scripts are clearly Christian. It seems most likely that the 'monotheistic' aspects of the Ge'ez version result from either an unwillingness to be too specific at this stage in the version primarily aimed at local readers, or perhaps from an uncertainty as to how to render the name of the Christian God in Ge'ez. In the end, the locutions 'Lord of Heaven' and 'Lord of All' employed in this inscription were replaced by a variant expression 'Lord of the Land', (*egzi' abher*), which name soon appeared on a silver coin as part of the legend, and remained the usual designation for the Christian God in Ge'ez ever afterwards.

LATOURETTE[162] asserted that Ezana "showed his zeal for his new faith by destroying pagan temples and killing pagan priests". This idea is presumably drawn from the inscription DAE 11 mentioned above, which recounts the course of the king's campaign against the Noba. The inscription does mention the details cited by LATOURETTE, but the impression is much more that this happened in the course of suppressing resistance as a military necessity during a foreign war, than that there was a deliberate anti–pagan slant to the campaign.

Aksum's rulers seem to have accepted Christianity fairly positively, though the country as a whole was probably not converted until some time later.[163] Political considerations[164], such as the lure of alliance with the Roman emperor, may have had some part to play in the adoption of

---

160 LITTMANN, DAE, Vol. IV, Berlin 1913.

161 F. ANFRAY, A. CAQUOT and P. NAUTIN, *Une nouvelle inscription grecque d'Ezana, roi d'Axoum*, Journal des Savants 70, 1970, pp. 260ff.

162 K.S. LATOURETTE, A History of the Expansion of Christianity, London 1953, Vol. I, p. 236. See also SERGEW HABLE SELLASSIE, in: The Church of Ethiopia; a panorama of history and spiritual life, Addis Ababa: Ethiopian Orthodox Church 1970, p. 5.

163 C.F. BROWN, The Conversion Experience in Axum during the fourth and fifth centuries, Howard Univ. Washington 1973.

164 I. GUIDI, *La Chiesa Abissina*, Oriente Moderno II, 1922, p. 126.

the new religion, but, if so, this does not appear to have been a motive strong enough to encourage Ethiopia to depart from its obedience to Athanasius when religious differences removed him temporarily, several times, from the patriarchal throne of Alexandria.

Constantinople doubtless had as much to gain as Ethiopia from a Romano–Aksumite agreement in the Red Sea; this may be one reason why Constantius himself took steps to supplement the political alignment with religious unity. Constantius II's letter of 356 was an attempt to sway the Aksumites towards his own religious policy. He sought the confirmation of Frumentius in his see by Bishop George of Cappadocia, who was installed at Alexandria from 356–361 to replace the exiled Athanasius. His letter, as copied by Athanasius, read as follows[165];

> Victor Constantius Maximus Augustus to Aizana and Sazana.
>
> It is our greatest care and study as God knows – I think in fact such things for all the human race – to lead them to a knowledge of God, transforming life by hope, and in nothing dissenting in respect of the search for the just and the true. I consider it right to assign to you the same treatment as to the Romans and the duty to use the identical doctrine in the Church. Therefore send Bishop Frumentius as quickly as possible to Egypt to the most honourable Bishop George and the other Bishops in Egypt who have the authority to ordain and judge affairs of this nature. You in fact know and understand though you pretend to be ignorant, you alone, of what is well noted by all, that Frumentius was promoted to his rank by Athanasius who is guilty of a thousand crimes which cannot be justified by any of the pretenses of the accused and has to–day been deposed from his office and is not found in any locality where it is possible to live. He goes as a vagabond from one region to another almost as a fugitive criminal. If Frumentius spontaneously obeys and renders account of the whole state of the case and in every way manifests that he has in no wise broken away from the law of the Church and of the faith it holds; and when he has been judged, having rendered an account of his whole life, and has furnished explanations to those who are competent to judge questions of this nature, it will be decided by them whether he is worthy to be considered a true bishop and to be ordained according to the law. If he prefers to procrastinate and to hide from justice, it will be evident that seduced by the villainous Athanasius, he feels impiously toward God and is infected like those already declared infected and is culpable. If Athanasius has the temerity to come to Aksum he will only corrupt you with his abominable and impious discourses; he will also confound and dis-

165 From S. PANKHURST, Ethiopia: A Cultural History, London 1955, pp. 58-9. Another trans. in J. STEVENSON, ed., Creeds, Councils, and Controversies, London 1975, pp. 34-5.

> turb the Church, blaspheming against God, and even more he will be the author of the slaughter and ruin of the entire nation. But I am certain the same Frumentius, informed of many things, will achieve great utility for the public good by consorting with the most venerable George and with the others of the first rank who are gifted in such teaching, and that he will return to his seat highly instructed in all things ecclesiastical. God keep you most honourable brothers.

There is, however, no indication whatsoever that this letter had any effect on the Aksumites' adherence to the orthodox Alexandrian creed as expressed by Athanasius. Frumentius may well have procrastinated, perhaps wisely, as both Constantius and George of Cappadocia were dangerous opponents, and the letter unquestionably indicated that he would have to suffer severe examination. Ammianus Marcellinus, in his history of the reign of Constantius, was briefly scathing to both emperor and bishop.[166] He commented that

> ...the plain and simple religion of the Christians was bedevilled by Constantius with old wives' fancies. Instead of trying to settle matters he raised complicated issues which led to much dissension, and as this spread more widely he fed it with verbal argument. Public transport hurried throngs of bishops hither and thither to attend what they call synods, and by his attempts to impose conformity Constantius only succeeded in hamstringing the post services.

As far as the 'venerable' George was concerned, Ammianus called him "a human snake, who had often made (the people of Alexandria) suffer from his poisonous fangs".

Though the Ge'ez tradition indicates that it was because of his work in Ethiopia that Frumentius came to be called Abba Salama, GETATCHEW HAILE[167] has suggested that actually Abba Salama I was a fifth–century preacher, not identical with Frumentius. This Abba Salama would have worked in the time of kings Abreha and Atsbeha in year 111 of the Martyrs. This works out, in the text that he uses, to 463 (Ethiopian Calendar), and would make the Synaxarium 's identification of Abreha and Atsbeha as the kings contemporary with Frumentius impossible. However, this theory depends on a Ge'ez text in which many dates have to be altered – even Diocletian's reign is incorrectly calculated – and which

---

166 Ammianus Marcellinus, "The Later Roman Empire" (A.D. 354-378), trans. W. HAMILTON, Penguin Books 1988, pp. 232, 246.

167 GETATCHEW HAILE, *A New Look at some Dates of Early Ethiopian History*, 1982, T 95, pp. 311-322.

mentions neither Abreha and Atsbeha nor Abba Salama, only the "coming of Christianity to the land of the Ag'azi (Ethiopia)". It is only an assumption that the text meant the introduction of Christianity by Abba Salama in Abreha and Atsbeha's reign, rather than some later evangelisation in the next century; for other dates attributed to the same event in other texts, see below.

Finally, there exists a book of the 'Acts' of Abuna Salama, summarised by SCHNEIDER[168] with the comment that it is, as rather to be expected, a muddle of legends, fanciful miracles and the like. The copy in question was written or copied in the year 1943–4/EC 1936, and has some curious features. Frumentius apparently questioned the incumbent bishop, Minas, in the reign of Kings Abreha and Atsbeha as to why Ethiopia, which already had circumcision and the faith of Christ, did not have baptism or the eucharist. The bishop replied that their Levite fathers had introduced circumcision, and the eunuch of queen Candace had brought the faith of Christ, but no apostle had been sent with the other ingredients. He suggested that Frumentius go to Alexandria and bring a metropolitan, a suggestion backed up in dreams by the Virgin and Christ themselves. Frumentius departed, was himself consecrated metropolitan, and returned to Aksum to baptise the people in the year 315. Such a version attempts to reconcile varying elements in the traditions about Christianity in Ethiopia. The presence of Jewish influences is explained, certain customs and attitudes supposedly harking back to the time of the first emperor, Menelik, son of King Solomon, and those who came with him to Ethiopia with the Ark of the Covenant. The story also confirms the adoption of Queen Candace as a queen of Ethiopia rather than of Meroitic Kush. It ignores, however, other tales about the preaching of St. Matthew in Ethiopia, and his conversion of its king.

7b. Theophilus 'the Indian'

Constantius' religious policy – later to be rejected by the victorious party in the dispute as it did not exclude Arians – was of sufficient importance to him to lead him to make another attempt to influence the Red Sea kingdoms. The date of the mission[169] of Theophilus the 'Indian' is not quite certain; it has been suggested that it was part of the episode noted by Athanasius around 356, or it may have occurred rather earlier.

Philostorgius, an Arian historian, recounts this missionary attempt in

168 R. SCHNEIDER, *Les Actes d'Abuna Salama*, AE XIV, pp. 153-65.

the 'Indian' regions. He claims some success for it in South Arabia, part of which was then included among the territories claimed in the Aksumite royal titulature. The account of Philostorgius is preserved in an eighth century epitome by Patriarch Photius of Constantinople. Many have doubted the whole story, Philostorgius being eager to aggrandise the role of Arianism, and expand its area of reputed influence.[170]

Theophilus, an Arian, bearing the title of bishop, was sent to the Himyarite kingdom by Constantius. His party, bearing rich gifts, supposedly succeeded in converting the population, who worshipped the sun, the moon, and various indigenous gods. The Jews, also present in Arabia, were compelled to retire. The local ruler assisted Theophilus in building three churches, one in the capital, Zafar, one at Aden and one at the mouth of the Persian Gulf. Theophilus then passed on to Dibos, his native island, and into other 'Indian' regions, already Christian, attending to religious questions as he went. Dibos may perhaps be Socotra or Sri Lanka – Gregory of Nyssa calls Theophilus a Blemmye, possibly intended as an insult, though others have suggested that perhaps he really came from the east African coastal region.[171] Then, from Great Arabia, he passed to the Aksumites, defined as Ethiopians named thus after their capital city. He is said to have regulated affairs there, to bring them to the Roman dominion again; this has been interpreted to mean that he delivered the letter of Constantius, with its attempt to influence the religious policy of the Aksumite kingdom, but there are problems here with the dating[172] Only DORESSE suggests that Theophilus was actually sent to replace Frumentius.[173]

SERGEW HABLE SELLASSIE[174] comments "He also mentions the courtesy of the (Aksumite) Emperor, and at the same time points out that Theophilus has not been in the capital city, Aksum". The note about the Ethiopian emperor stems from a misinterpretation of the text, which actually refers to the honours which Theophilus received from the Roman

---

[169] SERGEW, *Die Aethiopische Kirche*, p. 62, and in: The Church of Ethiopia; a panorama of history and spiritual life, p. 6.

[170] "The Ecclesiastical History of Philostorgius", as epitomised by Photius, trans. E. WALFORD, London 1855, p. 446. S.C.H. MUNRO-HAY, Aksum. An African Civilisation of Late Antiquity, Edinburgh UP 1991, pp. 17, 57; F. CABRAL, & H. LECLERCQ, Dictionnaire d'Archéologie chrétienne et de Liturgie, T. 5, Pt. 1, cols. 590-93.

[171] Gregory of Nyssa in "Contra Eunomium", PG XLV, col. 264; see also J. DESANGES, *Une mention alterée d'Axoum dans l'Expositio totius mundi et gentium*, AE 7, 1967, pp. 147-8; and CABRAL & LECLERCQ, DACL, col. 591-2.

[172] R. SCHNEIDER (in his review of KOBISHCHANOV's Axum) in: JES XVII, p.156, says that according to Philostorgius, Theophilus returned not long after 344 AD.

[173] J. DORESSE, Histoire Sommaire de la Corne Orientale de l'Afrique, Paris 1971, p. 100.

emperor Constantius II when he returned, though he received no particular bishopric as a reward. SERGEW HABLE SELLASSIE observes, however, that there is no definite statement that Theophilus reached Aksum, and his mission very likely met with little success in Ethiopia. Frumentius (Feremnatos) Abba Salama, also called *kesate berhan,* the 'Revealer of Light', seems to have died peacefully in Ethiopia, according to the Ethiopic *senkessar (Synaxarium).* This, though a relatively late text, probably combines information from Rufinus via Byzantine and Arab accounts with some Ethiopian traditional material. Rufinus, though he does not mention Frumentius' death, does imply – admittedly in formal phraseology which probably indicates that he had little definite information – that he had very great success in Ethiopia. There is no hint of troubles with the emperor and Bishop George. Very likely the Aksumite rulers simply delayed until the problem evaporated with Constantius' death in 361, and Frumentius never had to undergo any examination of his beliefs by the Arian ecclesiastical authorities in Alexandria.

8. Minas; Salama II

The successor of Frumentius, Minas, called Salama II[175], is accorded brief mention in the lists of metropolitans, and in one or two other Ge'ez works. Abba AYELE TEKLAHAYMANOT[176] asserts that "Abuna Salama was at the head of the Ethiopian Church until towards the year 361", mentioning a tradition – presumably from the *Gadla Aftsé*[177] – that a certain Minas succeeded him, and welcomed the Nine Saints (IIA: 12) when they came to Ethiopia. He also notes an alternative story that a Metropolitan Ya'qob is said to have welcomed the Saints in King Gebre Masqal's time, that is, in the mid–sixth century. The explanation probably lies in the fact that several Ethiopian metropolitans would have received different members of the foreign missionary community as they arrived from time to time during a period stretching from

174 SERGEW, AMEH, p. 101.

175 CONTI ROSSINI, Storia, pp. 157-8; The Dictionary of Ethiopian Biography, Addis Ababa 1975, p. 119 (R.K.P. PANKHURST).

176 AYELE TEKLAHAYMANOT *Egyptian Metropolitans*, p. 18.

177 The *Gadla Aftsé* mentions Minas, on fol. 33 of an unpublished ms. in the Institute of Ethiopian Archaeology (note 9, p. 116 of SERGEW, AMEH).

the later fourth century to the sixth century. TURLA[178] also offered a similar date for Frumentius' death; "On the death of Frumentius, in 360 there came to succeed him from Alexandria the monk Abba Minas, who assumed the name Salama II". Neither of these authors cites his source for the dating.

This Minas, according to SERGEW HABLE SELLASSIE, is said to have been an Egyptian. His appointment is thought to have represented the beginning of Egyptian jurisdiction over the Ethiopian Church. He is also supposed to have left certain literary compositions.[179] In another work[180], SERGEW HABLE SELLASSIE states that "about his origin nothing is mentioned"; and indeed, no further information about Frumentius' first successor is to be found in the usual sources. The idea that Minas was the first of the Egyptian metropolitans of Ethiopia is based on the extrapolation of the known arrangements as recorded in later times, back to the fourth century; there is no actual evidence for this bishop's place of origin. The name Minas, however, is a fairly common Coptic name.

9. Bishoprics in Ethiopia after Frumentius. Bishop Moses of Adulis and others

From the evidence of a Ge'ez inscription found at Aksum[181], SERGEW HABLE SELLASSIE nevertheless concludes that the bishops of Aksum continued to come from Egypt, and that sometimes other persons accompanied them. One such is supposed to be the writer of the inscription which reads "I David, the Egyptian, have written this; Lord have mercy on me". The inscription, numbered by LITTMANN as DAE 19, is carved on one of the thrones near the cathedral of Maryam Tseyon at Aksum. It has been cleverly paralleled by FIACCADORI with another transcribed by ROHLFS during his 1880–1 visit to Ethiopia, which, though included in MONNERET DE VILLARD's collection of documents, has previously never been deciphered.[182] FIACCADORI also comments that

---

178 A. TURLA, *La religione in Ethiopia*, Rassegna Sociale dell'Africa Italiana, II, 9, 1939, pp. 1068-73.

179 SERGEW HABLE SELLASSIE *et al.*, The Church of Ethiopia, Addis Ababa, 1971, p. 7; BROWN, *op. cit.*, p. 13.

180 SERGEW, AMEH, p. 110.

181 SERGEW, AMEH, p. 110.

182 G. FIACCADORI, *Per una nova inscrizione Etiopica da Aksum*, Egitto e Vicino Oriente IV, 1981, pp. 357-367; U. MONNERET DE VILLARD, Aksum, Rome 1938, pp. 36, 118.

the inscriptions could indicate the presence of ecclesiastics from Egypt who had come in the train of one of the metropolitans; but the dating, given the paucity of comparative palaeographic material, is extremely difficult.

It seems likely that bishops were soon appointed for the Ethiopian port of Adulis, doubtless under the primacy of the metropolitan bishop at Aksum. Bishop Moses of Adulis is the only one known by name, but the see appears in the *Notitiae Episcopatuum* (I: 5). Moses of Adulis was mentioned by Palladius.[183] He is apparently to be dated somewhere around the end of the fourth century, but almost nothing is known about him. DIHLE[184] conjectures that Moses might have been a successor of Frumentius at Aksum, erroneously attributed to Adulis by the compiler of the account, or a bishop ordained by Frumentius himself for Adulis. The last of these alternatives seems not improbable, particularly since the town of Adulis was a place where foreign Christian merchants and travellers, such as those mentioned by Rufinus in Frumentius' time, or Kosmas Indikopleustes and his companion Minas rather later, must have congregated.

Some other bishops are mentioned during the early period of the Ethiopian church, but always with tantalising vagueness (see below). It has been claimed that Socrates and Sozomen wrote that among the bishops who accompanied Patriarch Theophilus to Chalcedon in 403 for the Synod which temporarily deposed John Chrysostom there were some 'Indians'. This has been taken to mean Ethiopians; if so it would supply early evidence for bishops in that country, and for their presence at church councils. However, the suggestion depends on uncertain data.[185]

---

[183] J.D.M. DERRETT, *The History of Palladius on the Races of India and the Brahmanes*, Classica et Medievalia XXI, 1960, p. 108; U. MONNERET DE VILLARD, *Mose, Vescovo di Adulis*, Orientalia Christiana Periodica 13, 1947, pp. 613-23; B. BERG, *The Letter of Palladius on India*, Byzantion 44, 1947, pp. 5-16.

[184] DIHLE, *op. cit.*, pp. 49-50.

[185] The reference given is Socrates, " Historia Ecclesiastica", PG 67, VI. II; this chapter however concerns the death of Nestorius and the ordination of John Chrysostom. No reference to Ethiopian bishops appears in Socrates. NEALE, *op.cit.*, I, p. 220; BUTCHER, *op.cit.*, I, p. 233. She states that Theophilus set out in 403 "with a splendid retinue of Egyptian and Abyssinian bishops", duly arriving at Chalcedon and deposing Chrysostom. SERGEW, AMEH p. 110, cites Sozomen, "Hist. Eccl." VIII, 14; there is some confusion here, since this refers only to Theophilus' summoning bishops from the east to Constantinople. SERGEW says that Theophilus (385-412) came to Constantinople to take part in the second Ecumenical Council of 431 (i.e. that of Ephesus). Theophilus was long dead at this time, and Cyril was patriarch.

10. Bishop Theonius and other Bishops; 'Abba Joseph'

According to John of Nikiu, a certain Theonius was appointed bishop for 'India' by Emperor Honorius (395–423), through the influence of a lady called Theognosta. It has been assumed that the historian was referring to the Yemen, but he adds that "India, that is, the great India", had formerly been converted by Afrudit (Frumentius). However, it now seems probable that in fact the text refers to the conversion of the kingdom of Georgia. The *Synaxarium* also tells the tale of Theognosta, head of the harim of the king of 'India'; she converted the king, and eventually a bishop was consecrated for the region; in this version no name for the bishop is mentioned.[186]

It is possible that there was a bishop of 'Adulis' at the Council of Chalcedon in 451[187], but interpretations differ as to the whereabouts of the diocese concerned. The various manuscripts supply different readings for the name of the bishop's see *(doulou, doulu, botou, koptiton)* which resulted in a proposal that the title be interpreted as "bishop of the Koptites residing at Adulis". But it is also possible that another reading entirely is correct, and that the bishop came from the town of Buto or from Doulopolis, if not Koptos. HONIGMANN notes, too, that all the other bishops mentioned in the texts came from Lower Egypt; it seems extraordinary that one alone should have come all the way from Ethiopia.

A number of other Ethiopian bishoprics are mentioned in the lists of WANSLEBEN and CONTI ROSSINI, but the origins of these cannot be reliably dated (I: 5). Abba AYELE TEKLAHAYMANOT[188] quotes Kosmas as evidence for more than one bishop in Ethiopia; but Kosmas' account is very general:

> ..in Ethiopia (Aithiopia), at Axum and in all its environs, among the peoples of Arabia Felix who are called Omeritae, throughout Arabia and Palestine, Phoenicia, Syria and Antioch, down to Mesopotamia, among the Nobadae (Nobatas) and the Garamantes, in Egypt, Libya and Pentapolis, in Africa and

---

[186] John of Nikiu, CHARLES, trans., *op. cit.*, p. 69; BUDGE, Synaxarium, Vol. I. pp. 61-62. G. FIACCADORI, *Teofilo Indiano* (in two parts, in: Studi Classici e Orientali 33-4, 1983-4; Parte II, p. 281, n. 26.

[187] E. SCHWARZ, *Ein Bischof der römischen Reichskirche in Abessinien*, Philologus 91, 1936, pp. 356-7; E. HONIGMANN, *Un évêque d'Adulis au Concile de Chalcédoine*, Byzantion 20, 1950, pp. 295-301.

[188] AYELE TEKLAHAYMANOT, *Egyptian Metropolitans*, p. 20.

> Mauritania till Gadeir southwards, everywhere there are churches of Christians, bishops, martyrs, monks, and hermits, where the Gospel of Christ is announced.[189]

This gives plenty of scope for a multiplicity of bishops.

Later evidence for bishops in the country may be anachronistic, as when the *Acts of Yared and Pantelewon* refers to the condition of the church at the time of the arrival of the Nine Saints; the unity of the faith of the king, the metropolitan of Aksum, the priests and the bishops is stressed.[190]

SERGEW HABLE SELLASSIE notes a lamp found by PARIBENI at Adulis, bearing the words "Abba Joseph, Bishop"; his index refers to Joseph, Bishop of Adulis. However, the object is a votive lamp of the style of the one found by GRIFFITH in the Western Cemetery at Faras, commemorating St. Joseph, bishop and anchorite.[191] The inscription on such lamps reads **ΤΟΥ ΑΓΙΟΥ ΑΒΒΑ ΙωCΗΦ ΕΠΙCΚ**. The broken inscription of the Adulis lamp, **ΑΒΒ . Φ. ΕΠΙCΚΟ..** seems to belong to the same genre.

MEINARDUS briefly noted a certain monk, Musa, living in the late fourth century in the Egyptian desert (Scetis, the Wadi al-Natrun), but said to have been an Ethiopian. Perhaps an Ethiopian, on pilgrimage to Jerusalem, may have stopped in the desert to join one of the numerous hermitages and monastic institutions with which Egypt then abounded.[192] However, the designation Ethiopian may well simply mean that Musa was black, and he could just as easily have come from Nubia or some other African district.

---

189 VANTINI, OS, pp. 2-3 after PG 88, col. 170.

190 C. CONTI ROSSINI, ed., "Acta Yared et Pantelewon", CSCO, Scriptores Aethiopici, Series altera, T. XVII, Vitae Sanctorum Antiquorum, I, 1904, p. 40. "In regiis aedibus, una fide et in pace, cum rege et Metropolita Aksum, et sacerdotibus et episcopis, steterunt."

191 SERGEW, AMEH, p. 110 and index; F.Ll. GRIFFITH, *Oxford Excavations in Nubia*, LAAA XIV, 1927, pp. 73, and 111; pl. LXI 7; R. PARIBENI, Ricerche nel luogo dell'antica Adulis, Monumenti antichi, pubblicati per cura della Reale Accademia dei Lincei, Vol. XVIII, Roma 1907, col. 499-500; VANTINI, Faras, p. 236 refers to the lamp from Faras as a tombstone.

192 F. HEYER, Die Kirche Äthiopiens, Berlin/New York 1971, p. 180; O.F.A. MEINARDUS, Ethiopian Monks in Egypt, Alexandria, 1962; ID., *Ecclesiastica Aethiopica in Aegypto*, JES III, 1, 1965, pp. 30ff. See also FIACCADORI, *op. cit.*, p. 365, n. 42.

11. Bishop Thomas

A further bishop or metropolitan, associated with Ethiopia by a Georgian text, was a certain Thomas. He was dispatched by Patriarch Martyrius of Jerusalem (478–486) with messages to the Alexandrian patriarch. Thomas so impressed the patriarch that he was consecrated by him to the see of Aksum (Kusim), where he is supposed to have built many churches.

This information is from the Georgian version of the *Life of Cyriacus*, presumed to have been written by Cyril of Scythopolis, since it is lacking in the Greek version. The text[193] tells how Thomas took letters from Martyrius to the Alexandrian patriarch, and how the latter, seeing "the treasure that was in him", consecrated him "bishop over the land of the Abyssinians". Thomas then went to "the land of Kusim in Abyssinia" where he built many churches for Christ and "illuminated all Ethiopia with his virtues". Kusim in Abyssinia can hardly be anything other than Aksum.

This extract is of extreme importance for the history of the Ethiopian church. The Greek version of the text reports that Thomas was sent to the archbishop of Alexandria to collect the hangings or veils necessary for the coenobion of St. Euthymius, then under construction (479–482). Thomas must then have been sent to Alexandria whilst the monophysite Peter III Mongus was in hiding from Emperor Zeno's decree of exile, and Timothy Surus or Salafaciolus was in his second period of office as melkite patriarch (477–482). To whom, then, did Martyrius, accused of a certain inclination towards monophysitism like Anastasius his predecessor, write? It seems likely that since Martyrius' messenger was so well received, and, eventually, consecrated for Aksum by the Alexandrian patriarch, the two patriarchs would have agreed in their faith, but Martyrius' attitude seems to have been equivocal. Could it, then, have been Peter, in hiding in Alexandria, who sent Thomas to Ethiopia, rather than Timothy? If so, we thus have the first account of the sending of a monophysite metropolitan to Ethiopia. As GARITTE affirms, there is every sign

193 G. GARITTE, *La version georgienne de la vie de S. Cyriaque par Cyrille de Scythopolis,* Le Muséon 75, 1962, pp. 399-440: "Et accepit secum epistulas patriarchae Martyrii ad Alexandrinum patriarchem; et ivit ut perficeret ministerium diaconatus sui. Et ut vidit patriarcha sanctum hunc, non latuit eum thesaurus qui erat in eo, et consecravit eum episcopum super Abyssiniorum terram; et ut intravit Thomas in terram Kusim in Abyssinia, gratia quae erat apud eum splendidus, erexit ecclesias multas pro Christo; totam Aethiopiam illuminavit per virtutes suas".

that the addition in the Georgian version is correct; even the point that Alexandria had the right of appointment to Ethiopia is in order here.

CERULLI[194] held that there was no evidence for such a Bishop, Thomas being unknown in Ethiopian sources. However, there is one reference which seems hitherto to have escaped notice. The Syriac *Book of the Himyarites* preserves the name in the title of the now lost Chapter IV, that relating "How Bishop Thomas went to the Abyssinians, and informed them that the Himyarites were persecuting the Christian(s)".[195] This news resulted in an Abyssinian expedition under a certain Hiuna.[196]

There is no precise evidence for a date for this Bishop Thomas, nor is it specifically stated in the *Book of the Himyarites* that he was the Ethiopians' bishop. All that can be said is that he preceded the Himyarite war of Kaleb and was bishop at the time of the persecution of Najran in the late teens of the sixth century, with which events he had some fairly intimate connection. He could, then, easily be the same Thomas as the one consecrated between 479 and 482. If so, he must have died shortly after he had conveyed the news of the persecutions in Arabia to the Aksumite court, since by the time of King Kaleb's invasion of the Yemen there was another bishop, Euprepius, in Ethiopia (IIB: 14).

This bishop, Euprepius, is mentioned by name in year 830 of Alexander/519 AD (IIB: 13). He is alluded to by the monophysite author of the *Book of the Himyarites* as the 'holy bishop', just as Kaleb is called the 'believing king'; it seems likely, therefore, that he was a monophysite and that his predecessor, too, would have professed the same faith. SERGEW HABLE SELLASSIE[197] asserts that Thomas' name occurs in the *Acts of Azkir*, who was the legendary founder of the Christian faith in Najran in the reign of King Sarahbil of Himyar. There is, however, no mention of this in either the WINCKLER version he quotes nor in those of CONTI ROSSINI and JEFFERY. ISAAC[198] finds it significant that Kosmas, himself an Egyptian monk (at least

---

194 CERULLI, quoted by GARITTE, *op. cit.*, p. 406, n. 10.

195 A. MOBERG, The Book of the Himyarites, Lund, 1924, p. CI.

196 *Ibid.*, heading of chapter V;

197 SERGEW, AMEH p.111, quotes H. WINCKLER, *Zur Geschichte des Judentums in Jemen*, Altorientalische Forschungen I, III, 1897, pp. 328-36; this cites the "Acts of Azkir", but Thomas is not mentioned. See also J. RYCKMANS, *Le Christianisme en Arabie du Sud pre-islamique*, Atti del convegno internazionale sul tema, "L'Oriente cristiano nella storia della civiltà", Accademia nazionale dei Lincei, 361, 1964, pp. 422-32; C. CONTI ROSSINI, *Un documento sul cristianesmo nello Iemen ai tempi del Re Sarahbil Yakkuf*, RRAL, Ser.V, Vol. IX, 1920, pp. 705-750; A. JEFFERY, *The Acts of Azqir*, Moslem World 37, 1946, pp. 200ff.

198 ISAAC, *Ethiopian Church*, p. 246.

he became one later), did not mention "the presence of any Coptic Abuna in Ethiopia" at the time he was there – just before Kaleb's invasion of the Yemen. However, precious though Kosmas' snippets of information about Aksum are, they are hardly so extensive for this to be a major gap – perhaps he simply took the bishop's presence for granted. To him, the presence of a melkite bishop might have been the more worthy of comment.

12. The Nine Saints

The next significant event in early Ethiopian church history recorded by the sources does not specifically concern Alexandria, but it is of vital importance for the history of Christianity in the Aksumite kingdom. The arrival of the so–called 'Nine Saints' from 'Rome', meaning from cities somewhere in the Roman empire, including Syria – Constantinople, Caesarea, Antioch[199] – is generally accepted as an event that firmly ratified the predominance of monophysitism in Aksum. These missionaries, according to the hagiographies, came during the reign of the Ethiopian king Alameda, son of Sa'aldoba, perhaps in the late fifth century.[200] They continued their activities in the reign of Tazena[201] and were in some cases still living when Kaleb became *negusa nagast* of Aksum. Alternatively, one Ge'ez manuscript notes that they arrived in the time of Kaleb's son King Gebre Masqal and an otherwise unknown metropolitan called Ya'qob.[202] Sometimes, as already noted, they are associated with the metropolitan Minas (IIA: 8), or sometimes with Eleyas (IIB: 16).

The hagiographies therefore mostly indicate a late fifth to sixth century date for the Nine Saints' activities, though of course other 'Roman' missionaries may have previously come to Aksum. Their coming is attributed to purely religious enthusiasm, but it has been reasonably suggested that anti–monophysite persecution in Syria and other places in the empire, and the Nine Saints' refusal to accept Chalcedon, might have supplied extra incentive. Ethiopia at this time was by no means too far afield for travellers from the eastern Roman empire; Kosmas Indikopleustes in the early sixth century almost casually writes of merchants of Alexandria and

199 GUIDI, *op. cit.*, p. 126.
200 BUDGE, Synaxarium, Vol. IV, p. 1010; Vol. I, p. 117. SERGEW HABLE SELLASSIE, in: The Church of Ethiopia; a panorama of history and spiritual life, p. 7.
201 I. GUIDI, *Il Gadla Aragawi*, RRAL Atti...2, 1896, p. 63.
202 In a ms. in the Conti Rossini Collection in the Accademia dei Lincei, Rome.

Ela (Eilat) at Adulis. If the later hagiographical accounts are to be credited, the new arrivals found fellow–religionists in Ethiopia[203], and royal sponsorship for their Christanising work (IIC).

To the Nine Saints – Za–Mika'el Aregawi, Pantelewon, Garima, Aftsé, Guba, Alef, Yimata, Liqanos, and Sehma – and to other missionaries who entered Ethiopia at about the same time, is attributed a great deal of important work in disseminating their faith. This included translating the Bible and such works as the monastic Rule of Pachomius, or the lives of St. Anthony and St. Paul the Hermit, into Ge'ez. It may have been at this time, too, that the translation of the *De recta fide* of Patriarch Cyril of Alexandria (412–444) was undertaken. A collection of christological treatises by eminent churchmen was in due course assembled, which took its name, *Kerillos,* from the author of this work, which forms the opening chapter. The dissemination of such a work (pre–Chalcedonian, written when Nestorianism was the major heresy), can only have increased the respect of Ethiopians for the Alexandrian patriarchate.

ISAAC[204] suggests that there was a Judaeo–Christian Syrian element involved in this missionary activity, which explains how Aramaic words were introduced into the Biblical translations. Certainly, the missionaries who fled the Roman empire as persecutions mounted may well have come from several different milieux. Whatever their origin, the missionaries' work can be regarded as a 'second conversion' of the country. Their establishment outside the capital helped enormously in spreading Christianity into remoter districts.[205] From archaeological evidence, it seems that they found fertile ground on which to work in Ethiopia (IIC).

Tradition says that Za–Mika'el Aregawi, Pantelewon, and Garima came from Rome, Aftsé from Asia Minor, Guba from Cilicia, Alef from Caesarea, Yimata from Cosait, Liqanos from Constantinople, and Sehma from Antioch. Pantelewon and Liqanos are both today commemorated by churches marking the places where they are said to have established their hermitages, close by Aksum itself. Aftsé is said to have founded his hermitage at Yeha, Garima and Guba nearby at Medera, by Adwa, and Sehma to the southeast of Adwa. Aregawi was the founder of Debra Damo, Alef of the monastery of Halleluya. Yimata went to the mountainous region of Geralta, later famous for its rock–cut churches.

It appears likely that we may regard the royal conversion of the fourth century as largely restricted to the upper echelons of Aksumite society, the

---

203 See note 190. See also HEYER, *op.cit.*, pp. 154ff, 218.

204 ISAAC, *Ethiopian Church*, pp. 243-5.

205 E. ULLENDORFF, The Ethiopians, OUP, 1937, p. 97; J. DORESSE, *Ethiopia,* London, 1959, p. 81; BUDGE, History, Vol. I, p. 259-60.

king, his family and court, with perhaps certain others who through their contacts with foreign merchants, or for other reasons, knew Greek. However hard Frumentius and whatever (presumably Alexandria–trained) priests he brought with him in the episcopal train may have worked, they would surely have been limited because of the lack of translated material to such of the population who could follow the services in Greek. Frumentius himself could doubtless speak Ge'ez after his long sojourn in the country as a youth, and perhaps some of his assistants were quick in learning it. A local priesthood must have been established in due course, but we know nothing whatever about it at this stage. Nevertheless, even the royal exhortations to faith included with the legends on the late fourth and fifth century Aksumite coinage (except on coins of MHDYS and a few other anonymous issues – IIC) are all in Greek. Only with the Nine Saints and their colleagues, foreigners, but isolated in many cases in country districts where progress must have meant acquaintance with the local language, can we begin to really imagine a major attempt to teach Christianity in the vernacular. The cherished memory of these foreign teachers in Ethiopian hagiographical literature is a testimony to their eventual success in spreading their faith much further abroad than the relatively restricted confines that Frumentius and his successors in the Ethiopian episcopate are likely to have reached during the first one hundred and fifty odd years of Christianity in the country.

IIB. The Sixth Century

13. The Reign of Kaleb and the Himyarite War

By the time of King Kaleb of Aksum, who reigned over Ethiopia in the first half of the sixth century, the Christian faith was so well established that the country could launch itself into a religious war, one of the most famous events in Ethiopian history. According to the sources, Kaleb responded to an appeal to save the Himyarite Christians from persecution by the reigning Jewish king of Himyar, Yusuf Asar. The subsequent invasion was a victory for the Aksumite forces. After Yusuf's defeat and death Kaleb ruled the Yemen through a viceroy, Sumyafa' Ashwa' (Esimiphaios) from about 520–525.[206] A certain Abraha, an Ethiopian, then seized control through a military coup. He subsequently defeated Ethiopian attempts to depose him, remaining independent except for a formal agreement with Kaleb's successor

[206] This detail is supplied by Procopius, "History of the Wars", ed. and trans. H.B. DEWING, Loeb, London 1914, p.189-191.

to pay tribute. Abraha is best known for his church or martyrium, al–Qulays, at San'a, for his restoration work at the great dam at Marib, and for his purported expedition to Mecca in the Year of the Elephant, 570.

Accounts of the progress of the war with Himyar may be found in many sources[207], the content varying according to their biases or distance from events.

The position of the patriarch of Alexandria in the affair is obscure. The sources, according to the points they wish to emphasise, accord or

[207] The bibliography of this Arabian war of Kaleb, and of the martyrs of Najran, is enormous and still growing. An excellent summary is to be found in I. SHAHID, *The Martyrs of Najran, New Documents*, Subsidia Hagiographica no. 49, Bruxelles 1971, pp. 277ff; ID., *The Book of the Himyarites, Authorship and Authenticity*, Le Muséon 76, 1963, pp. 349-362; MOBERG, *op. cit.*; Ioannes Psaltes "Hymn on the Himyarite Martyrs", ed. R. SCROTER, ZDMG 31, 1877, pp. 400-405; "The Hymns of Severus and others in the Syriac version of ZDMG 31, 1877, pp. 400 – 403; "The Hymns of Severus and others in the Syriac version of Paul of Edessa as revised by James of Edessa", no. 154, VII. PO VII, 5, 1911, pp. 613-4; A. SCHER, ed., "Histoire nestorienne (Chronique de Séert)", PO VII, 2, 1911, pp. 99-201; Pseudo-Dionysios Telmahrensis; ed. I.B. CHABOT, "Incerti auctoris Chronicon anonymum pseudo-Dionysianum vulgo dictum", II. Accedunt Iohannis Ephesini fragmenta, curante E.W. BROOKS, CSCO 104 (1933) /Syr. 53 = Str. III, 2, textus. Also J.S. ASSEMANI, Bibliotheca Orientalis, I, Rome 1725, pp. 359ff; Ioannes Malalas "Chronographia", ed. L. DINDORF, L., CSHB, Bonn 1831, pp. 433-434. Also PG XCVII, 433, col. 639/640. For a translation from the Church Slavonic, mentioning Andas (Iadas) see SPINKA and DOWNEY, Bk. 18, 111. English version taken from VANTINI, OS, pp. 5-6. Nicephorus Callistus; "Historia Ecclesiastica", PG CXLVII, Liber XVI, Caput XXXII, pp. 301-302. Theophanes "Chronographia", PG CVIII, col. 487-8. See also col. 395-6 for Elesbaa and St. Arethas, and p. 531 for king Arethas. Cedrenus "Historium Compendium", PG CXXI, p. 715, ch. 656. Procopius Caesariensis, ed., and trans., H.B. DEWING, "History of the Wars", Loeb ed., London 1961, I, p. 189ff; "Chronique de Jean, Evèque de Nikiou", Texte Ethiopien, publiée et traduite par H. ZOTENBERG, Paris 1883, p. 391-2, and 157-8 (text). An English translation by R.H. CHARLES, London 1916; J.B. CHABOT, Chronique de Michel le Syrien, II, Paris 1905, pp. 183ff; W. WOLSKA-CONUS, La topographie chrétienne de Cosmas Indicopleustes, Sources chrétiennes, no 141, 159, & 197, Paris 1968 etc; BUDGE, Synaxarium, Vol. I, p. 289; "Acta Yared et Pantalewon", ed. C. CONTI ROSSINI, CSCO, Scriptores Syri, series altera, T. XVII, Vitae Sanctorum Antiquorum, p. 8; C. BEZOLD, *Kebra Nagast; Die Herrlichkeit der Könige*, Abhandlungen der Wissenschaften XXIII, Munich 1905; E.A.W. BUDGE, The Queen of Sheba and her only son Menyelek..., a complete translation of the Kebra Nagast with introduction, London 1922, p. 225; E. CARPENTIER, ed., "Commentarium preavis ad Martyrium Arethae", Acta Sanctorum, Oct. 24, tomus X, 1861, pp. 721-759. Simon Metaphrastes; BHG 167. PG CXV/2, cols. 1249-1290. Gregentius; His "Life" is preserved in later mss., (12th century etc.)

withhold mention to various details. Thus the Syriac report in the *Book of the Himyarites* by a monophysite author, possibly Simeon, bishop of Beth Arsham, attributes "the first coming of the Ethiopians" under a certain Hiuna to the report of Bishop Thomas (IIA: 11). The "second coming" was encouraged by one Ummayah, who delivered the news of the persecutions to Bishop Euprepius (see below) and Kaleb "the believing king".[208] However the Greek *Martyrium of Arethas* reports that Emperor Justin I (518–527) wrote to Timothy III (517–535), monophysite patriarch of Alexandria – his religious opponent – asking him to use his influence with the Ethiopian *negusa nagast* to persuade the latter to intervene on behalf of the Christians of Himyar.[209] The Ethiopian *Synaxarium* agrees with this account, adding the date of the fifth year of Justin, when John was archbishop of Jerusalem, Timothy of Alexandria, Timothy of Constantia, Euphrasios of Antioch, and Kaleb was king of Ethiopia.[210] Simon Metaphrastes' version of the *Acts of Arethas* declares that Justin wrote to one Asterius, patriarch of Alexandria[211], and the Armenian *Synaxary* tells of letters from Justinian (Justin) to Elesban (Kaleb) and to John of Jerusalem to ask him to encourage Elesban.[212]

However much truth there may or may not be in the assertion that the Alexandrian patriarch influenced the king of Aksum in his invasion plans, the real problem arises after Kaleb's victory, with the different accounts of the installation of a bishop. Naturally, any analysis of the

---

see A. Vasiliev, *The Life of St. Gregentius*, Vizantiyskiy Vremiennik XIV, 23-67, in Greek and Russian, and Justin the First, p. 298, n. 74; V. Christides, *The Himyarite-Ethiopian war and the Ethiopian occupation of South Arabia in the Acts of Gregentius (ca. 530 A.D.)*, AE IX, pp. 115ff; H. Zotenberg, trans., Chronique de Tabari, version Persane de.. Belami, Paris 1869, T. II, pp. 174ff; A. Guillaume, The Life of Muhammad a translation of Ibn Ishaq's Sirat Rasul Allah, OUP (Pakistan) 1955, pp. 14ff. For the inscription of Kaleb, R. Schneider, *Trois nouvelles inscriptions royales d'Axoum*, IV Congresso Internazionale di Studi Etiopici, Accad. dei Lincei, Quaderno 191, Roma 1974, T.I, p. 771. For Yusuf Asar, see S. Smith, *Events in Arabia in the 6th century*, BSOAS 16, 1954, p. 458, and Sergew, AMEH, p. 130.

208 Titles of the Chapters IV and XL, which are both missing; Moberg, *op. cit.*, pp. ci and civ.

209 Carpentier, ed., *op. cit.*, PG CXV/2, col. 1249-1290 (Simonis Metaphrastae); Ethiopic version ed. E. Pereira, Historia dos Martyres de Najran; Shahid, Martyrs, pp. 23ff; J.F. Boissonade, Analecta Graeca, Vol. V, Paris 1833.

210 Budge, Synaxarium, Vol. I, p. 289.

211 Simon Metaphrastes, PG CXV/2, col. 1280.

212 G. Bayan,, ed., *Le Synaxaire Armenien de Ter Israel*, PO XV, p. 347.

sources for these events needs to take into account the relative distance in time of the historians from the events that they narrate; but the events seem in this instance to have been recorded confusedly even in the sixth century. The names and dates cited are difficult to reconcile.

Nevertheless it is possible to ascertain a reasonably coherent sequence of events. In spite of the suggestions offered by certain scholars[213] it does not seem advisable to regard the accounts as referring to two separate occurrences.

The different sources name the two protagonists as follows:

- Aidog (Xenodon) and Dimion (John of Ephesus *apud* Pseudo–Dionysius of Tell Mahre);
- Andas and Dimnus (John Malalas);
- Andas and Damnus (John of Nikiu);
- Adad and Damianus (Theophanes and Cedrenus);
- David and Damnus (Nicephorus Callistus);
- Hellesthaeus and the Himyarite king (Procopius);
- Elesbaan and the Himyarite king (Kosmas Indikopleustes);
- Elesbas and Dounas (Greek *Martyrium Arethae*);
- Elesboam and Dounaa (*Life of Gregentius*);
- Elesbaa (*Nomoi ton Omeriton*);
- Elesbovman and Dunaas (Armenian *Synaxarium of Ter Israel*);
- Kaleb and Finhas (Ethiopic *Synaxarium, Acta Pantelewon, Kebra Nagast*);
- Kaleb and Masruq (*Book of the Himyarites*);
- Masruq also in the *Hymn of John Psaltes* and the *Chronicle of Se'ert*;
- *Al–najashi* and Yusuf Dhu Nuwas or Zur'a (al–Tabari and Ibn Ishaq), and on the inscriptions, the Aksumite *negusa nagast* Kaleb Ella Atsbeha and Yusuf Asar Yathar, king of Himyar, and of all the Tribes.

These variants appear to be mere distortions, through time and scribal error, of the originals mentioned at the end of the list above. The protagonists are the same; the event is the same; dates and names differ to varying degrees. One indication that the Aidog/Andas – Dimion/Damnus cycle is the same as the Kaleb Ella Atsbeha/Elesbaan *et var.*– Yusuf/Dounas *et var.* cycle, is that in both, despite the different names and dates, Abraham, Abraha or Abramos is the name of the later Himyarite king; John of Ephesus,

---

213 STEIN, *op. cit.*, II, pp. 103-4, considers that this occurred in the time of Anastasius. See also J. PIRENNE, *Le cadre chronologique de l'histoire éthiopienne du IV au VI siècle*, Etudes Sémitiques, Actes du XXIXe Congrès international des Orientalistes, Paris 1975, tables I and II.

Procopius, and al-Tabari all agree on this, and there is plenty of inscriptional evidence for Abraha's reign in Arabia.[214] Alparna occurs for Abramos in one source.[215] One or two of the chroniclers include elements of both the Andas and the Elesboas cycles. John Malalas (who may be identical with John the Scholastic, patriarch of Constantinople from 563–572) writes of Andas and Dimnus, but mentions elsewhere Elesboas, and his appointee in Arabia, Anganes.[216] Theophanes, a ninth century historian, who seems to depend much on Malalas for the time of Justin, describes, in 515, the martyrdom of Arethas, and the expedition of Elesbaa, king of the Ethiopians; in 535 he describes the war of Adad king of the Aksumites and Damianus king of the Himyarites (dated to year15 of Justinian, 542, by Cedrenus); and in 564 messengers were, he adds, sent to Arethas king of Ethiopia. Much of this confusion may be blamed on the fact that Kaleb, like all Ethiopian rulers, had a number of names, and that Yusuf Asar was also called by an epithet, Dhu Nuwas. These names, together with the errors caused both by their transposition into other languages, and the mistakes made by copyists or in dictation, have resulted in the varied forms detailed above.

14. The Historians of the War and the Bishops Euprepius, John Paramonarius and Gregentius

At the beginning of the reign of Yusuf Asar the Ethiopian metropolitan was 'UFRF, Euprepius, according to MOBERG's reading from the Syriac *Book of the Himyarites*.[217] Euprepius is also mentioned in the new (Syriac) letter published[218] by Irfan SHAHID, which is dated in different places with two different dates, the years 830 and 835 of Alexander, 519

[214] SERGEW, AMEH, pp. 148ff; p. 153.

[215] A. JEFFREY, quoting the Letter of Simeon. The Moslem World 36, 1945, p. 216.

[216] Translated in: SMITH, *op. cit.*, pp. 449-450.

[217] "The Book of the Himyarites" reads 'ufrf - the name is transcribed as Eupremius by VASILIEV, Eutropius by SERGEW HABLE SELLASSIE and Abba AYELE TEKLAHAYMANOT, and Eutrepius by CHRISTIDES. VASILIEV's version is in his *Justin the First* p. 294; SERGEW, AMEH, p. 131; CHRISTIDES, *op. cit.*, pp. 124-5, says that Eutrepius is supposed to have been sent from Ethiopia to South Arabia after the Dhu-Nuwas war; he adds that this is impossible, since authority to appoint bishops emanated only from Alexandria and the "Book of the Himyarites" explicitly states that only Ethiopian clergymen under the Ethiopian archbishop Eutrepius were sent to South Arabia. In fact, from the text (p. CXLI) it is indicated that Euprepius stayed in Ethiopia. MOBERG, p. XXXVI states "troops were left but no bishop" whilst the "Acta Arethae" mentions the leaving of the "holy bishop", presumably John Paramonarius or Gregentius.

and 524 AD. The former appears to be correct. The text reads;

> And in addition there being sent to your holiness a copy of the documents concerning the faith which have been written by the believing Cushites to the Orthodox Persians, together with a copy of the petition and the discourse which had been submitted by our humble person to the reverend AWFRFYS (Euprepius), the bishop of the Cushites, and to their believing king KLB (Kaleb), a copy of which we formerly sent to your Reverence.

It seems that Euprepius did not accompany Kaleb and his army to Himyar. In the *Book of the Himyarites*,Ch. XLVIII, after Kaleb's victory, the king is described deciding what to do about the Christian apostates. He says "When I was about to come to this land... . I asked our holy father, our blessed bishop Euprepius, if it was right that some of you who had denied and would repent should be accepted or not". It seems clear that the bishop was not on hand to judge them himself. His judgment as expressed by the king was; "Because these Himyarites are barbarians and a people for whom such conditions" – a many–years abstention from the sacraments – "would be too hard, they shall wait one year only and then be esteemed worthy of the Holy sacraments". Another hint that the was not with the expedition is supplied when the author of the *Book of the Himyarites* states in the same chapter that Kaleb "built many churches in that land, and appointed in them priests from those who were with him". He took with him from Ethiopia a supply of priests, ordained by Euprepius or his predecessors, since the bishop was not there himself to ordain them on the spot.

Some of the accounts of the war with Himyar are worth quoting *in extenso,* since they form the basis of the later chronographies. An early recorder of the Arabian war of Kaleb was John Malalas, writing not long after Kosmas Indikopleustes, and at about the same time as John of Ephesus, c. 580. Malalas records the history of King Andas of the Aksumites and Dimnus of the Himyarites. The relevant part (taken from the English version in VANTINI (see note207) reads;

> A war broke out between the Aksumite and the Ameritae Indians (Ameriton), on the following grounds. The king of the Ameritae (Omeritae) is closer to Egypt than the king of the Axumitae, who reigns over the inner regions. Some Roman merchants, on their way to Axum (Axuma) and to the inner kingdoms of the Indians, passed through the lands of the Ameritae (Omeritae)...Dimnos, king of the Ameritae, assailed the Roman merchants who were on transit through his kingdom for commerce, killed them, and carried away all their belongings. "Actually", he said, "the Jews who live in the territory of the

---

218 SHAHID, Martyrs, p. 63.

> Roman Christians, are vexed, and many are killed every year". Since then it was forbidden to carry out trade. The king of the Axumitae, writing to the king of the Ameritae, warned him "You have acted very badly", he said "in killing the Christian Roman merchants; you have also harmed my kingdom". This was a source of hatred between them, which later ended in a war. Under these circumstances, the king of the Auxumitae on his way to the war, bound himself with a promise saying: "If I succeed in vanquishing Dimnos, the king of the Ameritae, I shall become a Christian. For it is for the sake of Christians that I am waging the war". The king of the Auxumitae was victorious, seized (the king of the Ameritae) and slew him, defeated his army and occupied all his lands and kingdoms. After the victory, he sent two envoys accompanied by two hundred other prominent people to Alexandria. Through them he made a petition to Justinian asking that he appoint a bishop and clerics to teach him the elements of religion and the mysteries, after which he could be baptised. He also requested that all the territory of the Indians be taken under the empire of the Romans. The emperor, informed by Licinius, the Augustal of Alexandria, wrote back ordering that they might choose for themselves the bishop whom they wanted. The envoys of the Indians chose John, the Paramonarius of the Church of St. John in Alexandria, who was pious, unmarried, and about 62 years old. The envoys, having chosen thus a bishop and other clerics, took them to India, to their own king Anda.

This tale, repeated virtually word–for–word by pseudo–Dionysius of Tell Mahre's version of John of Ephesus and by John of Nikiu, sounds credible enough when it mentions the Roman merchants; the setting is clearly that of the Kaleb/Yusuf Asar war. Other aspects, particularly the king's reason for adopting Christianity, and his desire to hand over of the Indian kingdoms to Roman authority, are more suspect, but are not surprising in a rendering of the tale half–a–century later by a Christian Roman subject. In general the idea of a war over commercial affairs, coloured by the rescue of brothers in religion as was Kaleb's war, is by no means implausible. If we assume that the tale is a variant of that of Kaleb's war, rejecting the additions as the embroideries of a Roman Christian author, nothing in it seems particularly unlikely. Justin – or Justinian after the text, who was responsible for much of his uncle's imperial policy though he only ascended the throne in 527 – albeit following the principle that orthodoxy (the melkite, Chalcedonian faith) was the key to unity, was not inflexible towards monophysites.[219] It seems that Patriarch Timothy III of Alexandria remained in his office undisturbed (but see below), and through Kaleb the Roman emperor could hope to strike a

---

219 A. VASILIEV, Justin the First, Harvard 1950, is a useful source for the reign of Justin, and the nature of his policy in religious matters. The article *Justin I (518-527) and Abyssinia*, BZ 33, 1933, pp. 67ff is largely a preview of the later work in specific aspects.

blow at the Persians. The later embassies of Justinian to Kaleb [220] justify the assumption that the emperors were fully aware of the value of a Christian state in Arabia, and Aksumite co–operation, in their moves to undermine the Persian power in the Red Sea. Justin or Justinian, therefore, allowed the Aksumite envoys to select their own bishop. Naturally it is to be supposed that the emissaries of King Kaleb chose a monophysite, consecrated by Timothy III. Ethiopia's "normal relations with Chalcedonian Christians", cited by ISAAC[221], does not in any way indicate that the Ethiopians themselves must have been Chalcedonian in belief. Politics and commercial considerations transcended the religious question.

Another aspect of the story needs brief mention. The coins of the Aksumite kings, with their prominent, even gold–inlaid, crosses, and with emphatically Christian mottoes forming the legends, offer absolutely firm evidence that there was no return to paganism by the Aksumite royal house after the first conversion of Ezana in the fourth century.[222] There is no hint of any such apostasy; the sequence shows that all the kings from Ezana to Kaleb were Christians. Accordingly, the tale of the king's conversion appears as just an extra embroidery by later historians, their copyists or continuators.[223]

John of Ephesus, in an extract preserved by pseudo–Dionysius of Tell Mahre, mentions two wars. The first war, in year 4 of Justin, 521, was fought between the king of the Indians, Xenodon or Axenodon, and Aidog, king of India Interior; the text reads, in translation:[224]

> About the same time [i.e. contemporary with Athanasius or Justin] it happened that war broke out between the kings of the Indians, that is, between Xenodon, king of the Indians, and Aidog, king of Interior India, who was a pagan. When the latter had settled matters with Xenodon, he moved against Dimion, king of the Himyarites, who are also Indians, the cause of the war being as follows...

It is evident that here 'King Xenodon' is an erroneous rendering of the title 'the king of the Aksumites' *(Aiksoumiton basileus)* which occurs in

---

220 Those of Julianus, recorded by Procopius, and perhaps also by Malalas, and Nonnosus; for references see SERGEW, AMEH, pp. 137-140 and Y.M. KOBISHCHANOV, Axum, Pennsylvania and London 1979, pp. 103ff.

221 ISAAC, *Ethiopian Church*, p. 246.

222 S.C.H. MUNRO-HAY, The Coinage of Aksum, New Delhi 1984.

223 I. SHAHID, *Byzantium in South Arabia*, Dumbarton Oaks Papers 33, 1979, p. 43 n. 51, p. 64.

224 ASSEMANI, *op. cit.*, (n. 207), I, p. 359ff.

the same place in Malalas[225]; the two texts undoubtedly use the same source for this section. John of Ephesus' second war, between King Aidog of Interior India (Ethiopia) and Dimion, king of the Himyarites, is the real war, that between Kaleb and Yusuf. The story continues as follows, after an explanation about the *casus belli,* the damage to trade inflicted by Dimion's interference with the Christian Roman traders;

> Therefore enmity rose between them and war broke out. When they were gathered ready for battle, Aidog, king of the Ethiopians, declared "If it is granted to me that I conquer this bandit, the king of the Himyarites, I shall become a Christian; it is the Christian blood that he has shed that I want to avenge"...

Thus the Ethiopian *negus* was not yet, according to this text also, a Christian. John of Nikiu, in a garbled late–seventh century version of the same events, mentions that Andas, king of the Indians, worshipped Saturn, but attributes the war with Damnus 'king of the Jews' to an unnamed 'king of the Nubians'. Pseudo–Dionysius' version of John of Ephesus continues with a description of the victory of Aidog, and then goes on to add;

> Soon after this victory, he did not delay in fulfilling his vow, but sent two of his nobles to the emperor Justinian [i.e. Justin?], requesting him that he send to him a bishop and clergy. He (the emperor), very joyful at this, ordered that whatever bishop they chose should be sent. The envoys made diligent enquiries, and asked that John, paramonarius (watchman) of St. John, a chaste and pure man, be ordained bishop for them. So they received him and many clergy with him, and returned to their country with wonderful joy, and King Aidog welcomed them, together with the bishop and the priests who came with them, with equal happiness. He himself was instructed in the holy catechesis, received baptism, and became a Christian, together with all the nobles of the kingdom....

Essentially this is the same story as in Malalas, repeated by Theophanes in the ninth century, and by Michael the Syrian, monophysite patriarch of Antioch, in the twelfth century. Michael recounts that John Paramonarius was sent to Ethiopia, and that an anonymous prelate, a monophysite appointee of Timothy III, was sent to Arabia. John of Ephesus and John Malalas would both seem to imply that John Paramonarius was sent to Aidog/Andas in Ethiopia, but if the story in the *Life of St. Gregentius*[226] is correct, and Kaleb (Elesboam in the *Life*) remained three years in Arabia, John could have been sent to him there, as bishop for Arabia rather than for

---

[225] PG XCVII, 433, col. 639/640.
[226] A. Vasiliev, *op.cit.,* (n. 219), p. 297.

Aksum. However, the *Book of the Himyarites,* the most reliable text, only allows Kaleb seven months in Arabia.[227] There is no evidence for the date of death of either John Paramonarius or the Ethiopian bishop Euprepius.

The order of events is muddled by John of Ephesus, who next declares that the king of Arabia, the Christian king established by the Ethiopian king (Kaleb), died, and the Jewish king took over. The king of Ethiopia again attacked and defeated the king of Himyar, this time setting Abraham (Abraha) on the throne. The actual events are clearer from the Arab sources and Procopius; the rebellion of Abraha, which resulted in the deposition of Esimiphaios, called Sumyafa' Ashwa' in his inscriptions[228], was followed by an expedition, or perhaps two, to depose Abraha. The Ethiopians failed to dislodge him from his new throne; in the end they agreed to leave him there. The interesting point here is that, after the establishment of Abraha, John of Ephesus adds that another bishop was sent for by Kaleb from Alexandria. It is fairly certain that, since John of Ephesus has doubled the events, he has also doubled the bishop; this new bishop is therefore the already–mentioned John Paramonarius. ASSEMANI, however, taking into consideration the doubtful evidence from the *Life of Gregentius* (see below) considered him to be "certainly St. Gregentius, bishop of the city of Taphar"[229] – Taphar stands for Zafar, the ancient capital of the Himyarite kingdom.

The text after Pseudo–Dionysius of Tell Mahre reads;

> He then sent to Alexandria for a bishop, and received one from there before the (doctrine of the) Chalcedonian Synod had penetrated those parts. This bishop, after governing that region briefly, paid his debt to nature.

After the bishop's death, difficulties occurred;

> And the king of the Himyarites [i.e. Abraham] having learned that the (doctrine of the) Chalcedonian Synod had been introduced into the city of the Alexandrians and that Theodosius had been expelled on account of his faith and deposed because he recoiled from embracing the Synod [he was exiled in 536; in 541 Paul was installed in Alexandria], (the king), himself offended by this, refused to accept a bishop from the city of Alexandria.

---

227 SHAHID, *Byzantium in South Arabia*, p. 61 n. 103.

228 H.St.J. PHILBY, *Note on the last Kings of Saba*, Le Muséon 63, 1950, p. 272; G. RYCKMANS, *Une inscription chrétienne sabéenne aux Musées d'Antiquities d'Istanbul*, Le Muséon 59, 1946, pp. 171-2.

229 ASSEMANI, *op. cit.*, I, p. 383, n 1; for the text, see pp. 383-6.

The story according to Pseudo–Dionysius continues,

> At that time, the lack of a bishop became immensely detrimental to the kingdoms of the Ethiopians, Himyarites and Indians. In fact, every year without fail they sent to the emperor Justinian ambassadors with lavish gifts, requesting thereby that he give them a bishop who would not, under any circumstances, accept the Council of Chalcedon. For his part, although incessantly solicited regarding this matter, the emperor, as a zealous supporter of the Synod, kept on urging and admonishing them to receive a bishop who had embraced the Synod and was still waiting in Alexandria. They, however, replied that on no account would they be persuaded to receive anyone who approved the Synod; conversely they would welcome a bishop who condemned the Synod. Yet the emperor would not accede to their wishes. Thus every year the ambassadors of the three aforesaid kingdoms came to the emperor, and, having accomplished nothing, were dismissed by him. This contention lasted about twenty–five years until finally all the priests of those peoples had died out. Since they had struggled for so long to have a bishop opposed to the Synod, and had not obtained one, they eventually reached the point that, against the prescription of the canons, the presbyters, having convened, held the Gospels over the head of one of their order, thus investing him with the episcopacy; for they thought that in this way the laying–on of hands on a bishop had been performed – they who had not even the authority to ordain laymen. But most people were offended by such a laying–on of hands, rejected it and did not acknowledge its legitimacy. Hence great dissension arose among them. So, because of the lack of a bishop, a further error and heresy came to prevail in those lands: that of the Melchizedekians, who rashly asserted the identity of Melchizedek and Christ. Owing to the conduct of that particular people, not only was the Church divided, but the kingdom also was split into two parts; and wars, schisms and seditions were to spread throughout those regions for a long time to come. Lastly, Phantasiasts from the sect of Julian and Gaianus poured into those provinces and completely infected them with errors.

This is John of Ephesus' gloomy description of the state of affairs in the 'three' kingdoms of Ethiopia, Himyar, and the Indians, after the death of the unnamed bishop. ASSEMANI notes[230] that if Bishop Gregentius really held his see for thirty years as the *Disputatio cum Urbano Judeo* claims, this dispute with Justinian can hardly have continued for about twenty–five years of the same reign. He also comments that the unnamed bishop's episcopate was brief; the span of time from Abraha's advent until some time after the deposition of Theodosius is available for it, from about 530 to 536 (see also SHAHID).[231]

The *Nomoi ton Omeriton,*[232] purportedly a legal code prepared for

[230] *Ibid.*, p. 385, n. 1.

[231] SHAHID, *Byzantium in South Arabia*, p. 90.

the Himyarites by their Ethiopian conquerors, and part of the *Life of Gregentius,* describes the coronation of the new king Abraam. It quotes the rather studied–sounding acclamations of the army, in such a way that the status of the three chief personages is represented. They shout;

> Let there by many joyful years to Elesbaa, most holy king of Ethiopia....let there be many years to Abraam the Christ–loving king of the Himyarites, best and pious....let the years of the most pious kings Elesbaa and Abraam be long, and let the years of our most holy archbishop and peaceful shepherd, Gregentius, be healthy and whole, many and good and holy.

A minor difficulty here is that Abraam, presumably Abraha, was not the king at the time; most probably Sumyafa' Ashwa' has simply been ignored and the much better–known Abraha was substituted by the writer – here we are not dealing with a reliable source, even the Gregentius who gives the work its name being apparently fictional (see below) – or, far less likely, Abraam was a name adopted by Sumyafa' on his accession.[233] By the time the tale was written down, Abraha was famous for his deeds as king of Himyar, while the ephemeral Sumyafa' had probably been forgotten.

The second bishop mentioned by John of Ephesus may, as we have indicated above, have been John Paramonarius, if the confusion of events has resulted in double reporting. SHAHID suggested that this bishop might be identical with Euprepius[234], but Euprepius is known to have been bishop already before the war. If the *Life of Gregentius* is to be credited, he may alternatively be identical with Gregentius (see below). Gregentius, in fact, must fit here if there was an approximately twenty–five year gap because Justinian blocked the next monophysite appointment to the Arabian/Ethiopian bishoprics after the expulsion of Theodosius in 536. Since both Arabia and Ethiopia were supposedly affected by this blocking, it may be assumed that whether John Paramonarius was bishop in Ethiopia and Gregentius bishop in Arabia (Zafar), or whether they represent one single bishop or successive bishops of Zafar, they were both dead by the time this contretemps with Justinian arose.

Gregentius is a very obscure character. Indeed, his very existence is questioned by various scholars. SHAHID thought that Gregentius' *Life* contained a mixture of fact and fiction, the latter element including his name,

---

232 Gregentius, "Nomoi ton 'Omeriton", PG LXXXVI/I, col. 570.

233 SHAHID, *Byzantium in South Arabia*, pp. 34-5.

234 *Ibid.*, p. 90.

western origin and religious affiliation;

> ...as far as the *Vita* is concerned, it is certain that the bishop, consecrated for the newly conquered South Arabians, was not called Gregentius, that he did not hail from the Occident but from the Orient, and that he was a Monophysite, not an Orthodox Chalcedonian.

This last point may not be important if, as is not entirely impossible, South Arabia under Abraha moved away from monophysitism as it moved away politically from Ethiopia. Two hierarchies may even have existed at the same time[235], as they did, uneasily, in Egypt and other eastern regions. In the *Nomoi ton Omeriton* Gregentius is promoted to archbishop of Zafar, who consecrated other bishops.[236]

In spite of the complexities in the sources for the history of Kaleb's war, it seems clear enough that, on the death of the metropolitan bishop of Ethiopia, Euprepius, who was already incumbent by 519, another bishop, probably John, was sent by the monophysite patriarchate following the principle of Alexandria's right to appoint the Ethiopian primate. This seems to have occurred about 520 AD. Bishop John was in his sixties when he was sent south, and very likely he did not live long after; possibly he was succeeded by one of the other metropolitans mentioned in Ge'ez sources as contemporaries of Kaleb, Qerlos or Eleyas (II: 16). GETATCHEW HAILE makes a tentative suggestion that one of the homilies in the manuscript EMML 1763, of 'Yohannes bishop of Ethiopia' about the Holy Virgin Mary, might conceivably, after due study, prove to belong to John Paramonarius.[237]

15. The Melkite Patriarchs 'Asterius' and 'Proterius'

For the melkite patriarchs, whose sequence had lapsed after John Talaia's election in 482 there is confusing evidence. Ibn Rahib states that Justin replaced Timothy III by Apollinarius. The enigmatic figures Asterius and Proterius are also supposed to have been melkite patriarchs during Timothy's episcopate, 517–535; Asterius was apparently appointed by Justin on the death of Dioscorus in c. 519. For the next monophysite episcopate, that of Theodosius, 535–567, Justinian set up Paul, 541, Zoilus,

[235] *Ibid.*, pp. 30ff, 47 n. 63, 87 n. 201.

[236] *Ibid.*, p. 45 n. 54.

[237] GETATCHEW HAILE, *A New Ethiopic Version of the Acts of St. Mark*, Analecta Bollandiana, 1981, p. 120.

and Apollinarius 550–570 on the melkite side. Ibn Rahib's Apollinarius might be an error for the later Apollinarius.[238]

Though it seems from VASILIEV's comments that Justin left the patriarchate of Timothy to run its course without interference, there are some anomalies in the records, particularly with regard to the mysterious Asterius or Proterius. Proterius is supposed to have consecrated Gregentius; indeed, he is only mentioned with Gregentius (in his *Life*). CHRISTIDES[239] noted that the two Greek sources, the *Acts of Gregentius* and the *Martyrium of Arethas* present an orthodox (melkite) viewpoint, although Gregentius himself was "probably" monophysite. Proterius must be seen as a melkite anti–patriarch, inserted, CHRISTIDES suggested, to "orthodoxize" the former work. NEALE[240] commented that

> Gregentius, the successor of John, is not only commemorated in the Menology, but seems, from a fragment of his writings, to have been a Catholic. On the other hand, Dionysios, Patriarch of the Syrian Jacobites, affirms, quoting John of Asia, ... that when the Orthodox succession was restored to Alexandria, it was rejected by the Homeritae. The fact that Elesbaan received a bishop from Alexandria is not convincing for two reasons – that the appeal was made through Justinian, and that the Patriarch of Alexandria is called, not Timothy, but Asterius. LE QUIEN excuses S. Elesbaan for applying to Alexandria, on the ground of his being unable to know the real heresy of this See through his separation from the rest of the Catholic world.

That Kaleb would have tolerated an 'orthodox' (Chalcedonian) bishop in South Arabia seems curious, though many of the sources implicitly accept a burying of differences in the period of the Ethiopian war – indeed, for the entire reign of Justin, if VASILIEV is right in his interpretation of the emperor's political and religious attitudes (see above). Nevertheless, the very vagueness of the orthodox appointee of Justin to Alexandria, Asterius, or perhaps Proterius[241], seems instead to favour the likelihood of an incumbent in Arabia appointed with Kaleb's approval by Timothy III.

For the identity of Proterius and Asterius, and their possible historical

---

[238] For notes on this, see ASSEMANI, *op. cit.*, (n. 219), I, p. 382, note 1; BUTCHER, *op. cit.*, I, pp. 322ff; VASILIEV, Justin the First, p. 285, note 47, p. 298, note 74. Petrus Ibn Rahib, "Chronicon Orientale", ed. P.L. CHEIKHO, CSCO, Scriptores Arabici, versio, ser III, T.I, Paris 1903.

[239] CHRISTIDES, *op. cit.*, pp. 117, 123, 125.

[240] NEALE, *op. cit.*, II, p. 32.

[241] CHRISTIDES, *op.cit.*, p. 123, 136ff; VASILIEV, *op. cit.*, p. 298, n. 74; NEALE, *op. cit.*, II, p. 32 and n. 4 for references to Simon Metaphrastes and S. Arethas.

validity, much ingenuity has been exercised. VASILIEV supplies an excellent bibliography. The outcome seems to be the excision of both from the record. It may perhaps be that the whole problem of Proterius originated from the confusion, in the later redactions of the *Life of Gregentius,* between the patriarchs of two periods; it is striking to notice that the Proterius who held the melkite episcopate 451–457, was also interposed between a Patriarch Dioscorus (I, 444–454), and a Timothy (II, 458–480). The suggestion that the name of Proterius was inserted into the story of Saint Gregentius because its compiler was of the orthodox (melkite) belief, and hesitated to name the monophysite Timothy III, has been noted above;[242] exactly the opposite suggestion has been offered to explain the replacement of the name Asterius by that of Timothy.[243] VASILIEV very plausibly sought to identify the two, Proterius being a corrupt form of Asterius, himself of doubtful existence.[244]

An Arabic text[245] (from a manuscript in the library of the Maronite College in Rome) is relevant to the study of the Ethiopian church and its Alexandrian mother–church in this period. The text, which ASSEMANI quoted, is anachronistic, as will be evident;

> And when Theodora the queen, Justinian's wife, heard that the metropolitan of Ethiopia (matran al–Habasha) was dead, and that the Melkites had consecrated another over the land of the Habasa, she sent to the Copts to tell them this; and they wrote to Mar Ya'qub al–Barad'a (Jacob Baradeus) and told him about it. And they told him that the king of Suakin held the door of Habasa. And when this Roman Melkite metropolitan reached him (the king of Suakin) and with him a thousand cavalry and weighty gifts, and that metropolitan began to show the king of Suakin the gifts and the decrees and the robe of honour, he kept him with him for a month, and he served him and treated him as a guest. And when, on a certain day, he thought to send him on his journey, a letter from Queen Theodora came, and a sealed decree of the king. There was stated in it "There will come to you a rich metropolitan and a poor metropolitan. Hold and delay the rich metropolitan and let the poor metropolitan travel on, and do not hold him back". And he directed him quickly, and he speedily arrived at the land of Habasha. But as for the other, when he arrived amongst them (the Ethiopians) and they read his writings, they saw that his beliefs were those of Arius the heretic, and they killed him and burnt

242 CHRISTIDES, *op. cit.*, p. 123.

243 VASILIEV, *op. cit.*, p. 285, n. 47, quoting J.B. COULBEAUX, Histoire politique et religieuse d'Abyssinie, depuis les temps les plus reculés jusqu'à l'avènement de Ménélick II, Paris n.d (preface dated 1928).

244 *Ibid.*, p. 298, n. 74.

245 ASSEMANI, *op. cit.*, I, p. 384. Quoted also in LE QUIEN, Oriens Christianus, II, pp. 646-7. See also NEALE, *op. cit.*, II, p. 37, who believed that Jacobitism was first preached in Ethiopia by the exertions of Theodosius when in exile (p. 36, n. 1).

him. And so the Ethiopians continued in the belief of Mar Ya'qub until now.

This cannot fail to recall the similar rivalry between the melkite and monophysite ecclesiastical missions apparently sent to Nubia by Justinian and Theodora. Most probably the text refers to the same incident, in a slightly garbled fashion. Ethiopia and Nubia are similarly confused by Abu Salih, for example. If the incident is applied to Ethiopia, in the lifetime of Theodora (d. 548) and Jacob Baradeus (d. 578), it would fit in the period without metropolitans cited by John of Ephesus, which ended with an illegal election. The text transports the incident into a period when the coastline of what is now Ethiopia and the Sudan had fallen under the control of local Muslim rulers.

Some of the events of the time of Patriarch Theodosius I, 535–567, have already been mentioned.[246] NEALE also states[247] that Theodosius sent a disciple, Julian, to Ethiopia while SERGEW HABLE SELLASSIE adds that the exiled patriarch sent 'Dionysios of Halicornasus' to Ethiopia to strengthen the Christians in their faith.[248] Julian was the missionary sent by Theodora to convert Nubia; only GETATCHEW HAILE[249] suggests that he "might have extended his mission to the king of the Axumites after «converting Silko, king of the Nobatae»". This idea derives from the name Luleyanos, bishop of Aksum, author of a homily in the manuscript EMML 1763; a name which GETATCHEW HAILE notes as "Julius?" with a comment that the form is Syriac. 'Dionysios of Halicornasus' is perhaps a reference to Julian of Halicarnassus, whose heretical teachings later entered Nubia from Aksum (I: 3a).

The entry of heresy into Ethiopia as a result of the lack of communication with the head of the monophysite church is related by John of Ephesus.[250] In describing the conversion of Alodia in c. 580, he com-

---

246 NEALE, *op. cit.*, II, p. 36; quoting LE QUIEN, *op. cit.*, II, 646, and ASSEMANI, *op. cit.*, I, p. 384.

247 NEALE, *op. cit.*, II, p. 37, quoting GREGOR, Bar Hebraeus, ap. Assemanus, *op. cit.*, II, p. 326.

248 SERGEW, AMEH, p. 142.

249 GETATCHEW HAILE, *A New Ethiopic Version of the Acts of St. Mark*, Analecta Bollandiana, 1981, p. 120-1.

250 John of Ephesus, trans., PAYNE-SMITH, p. 323. The comment is in a letter which Longinus conveyed to the king of the Nobatae, Awarfiula (Orfiulo), to be forwarded to the illegally-elected patriarch, Theodore, installed by Longinus himself in 575. This patriarch, in his anomalous position of monophysite anti-patriarch to Damianus 569-605 and to John 569-79, had become, through the missionary activities of Longinus, the head of the church as far as the Nobadae and the Alodaei were concerned. It could not have been Peter IV, 567-9, who deposed Longinus (TRIMINGHAM, Sudan, p. 55 note 4) nor was he a melkite. Longinus was deposed between 576 and 578 when Damianus was monophysite patriarch, Theodore anti-patriarch, and John melkite patriarch.

ments that Bishop Longinus found that there were already certain heretical beliefs in the country, imported by Aksumites, crediting the opinions of Julian of Halicarnassus. Perhaps the Gaianites, who after all accepted the basic tenets of the monophysite faith, were not unwelcome in Ethiopia. JARRY[251] suggests that Julianist ideas may have permeated into Arabia through the Ethiopian invasion, since he assumes that the Ethiopian church was under the influence of an Egyptian clergy well imbued with Julianist ideas.

CHRISTIDES[252] supposed, after the text of John of Ephesus quoted above, that the monophysite Himyarites refused to accept a bishop from Patriarch Theodosius after the death of the previous bishop, since Theodosius was orthodox. Theodosius, however, was not orthodox except as a monophysite who was not a follower of the heresy of Julian of Halicarnassus; he was himself eventually expelled from Alexandria for his monophysite adherence. Theodosius[253], it is true, was installed by the imperial prefect Dioscorus and the *dux* Aristomachus, which demonstrated Imperial support, but that support was through Theodora rather than Justinian. The installation of Gaianus, a monophysite heretical follower of Julian of Halicarnassus, was achieved by force, but his patriarchate only lasted for 103 days before the authorities ejected him. Then the imperial commissioner Narses arrived, and the Severan monophysite Theodosius was re–installed. Theodosius, supported only by the military force of the empire, and hated even by his co–religionists, was asked to accept Chalcedon by Justinian in 536. By the end of 537 he had been deposed as a heretic; it was presumably this situation which made the monophysite Himyarites refuse to accept a bishop from any other patriarch, rather than Theodosius' 'orthodoxy'. Theodosius, after a brief exile, returned to

251 J. JARRY, Hérésies et factions dans L'Empire Byzantin du IVe au VIIe siècle, Le Caire 1968, p. 86 states that Christianity at Najran "subit certainment l'influence des idées julianists. N'oublions pas qu'elle fut sauvée par une expédition éthiopienne à une époque où l'église éthiopienne était sous l'influence d'un clergé égyptien en bonne partie julianiste. N'oublions pas non plus que les missionaires julianistes d'après Michel le Syrien s'aventurèrent égalment dans le pays de Kush, c'est-à-dire en Ethiopie (note 3). Les idées julianistes par conséquent ont pu parvenir en Arabie non seulement par l'intermediane de Sergius [a bishop consecrated by Eutropius, a Julianist bishop] mais aussi par le canal des envahisseurs éthiopiens". Note 3 adds " En 580 encore Longin trouva en Abyssinie (*sic*) des Axumites qu'il sauva de la phantasie de Julien."

252 CHRISTIDES, *op. cit.*, p. 125.

253 E.E.A. STEIN, Histoire du Bas Empire, Paris-Bruxelles-Amsterdam 1949, pp. 380-1.

Alexandria and lived there quietly until his death in 566. Melkite restoration in Egypt only occurred with Paul of Tabennesis in 537; abbot of a monastery whose monks had expelled him for Chalcedonian leanings, he was then at the imperial capital, and came back as patriarch. He only lasted until 542, when intrigues drove him also from the patriarchal throne, to be succeeded by Zoilus.

16. The Metropolitans Qerlos and Eleyas

Finally for the reign of Kaleb there are two metropolitans whose names are mentioned in Ge'ez texts. According to AYELE TEKLAHAYMANOT[254], a note in one of the lists mentions a metropolitan named Qerlos (Cyril) who lived in Kaleb's time. The king and the metropolitan are both supposed to have "agreed in the faith" and together led an expedition against "Tanbalat".

In the last years of Kaleb's reign and the beginning of that of Gebre Masqal (as the Ethiopic texts call Kaleb's son and successor), the *abuna* Eleyas, who is supposed to have been accused of simony by the 'Apostle of Eritrea', Libanos, is said to have been the metropolitan of Aksum.[255] This accusation resulted in King Za–Gabaza–Aksum (possibly to be identified with the Gebre Masqal of Ethiopian tradition, and the Ella Gabaz of the coinage?) exiling Abba Libanos. Homilies supposedly composed by Eleyas appear in two manuscripts[256] which also mention other bishops not included in the lists; Tewoflos, Luleyanos.

Abba Libanos is supposed to have been a monk with the great Egyptian monastic leader Pachomius, who later sent him to Ethiopia. However, Pachomius died in 348, and Libanos must have encountered Eleyas some two hundred years later; the records probably indicate that Libanos was reared in the Pachomian monastic tradition before journeying to Ethiopia.

---

[254] AYELE TEKLAHAYMANOT, *Egyptian Metropolitans*, p. 19; the list: Conti Rossini collection, no. 7, Accademia dei Lincei.

[255] For Elias (Eleyas), see C. CONTI ROSSINI, *Il Gadla Libanos*, Ricordi di un soggiorno in Eritrea, Asmara 1903, III; *Dictionary of Ethiopian Biography*, pp. 55, 103; AYELE TEKLAHAYMANOT, *Egyptian Metropolitans*, p. 19.

[256] SERGEW HABLE SELLASSIE, *A New Literary Source for Aksumite History; the Case of EMML 8509* paper read at the Seminar on Aksum, Addis Ababa University, Oct. 4th-5th, 1989; GETATCHEW HAILE, *A New Ethiopic Version of the Acts of St. Mark*, Analecta Bollandiana, 1981 (EMML 1763, ff. 224r-227r).

IIC. Archaeological evidence for Christianity in Aksumite Ethiopia

Material evidence for the spread of Christianity in Ethiopia comes from a number of categories of objects found during archaeological excavations. Although archaeological research in Ethiopia is not well developed, an impressive number of indications as to the prevalence of Christianity have already been identified from the Aksumite period. This does not include the several hundred rock–cut churches or monastic sites, difficult to date but doubtless often originating from pre–Zagwé times, to be found in Tigray and other places.

A hint that the depiction in the Ge'ez hagiographical literature of Christian rulers encouraging the spread of Christianity in Ethiopia during the fifth century (IIA: 12) may be substantially true comes from two important primary sources. From the fourth century coins and inscriptions[257] served as public demonstrations of the religious policy of the monarchy. The dedication of inscriptions to the old pantheon was altered to Christian phraseology; though as yet there is no clear evidence for biblical quotations in the early inscriptions, which would have been an interesting sign as to the progress of translation of the Bible into Ge'ez. The cross replaced pagan symbols on the coins. Later in the fourth century, Christian legends were also inscribed on the coins. The earliest ones read, in Greek, around a cross, 'May this please the people'. They were probably first struck in Ezana's time. Ouazebas followed this example, and MHDYS (Mahadeyis?) employed a version of Constantine I's famous phrase *In hoc signo vinces*. His coins depict a cross with the Ge'ez legend 'By this cross (masqal) he will conquer'. Another anonymous type of approximately the same period – the royal name is not preserved – employs the Ge'ez word for the Christian God., *egzi'abher*. Fifth century coins often used the phrase *Theou eukharistia,* 'By the Grace of God' written after a cross.

On large numbers of pottery vessels dating apparently from the fourth to the seventh century, found at all the main Aksumite sites excavated[258], depictions of the cross appear. These, in a multitude of forms, were sometimes stamped, sometimes incised, and sometimes painted. The earlier examples come from royal tombs (chiefly, so far, from the Tomb of

[257] S.C. MUNRO-HAY, The Coinage of Aksum, New Delhi, 1984; E. LITTMANN, *et al.*, DAE, Vol. IV, Berlin 1913.

[258] See for example R. PARIBENI, *Richerche nel luogo dell'antica Adulis*, Monumenti Antichi, Reale Accad. dei Lincei XVIII, Rome 1907, pp. 438-572; F. ANFRAY, *La poterie de Matara*, RSE XXII, 1966, pp. 5-74; R. WILDING in: S.C. MUNRO-HAY, Excavations at Aksum, BIEA, London 1989. For the Matara treasure see F. ANFRAY and G. ANNEQUIN, in: Annales d'Ethiopie, 1965, pp. 69-70, and Pl. LXIX.

the Brick Arches) in the central necropolis of Aksum, and apparently date from the period when Christianity was limited to the ruling strata of the kingdom. But from other sites, at Aksum itself, Matara, or Adulis, the cross soon becomes one of the commonest of all decorative motifs. Such evidence, far more than the 'official' manifestations of the adoption of Christianity constituted by the coins and inscriptions, suggests that Christianity rapidly became popular, at least in the major Aksumite towns. The 'Matara treasure', consisting of chains, gold coins and two crosses of gold, possibly dating to the sixth century, might even, ANFRAY suggests, have been the property of a bishop.

Ecclesiastical buildings are also known from the Aksumite period.[259] Ethiopian legends attribute to kings Abreha and Atsbeha (IIA: 7a) the construction of the cathedral of Maryam Tseyon at Aksum on land which Christ miraculously dried up from a former lake for the purpose.[260] However, archaeology indicates that two earlier Aksumite buildings preceded it; the podium of the present cathedral rests on yet another Aksumite structure, possibly an earlier church.[261] The cathedral described by ALVARES (see below) which we may presume was built in Aksumite times (unless the armies of queen 'Gudit' had already partially ruined the original one in the tenth century –IV: 31) was a large 'five–aisled' – nave and four aisles – basilica. It was eventually destroyed in the sixteenth century by the Muslim armies under the *amir* of Adal, Ahmad Gragn, but Francisco ALVARES'[262] description of the ancient church, the only record we have, survives;

> ...a very noble church, the first there was in Ethiopia: it is named Mary of Syon. They say that it is so named because its altar stone came from Sion. In this country (as they say) they have the custom always to name the churches by the altar stone, because on it is written the name of the patron saint. This stone which they have in this church, they say that the apostles sent it from Mount Sion. This church is very large; it has five aisles of good width and of great length, vaulted above, and all the vaults closed, the ceiling and sides all painted. Below, the body of the church is well worked with handsome cut stone; it

259 For references see MUNRO-HAY, Aksum. An African Civilisation of Late Antiquity, EUP 1991, Ch. 10: 5).

260 C. CONTI ROSSINI, *Liber Axumae*, CSCO, Script. Aeth., series altera, T. VIII, 1909.

261 H. DE CONTENSON, *Les fouilles à Axoum en 1957, Rapport préliminaire*, AE III, 1959, pp. 25-42, and *Les fouilles à Axoum en 1958, Rapport préliminaire*, AE V, 1963, pp. 1-40; F. ANFRAY, *Chronique archéologique, (1960-1964)* AE VI, 1965, pp. 3-26.

262 C.F. BECKINGHAM and G.W.B. HUNTINGFORD, eds., *The Prester John of the Indies*, Hakluyt Society, Cambridge 1961, p. 151.

> has seven chapels, all with their backs to the east, and their altars well ornamented. It has a choir after our fashion, except that it is low, and they reach the vaulted roof with their heads; and the choir is also over the vault, and they do not use it. This church has a very large circuit, paved with flagstones like the lids of tombs. This consists of a very high wall, and it is not covered over like those of the other churches, but is left open. This church has a large enclosure, and it is also surrounded with another larger enclosure, like the enclosing wall of a large town or city. Within this enclosure are handsome groups of one storey buildings, and all spout out their water by strong figures of lions and dogs of stone [of different colours]. Inside this large enclosure there are two mansions, one on the right hand and the other on the left, which belong to the two rectors of the church; and the other houses are of canons and monks.

Presumably this description reflects the result of continual refurbishing or even partial rebuilding of the original church from the fourth century onwards.

Copies of land charters detail territory purportedly granted to Maryam Tseyon church by Aksumite kings; Abreha and Atsbeha, Gebre Masqal, and Anbessa Wudem.[263] An account of the church's magnificence in late Aksumite times was apparently related to the prophet Muhammad by two of his wives, Umm Habiba and Umm Salama, who had lived in exile in Ethiopia in the 620s. It seems that the church's walls were covered with paintings, a type of decoration that later became standard for Ethiopian churches. Unfortunately, no such early paintings have survived, or at least none have been found to date.

To the east of Aksum, the church of Abba Pantelewon seems to have succeeded a pre–Christian sanctuary. It is supposed to have been built on the site where the saint decided to settle, and where later King Kaleb retired after his abdication.[264]

The Aksumite churches[265] which have so far been excavated in Ethiopia were apsidal basilicas, contrasting sharply with the round churches of the present day. These latter are probably based on a local African architectural tradition. Two basilicas have been found on the hill called

---

263 G.W.B. Huntingford, The Land Charters of Northern Ethiopia, Addis Ababa 1965.

264 E. Littmann *et al.*, DAE, Berlin 1913. see Vol. II, p. 90 for Abba Pantelewon, and Vol. IV for inscriptions.

265 For references see Munro-Hay, Aksum. An African Civilisation of Late Antiquity, EUP, Ch. 10: 5; L. Ricci, *Communication* AE X, 1976, pp. 327-8; H. de Contenson, *Les fouilles à Haoulti-Melazo en 1958*, AE IV, pp. 39-60; F. Anfray, *Deux villes Axoumites; Adoulis et Matara*, VI Congresso Internazionale di Studi Etiopici, Rome 1972, Rome 1974, pp. 745-65; Paribeni, *op. cit., loc. var.*; S.C.H. Munro-Hay, *The British Museum Excavations at Adulis, 1968*, The Antiquaries Journal 69i, 1989, pp. 43-52.

Beta Giyorgis rising above Aksum to the north. Another was excavated nearby at Enda Cherqos. Churches of the same basic plan have been excavated at Matara and at Adulis. Two of the latter included marble columns and screens which probably came from the eastern Mediterranean.[266] Such church furniture may have been gifts from the Roman/Byzantine empire; they seem to date from the period of vigorous contact during the reigns of Kaleb and Justinian. Kaleb himself may have been something of a church–builder. His inscription mentions that he built a church in Himyar, and also refers to a *gabaz,* possibly in Himyar, possibly at Aksum. The *Life of Gregentius,* which for its list of churches, as SHAHID argues, may have had a more reliable source than for much of its other information, claims that Gregentius built and restored churches at Zafar, Qana, Najran, Atarph and Legmia.

Other Aksumite churches are known from Agula and Qwiha, and possibly more exist at Tekondo and Qohayto. A church, possibly of the early sixth century, was built within the ancient pre–Aksumite temple at Yeha, and another magnificent church, reputedly originally of Aksumite construction though rebuilt, still survives at the monastery of Debra Damo.

Some of the rock–cut Tigray churches[267] may also date from Aksumite times; certainly many have Aksumite architectural features. They preserve other elements, too, which are not generally considered 'Aksumite', such as arches and cupolas. It has long been recognised that there are Aksumite elements in some of the surviving old churches, but now that the arch and barrel vaulting are also known from structures of certainly Aksumite date[268], it may be that other features will be seen to have an even earlier pedigree. A few churches have already been tentatively dated to the ninth to twelfth century. LEPAGE's dating[269], based largely on research on the paintings, suggests; Debra Damo 6th–9th century; Zarema 9th century; Agobo 10th–11th or 12th century; and Yemrahana Krestos 12th century. LEPAGE notes that if Zarema, Degum, Abreha and Atsbeha, and Yemrahana Krestos churches really belong, as he suggests, to this period of the so–called obscure centuries, then they reveal a high level of civilisation, capable of continuing the Aksumite architectural tradi-

266 Cf. MUNRO-HAY in: The Antiquaries Journal 69; 1989, pp. 43-52

267 R. PLANT, Architecture of the Tigre, Ethiopia, Worcester 1985.

268 S.C.H. MUNRO-HAY, Excavations at Aksum 1972-4, London 1989.

269 C. LEPAGE, *Bilan des Recherches sur l'Art Médiéval d'Ethiopie; Quelques Résultats Historiques*", Proceedings of the Eighth International Conference of Ethiopian Studies, Addis Ababa 1984, Addis Ababa 1989, Vol. 2, p. 55.

tion, and of combining this with artistic borrowings from neighbouring lands. ANFRAY perceptively writes[270] of the ancient churches of Tigray, after noting how accurate a memory their creators had of Aksumite architectural forms – “Pas plus qu’ils n’en était éloignés dans l’espace, ils ne devait pas l’être dans le temps”.

It may even be asked whether Lalibela itself should be looked at again from a dating point–of–view. The construction of the famous rock–hewn churches there is attributed by the Ge‘ez documents to the miraculous intervention of angels, and by historians sometimes to the influx of Coptic workers fleeing from religious persecution in Egypt, at the time of King Lalibela. But may they not date, in part at least, with their strong display of Aksumite architectural features, from a rather earlier period? The evidence which assigns them all to the late–twelfth/early thirteenth century – many hundreds of years after the Aksumite structures they so faithfully imitate – is in fact very slight.

A second type of Aksumite ecclesiastical structure was the baptistery[271], either included in a church or possibly as a separate building. The enigmatical structure at Wuchate Golo, just west of Aksum, may be an early example of the latter. It consisted of a podium approached by steps and surrounded by corridors, on which the main feature was a circular cistern paved with a large rounded stone. Small stelae, benches and basins lay around the main building, which was flanked by a lesser structure containing five rooms. Coins dated to the sixth or even early seventh century, and pottery fragments bearing crosses, were excavated there.

Other baptisteries, in churches, are known from Yeha, Adulis and Matara. Access was by staircases descending into the cisterns. The Matara example was fed from outside by pipes made from broken amphorae fitted one within the other. Baptisteries also appear in some of the rock–cut churches.

As noted above, King Kaleb is said to have built several churches in Himyar and his inscription[272] found at Aksum records the building of a *gabaz*, possibly a church. Conceivably it refers to improvements by Kaleb at the cathedral of Maryam Tseyon at Aksum.

---

270 F. ANFRAY, Les anciens Ethiopiens: Siècles d’histoire, Paris 1990, p. 185.

271 For baptisteries see: H. DE CONTENSON, *Les fouilles à Ouchatei Golo près d’Axoum en 1958*, AE IV, 1961, pp. 3-16; and the references cited above in note 217.

272 R. SCHNEIDER, *Trois nouvelles inscriptions royales d’Axoum*, IV Congresso Internazionale di Studi Etiopici, Accad. dei Lincei, Rome, 1974, pp. 767-86.

CHAPTER THREE

Ethiopia and *The History of The Patriarchs* from the Seventh to the Mid–Tenth Century

Introduction

From the mid–sixth century there is very little information available about either the history of the Aksumite kingdom, or its ecclesiastical affairs. An increasingly debased coinage bearing the names of numerous kings of Aksum, with the usual Christian symbolism and mottoes, attests to the continuance of the monarchy at Aksum, but eventually even this coinage ceased to be issued. It seems that the ancient centre of Aksum was abandoned as a capital city at about this time, perhaps around 630 AD, owing to a number of circumstances already noted above (II: Introduction).

The next Ethiopian capital city mentioned (this time exclusively in Arabic texts) is Ku'bar, whose location is still uncertain; the earliest reference to it is that of al–Ya'qubi in the later ninth century. Despite CONTI ROSSINI's attempt to read in this name the name of the former capital, Ku'bar does not seem to be Aksum. The term 'Aksumite' therefore seems unsuitable for this phase of Ethiopia's history, and will no longer be employed here for this period except in direct quotations from other authors.

The abandonment of the former capital, and the major reorientation which Ethiopia had to make when the Red Sea trade with the Roman world no longer brought wealth to the country, did not necessarily mean that post–Aksumite Ethiopia was reduced to desperate straits. The land's intrinsic productivity, combined with a continuing trading connection with the Arabs, evidently allowed it to maintain a certain prosperity, for Arab writers continue to note the vast territories of the *najashis* of Habashat (as they called the Ethiopian rulers from their title of *negus* or its enlargement *negusa nagast,* 'king of kings'.) It was only during the destructive war waged by the queen of the Bani al–Hamwiyya in the mid–tenth century that we have accounts indicating that the country had fallen into a depressed condition (IV: 31), but even then some sort of recovery was possible after the queen's removal.

Connections were re–established with the patriarchate of Alexandria, and the metropolitans continued to be sent as before.

From the seventh century our knowledge of the relations between the Ethiopian church and the patriarchate is based largely on the biographies of the patriarchs of Alexandria[273], which Severus of Ashmunein and his continuators, Mawhub ibn Mufrah, Michael of Tinnis and others preserve up to the end of the eleventh century. Only when messengers of the Abyssinian kings arrived at Alexandria or later at Cairo do we learn anything about the current history of the Ethiopian kingdom. For a long while, the history of the metropolitanate becomes, for us, the history of Ethiopia itself.

17. Patriarch Benjamin I (623–662) and the Rise of Islam

From Patriarch Benjamin's episcopate the brief scenes involving the Ethiopian metropolitanate are played out against a new background and with a new political emphasis. Events occurred during the patriarchate of Benjamin which were of the utmost importance to the Egyptian monophysite church – and as a corollary, to its dependent daughter churches in north and northeast Africa.[274]

Byzantine support told against the melkite party when the Roman/Byzantine emperors' hold on Egypt began to weaken. It is even possible that for certain Egyptians, invaders were welcomed to some extent as deliverers from religious oppression, though there seem to have been other reactions as well; resignation as a punishment from God, flight, even resistance. Just before Benjamin, the behaviour of the melkite patriarch, John the Almoner, towards his monophysite contemporaries Anastasius and then Andronicus, was beginning to mend the breach between the two churches a little. But when the Sassanian ruler Khusrau II's Persian invasion force arrived to occupy Egypt between 617–628, both the Byzantine general in charge, Niketas, and Patriarch John fled. The field was left clear for the Coptic church, under foreign rulers not involved in the religious quarrels of Christendom.

---

273 For a study of the information about Ethiopia in the "History of the Patriarchs, see S. Tedeschi, Etiopia, pp. 232ff. He continues his survey until 849 A.D.

274 General account of the history of the period in S. Lane-Poole, A History of Egypt in the Middle Ages, 4th Ed., London 1968. For the attitude to the Persian conquest, A. Vasiliev, History of the Byzantine Empire, Madison 1952, p. 196.

Both churches eventually elected new patriarchs. John the Almoner had died in 620, but the melkites elected their new patriarch, George – without imperial nomination – only when the Coptic church chose Benjamin to succeed Andronicus, who died in 622. Benjamin's patriarchate saw a complete change in the political situation of the church. At first, after the re–conquest of Egypt by Emperor Heraclius in 629, there was an attempt to mend religious differences by the Act of Union, which evolved the monothelite heresy, avoiding any mention of Chalcedon. Cyrus, bishop of Phasis, became patriarch of Alexandria in 630 in succession to George – whose future history is unknown. The new patriarch was sent off to collect the signatures of church dignitaries for the Act of Union. Many monophysites agreed, but the melkites did not favour the Act and Benjamin himself was not to be drawn. Attempts to force him to acceptance drove him to the Thebaid; a retreat that spelled the end of any hope of church peace. The account of Benjamin's life, as told by Severus of Ashmunein[275], presents his retreat as the result of the enmity of Emperor Heraclius and the mysterious figure called al–Muqaqis. This al–Muqaqis may be identical with Cyrus himself, whom Severus thought was made both patriarch and governor of Egypt by Heraclius. BUTLER's discussion[276] favours this identification. This was the position at the time of the arrival of the Arab armies in 641.

18. The Muslim Conquest of Egypt: The Melkite Succession

Patriarch Benjamin, still in exile, was allowed to return and to take up his office by the Arab conqueror of Egypt, 'Amr ibn al–'As, while guarantees for the liberty and safety of the Christians were given. Interestingly, 'Amr himself possibly knew something of Ethiopia. He is reputed to have been one of the emissaries sent by the Quraysh to Ethiopia, to the court of the *najashi* or *negus*, to obtain the extradition of the Muslims who had fled there. In the event, he was sent back empty–handed, but later he returned to Ethiopia where he is supposed to have avowed his allegiance

[275] PO I, 4.

[276] A.J. BUTLER, *On the Identity of 'Al Mukaukis' of Egypt*, Proceedings of the Society for Biblical Archaeology 23, 1901, pp. 275-90, and a later revised version in his: The Arab Conquest of Egypt, Oxford 1902, Appendix C, pp. 508-526. The latter reprinted, P.E. FRASER, ed., 1978.

to Islam before the *najashi* himself, who acted as Muhammad's representative in accepting it.[277]

From the melkite point–of–view, the death of Patriarch Cyrus in 642, and the election of Peter as melkite patriarch, had little effect; the influence of the Byzantine church was waning, and after the retirement of Peter to Constantinople, an hiatus in the melkite succession occurred. This state of affairs, mentioned by Eutychius[278] and later by al–Maqrizi,[279] combined with the end of state support for the melkites, gave the ultimate victory in Egypt, and therefore also in both Abyssinia and Nubia, to the monophysite church. Al–Qalqashandi (d.1418) commented;[280]

> ...after the death of Patriarch Benjamin, the (seat) of the Patriarchate remained in the sole hands of the Jacobites, who prevailed all over Egypt. They appointed Jacobite bishops to all their sees and sent their bishops to the Nuba and the Habasha so that these became Jacobites...

> In this time [Patriarch Agathon's episcopate, 661–677] the churches of the Melkites were taken over by the Jacobites...A patriarch was (later) appointed for the Melkites, after they had been without a patriarch about 100 years, since the time of the caliphate of Omar. (But) the supreme patriarchal power remained in the hands of the Jacobites; it was they who sent bishops to the districts and since that time [or, therefore], the Nubians and those Habasha who live beyond them became Jacobites.

Only in c. 737, with Patriarch Kosmas' election, was the melkite succession restored.

19. Relations between Muslims and Christians

Relations between Islam and Ethiopia are supposed to have been excellent, according to Arab historians. Muslim accounts declare that the

---

277 A. Guillaume, The Life of Muhammad, Oxford 1955, p. 484. See also J.B. Glubb, The Life and Times of Muhammad, London 1970, pp. 121-2; Isaac, *Ethiopian Church*, p. 245, n. 77.

278 PG CXI, pp. 1122-23; Vantini, OS, p. 110.

279 H.F. Wüstenfeld, ed., Macrizi's Geschichte der Kopten, Gottingen 1845, pp. 22, 57. Eutychius and Maqrizi are quoted and discussed by Kirwan, Firka, p. 49. (in Appendix II, *The Nature of Nubian Christianity*).

280 Vantini, OS, pp. 575-6.

prophet himself, who died in 632, had great admiration for the *najashi*[281], whom the Arab sources name Ashama ibn Abjar[282], and for the justice of his rule. According to these accounts, he mourned the *najashi* 's death in 630, performing the *salat* for him. Ibn Ishaq, as his text preserved by al–Tabari relates, wrote of the examination of Ja'afar before the *najashi* and the bishops of Ethiopia[283], describing the favourable reception of Islam there. The Muslim writers, indeed, claim that Ashama ibn–Abjar accepted Islam, but secretly;[284] the same tale as was told later by al–'Umari and al–Qalqashandi about 'Amda–Tseyon.[285] Both Ethiopian rulers are said to have retained their kingship by dissembling their conversions.

The story about the *najashi*, weeping until his beard was wet, and his bishops, weeping until their books were soaked, so moved were they by Muhammad's revelations, may be of uncertain validity.[286] It is, however, a single vignette which allows us to amplify a situation in which we may be confident only of one thing; that Ethiopia remained Christian during the long period, for which we have no other information whatsoever, between the reign of Kaleb and the ninth and tenth century metropolitans. It is certain that when the story resumes, the metropolitans of Ethiopia still come from Egypt, and are consecrated by the Coptic patriarch of Alexandria.

In conquered Egypt the political background varied within the basic pattern of Islamic supremacy. Egypt was first a province of the Umayyad and Abbasid caliphates of Damascus and Baghdad (641–868), then an independent state under the Tulunids 868–904. From 905–935, Abbasid governors were again in control, followed by the Ikhshid dynasty 935–969, the Fatimids 969–1171, and the Ayyubids 1171–1250. Then followed the

---

281 H. ZOTENBERG, ed., Chronique de Tabari, p. 416. GUILLAUME, *op. cit.* (n. 277), p. 146.

282 GUILLAUME, *op. cit.*, p. 657. Tabari had the tradition via Salama.

283 GUILLAUME, *op. cit.*, p. 151.

284 *Ibid.*, p. 155.

285 Al-'Umari, "Ta'rif", Cairo 1312, p. 30, cited by M. GAUDEFROY-DEMOMBYNES, ed., Ibn Fadl Allah al-'Omari, "Masalik el Absar fi Mamalik el Amsar", Paris 1927, p. 32; al-Qalqashandi is quoted in note 6, p. 24, of the same work, he too citing from the "Ta'rif"

286 W. RAVEN, *Some Early Islamic Texts on the Negus of Abyssinia*, Journal of Semitic Studies XXXIII/2, 1988, p. 199. RAVEN considers, p. 209, that the Negus, "far from being a historical figure, ...began as a semi-legendary king and gradually turned out to be employable for a variety of religious and political purposes". He also adds, p. 218, that the Negus had a further role in Islamic legend - "that of a plausible and prestigious donor of a "foreign" object".

Mamluk rule, the Bahri Mamluks, including Baybars from 1260–77, the house of Qala'un from 1279, the Circassians, 1382–1517, then the Turkish conquest. The Nile valley and eastern desert were controlled by the Christian kings of Nubia and the Beja tribes, though the Arabs and their successors were sometimes able to gain considerable influence there.[287]

The chaotic state into which Nubia at times fell must have made the maintaining of the Ethiopian contact exceedingly difficult. Nevertheless, the worst might have been avoided, the Red Sea being perhaps the easiest and safest route for travellers between Egypt and Ethiopia. Contact with Ethiopia persisted, and was valued by the Copts. Coptic writers, conscious of the importance of their reiteration of the community of monophysitism on an international scale, mentioned whenever possible the connections of their church outside Egypt. In particular, as has already been noted, they remark on the pre–eminent position of the patriarchate of Alexandria vis–à–vis the independent Christian kingdoms of the south. The assertion of the unity of faith with independent foreign lands must have helped to maintain the confidence of Christian Egypt;

> there was known amongst all the people the genuiness of the agreement of the Copts and the Armenians, the Syrians and the Abyssinians and the Nubians,

the historian of the patriarchs proclaims, speaking of the visit of Gregory, the Armenian patriarch, in the episcopate of Cyril II.[288] Such claims, whilst upholding their particular faith against the Byzantine church, also served as reminders that the Egyptian church was not totally impotent politically. Reports about Muslim persecutions of the Copts occasionally mention the intervention of the southern kingdoms to alleviate the lot of their co–religionists in Egypt.

The political power of the caliphate was represented in Egypt by the governors appointed there, each holding office for a fairly brief span of time. Zambour[289] lists twenty–nine changes in 109 years under the Umayyads, followed by over eighty changes in 118 years under the Abbasids. It became necessary procedure for the kingdoms under the spiritual authority of the

---

[287] A useful summary of this in Yusuf F. Hasan, The Arabs and the Sudan, Khartoum 1973.

[288] "History of the Patriarchs", II, III, p. 346.

[289] E. de Zambour, Manuel de généologie et de chronologie pour l'histoire de l'Islam, Bad Pyrmont 1955, pp. 25ff. Also see Lane-Poole, *op. cit.*, p. 30, n. 1 for a slightly different total.

patriarchate of Alexandria to seek permission from these Arab administrators for the consecration of their metropolitans. This was, of course, an opportunity for the exaction of 'gifts'; but the rulers of Egypt regarded the influence of the patriarchs in the southern kingdoms very cautiously (see also VII: 65). In general, the situation does not seem to have been any worse for the Ethiopians than it had been under Byzantine rule in Egypt. Indeed, there are no reports indicating that the new political authorities ever caused an impasse such as that related by Pseudo–Dionysios in Justinian's time (IIB: 14). As a foil to the power of the Muslim authorities over the patriarch, the histories often recall occasions when the southern kings issued threats, or even acted, in defense of the patriarchs. Protesting embassies, military threats or campaigns, reprisals against Muslims, even the curious threat of diversion of the Nile (V: 41), occur in the pages of the historians. These embassies, and others sent to apply for new metropolitans, constitute virtually the only reported external contact of the Ethiopians outside their own border wars for many centuries.

20. The Metropolitan Cyril

A connection between Patriarch Benjamin and Cyril, the twenty–fourth Ethiopian metropolitan, has been claimed by several scholars.[290] RENAUDOT

[290] NEALE, *op. cit.*, II, p. 74. MEINARDUS, *Abunate*, p. 42. LE QUIEN, *op. cit.*, pp. 647-8. They quote E. RENAUDOT, Historia Patriarcharum Alexandrinorum Jacobitarum a D. Marco usque ad finem saeculi XIII, Paris 1713, p. 170-1, where we read that Benjamin's memory was celebrated because..."Metropolitam Cyrillum nomine in Aethiopiam miserit...." and "Teklahaimanot qui apud eos pater existimatur Vitae monasticae, a Benjamino missus ad eos fuerit..." TEDESCHI, *op. cit.*, p. 254, n. 1, commenting that the mission of the time of Simon by the black Indian priest seems to be the first after Frumentius recorded in contemporary sources, briefly mentions the incident of Cyril and Benjamin; "la notizia venne dapprima pubblicata nel XVII sec. dai gesuiti portoghesi; E. d'ALMEIDA, Historia Aethiopiae, in C. BECCARI Rerum Aethiopicarum Scriptores Occidentales Inediti, V, Roma, 1907, p. 174, 192; B. TELLEZ, Historia geral de Ethiopia a alta, Coimbra 1660, p. 84; E. RENAUDOT, Historia Patriarcharum Alexandrinorum Jacobitarum a D. Marco usque ad finem saeculi XIII, Parisiis 1713, p. 170-171. Questi autori la trassero dagli Atti di Takla Haimanot, fondatore di Dabra Libanos in Scoia, nel XIII sec.; tuttavia l'opera fu scritta solo nel XV sec. ed a inoltre di valore assai insicuro sotto il profilo dell'esatezza storica. La notizia non trova comunque conferma nella vita di Beniamino I contenuta nella "Storia dei patriarchi". TEDESCHI does not pursue the matter, as outside the province of his article.

commented that Benjamin was remembered by the Ethiopians as the patriarch who sent Metropolitan Cyril to Ethiopia, and he also supposed that Benjamin sent Tekla–Haymanot, the great Ethiopian saint whom Cyril ordained as a deacon.[291] RENAUDOT further noted that in the *Life* of Tekla–Haymanot it is said that the future saint was taken at fifteen years of age to Cyril, metropolitan of Ethiopia, when Benjamin presided over the Alexandrian church.

Evidently confusion has arisen here. Though the extraordinary discrepancy in dates has sometimes passed without comment, other writers have observed the anomaly and attempted to reconcile the traditions. The link between a Metropolitan called Cyril and St. Tekla–Haymanot seems fairly secure. The *Synaxarium*[292] relates; "And then he took him to the bishop, Abba Cyril, who made him a deacon..." – presumably, in later Zagwé times (V: 36). GUIDI's list II[293] has the note, under no. 24, "Gerillos, in whose time was Tekla Haymanot". GUIDI suggested that the author of the list added the note by the name Gerillos, aware from such records as the *Synaxarium* entry quoted above that there had been a metropolitan called Cyril in the time of Tekla–Haymanot. The other Cyril (Qerillos) of the list, no. 32, occurs after a note mentioning Abba Ewostatewos who lived in the time of Metropolitan Ya'qob. Accordingly, since this saint died in c. 1332, and since the *Synaxarium* text uses the same spelling Gerillos instead of Qerillos, the compiler or copyist of the list would have preferred the first of the Cyrils as the most likely candidate. The 62nd metropolitan, Qerillos II is even more remote according to the compiler's arrangement, though DILLMANN[294] suggested that it was he who was contemporary with Tekla–Haymanot. Finally, however, outside the arrangements of the lists, a *liqa–pappasat* Cyril is mentioned[295] in a land grant of King Yekuno–Amlak of 1269/70, a contemporary of

---

291 RENAUDOT wrote that "In ipsius vita [Teklahaimanot], ... dictur eum anno aetatis 15 a parentibus ductum ad Abba Cyrillum qui Metropolita Aethiopiae fuit, quando Benjamin Alexandrinae Ecclesiae praesidebat". NEALE, *op. cit.*, II, p. 74; BUTCHER, *op.cit.*, I, p. 384.

292 BUDGE, Synaxarium, Vol. IV, p. 1242.

293 I. GUIDI, *Le Liste dei Metropoliti d'Abissinia*, Bessarione, N. 37-8, Anno IV, 1889, pp. 1-16, especially p. 4 and pp. 14-15.

294 A. DILLMANN, *Zur Geschichte des Axumitischen Reichs im vierten bis sechsten Jahrhundert*, Abhandlungen der K. Preussische Akademie der Wissenschaften zu Berlin, Berlin 1880, p. 22.

295 The Dictionary of Ethiopian Biography, Addis Ababa 1975, Vol. I, p. 135, notes two people called Qerelos, Cyril. Both the references probably apply to the same Qerelos.

Tekla–Haymanot, and in the *gadla of Samuel of Debra Wagag*, and others. Samuel was ordained deacon by Cyril, Gerellos, during Tekla––Haymanot's lifetime.[296]

GUIDI, noting that his list II included only twenty–one metropolitans (no. 11 is left blank) in nine centuries from Frumentius to the Cyril noted as a contemporary of Tekla–Haymanot, commented on the inability of the Ethiopians to elect one of their own nation, and the long vacancies that accordingly ensued. He envisages these few metropolitans holding office at different periods scattered through the centuries. An interesting parallel from Nubia, which may offer a comparative guideline, is provided by the Faras list of bishops.[297] The twenty–eight bishops named in it from Aetios to Jesu II occupy the period c. 625 - c. 1175; some of them, indeed a remarkable number, died at extreme old age, occupying the episcopal seat for several decades. Thus even if the Ethiopian metropolitans were equally long–lived – and Michael, Habib al–Atfihi, was certainly "old and advanced in age" (V: 43–VI: 45), whilst the uncanonically–appointed successor to Metropolitan Peter was installed under Kosmas III (d. 934), living on until Patriarch Philotheus' time, after 979 (III: 29, IV: 30) – one would have to assume very long periods in Ethiopia without a metropolitan to fit the GUIDI list. Between Tekla–Haymanot and Ewostatewos, a very brief period, many more metropolitans than usual would have arrived in impossibly quick succession. The value of GUIDI's list II itself is doubtful, directly opposed as it is to other lists in most of its content. The lack of Aksumite ecclesiastics at the church councils of the fourth and fifth centuries, which DILLMANN[298] notes, does not really imply that there were no bishops in Ethiopia then; merely that, even if they ever received a summons, they were unable to come, doubtless because of the distance or difficulties of travel.

It is when the Metropolitan Cyril discussed above, with his firm thirteenth century context, is associated with Patriarch Benjamin of Alexandria, 623–662, that the evident anomaly begins. SERGEW HABLE SELLASSIE[299] merely mentions that Benjamin selected one Cyril to be metropolitan of Ethiopia, without adding any remarks about St. Tekla–Haymanot. Of the two refer-

[296] S. KUR, trans., "Actes de Samuel de Dabra Wagag", CSCO, Scriptores Aethiopici, T. 50, Louvain 1968, p. VII, p. 5.

[297] S. JAKOBIELSKI, *La liste des évêques de Pakhoras*, ET I, 1966, pp. 151-70; ID., *Nouvelle lecture d'un nom de la liste des évêques*, ET V, 1971, pp. 193-9; ID., Faras III.

[298] DILLMANN, *op. cit.*, p. 21.

[299] SERGEW, AMEH, p. 193.

ences he quotes, MEINARDUS[300] and NEALE[301], the latter, with BUTCHER[302], states that Benjamin is said to have sent Tekla–Haymanot. However, this suggestion evidently has no historical justification.

Balthasar TELLES[303], quoting Don Alfonso Mendes, the Catholic patriarch of Ethiopia, indicates that Mendes believed that Tekla–Haymanot lived in the 6th century. Mendes worked out that the succession of holy men from Anthony to Tekla–Haymanot indicated that the latter was born about 515 or 520, which, he continues,

> is prov'd by an undeniable Argument drawn from his Life, in which it is written, that he being 15 years of Age, was carry'd by his Parents to the Abuna Kirilos, who was Patriarch in Ethiopia when Abba Benjamin was so at Alexandria.

TEDESCHI noted[304] that the originator of this idea seems to be Emmanuel d'ALMEIDA, who took it from a fifteenth century *Gadla Tekla–Haymanot*. TADDESSE TAMRAT[305], commenting on the lack of attention to the Muslim factor in the saint's life in the *Gadla Tekla–Haymanot,* adds; "This was one of the reasons that led ALMEIDA to date him between the 7th and 8th centuries". Further comments on the question occur in the *Dictionary of Ethiopian Biography.*[306]

---

300 MEINARDUS, *op. cit.*, p. 42.

301 NEALE, *op. cit.*, p. 74.

302 BUTCHER, *op. cit.*, p. 384.

303 TELLES, *op. cit.*, pp. 95-6; see also E. d'ALMEIDA, The History of High Ethiopia or Abassia (Historia de Ethiopia a alta, o Abassia), ed. C. BECKINGHAM and G. W. B. HUNTINGFORD, London, 1954, Hakluyt Soc.

304 TEDESCHI, *Etiopia*, p. 254, n. 1, and E. d'ALMEIDA, Bk. II, Ch. 18, ed. V. BECCARI, pp. 174, 192.

305 TADDESSE TAMRAT, *op. cit.*, p. 170, n. 1.

306 Dictionary of Ethiopian Biography, p. 135. The two entries read: QÉRELOS, Abuna (perhaps fl. 7th century AD), was a Metropolitan of Ethiopia consecrated by Benjamin, Patriarch of Alexandria 620-665 AD. This is the first clear indication in Coptic sources of the consecration of an Egyptian Metropolitan to Ethiopia. SERGEW HABLE SELLASSIE, for this entry, cites the same references as above. notes 300-301. The second entry, by BELAYNESH MICHAEL, reads: QÉRELOS, or GÉRELOS, Abba (fl. 13th century AD), was the bishop, or pappas, "in the country of Amhara, during the Zagwé kingdom" who first made St. Täklä-Haymanot a deacon, "in the days when Abba Benyamin was Archbishop of Alexandria". A reference to an archbishop or liqä-pappasat Qérelos, appears in a land grant given by Emperor Yekuno-'Amlak in 1269/70. Other references to the same person are found in unpublished MSS of the Gädlä Zéna-Marqos and Gädlä Qäwestos at Däbrä Libanos.

In fact, as we have seen, there is no warrant for a Metropolitan Cyril contemporary with Patriarch Benjamin I. Benjamin II, 1327–1339, though appreciably closer in time than Benjamin I, was not a contemporary of Tekla–Haymanot, who died around 1312. What the "clear indication in the Coptic sources" quoted by SERGEW HABLE SELLASSIE is, remains uncertain.

No version of the *Gadla Tekla–Haymanot*[307] mentions that Patriarch Benjamin had sent him; on the contrary, the accounts are full of the events of his early life in Ethiopia, and later of his apostleship of Shewa. Even the traditions associating him with important achievements in the national sphere during the reign of Yekuno–Amlak are likely to be later additions by politically motivated writers. A possible solution is noted below (VI: 59).

It seems, however, that there were bishops in Ethiopia in Benjamin I's time, and we may assume that there was a metropolitan as well. Ibn Ishaq wrote that the *najashi* Ashama ibn Abjar debated with the Muslims surrounded by his bishops. The name or see of none of these is known. The information may, of course, not be valid, a set piece or an embroidery of a basic story by a later historian – the *najashi* became a favourite figure for legendary tales among Arab writers; but it is possible.

21. Patriarch Isaac I (690–692); the Dispute between the Nubian Kingdoms

Patriarch Isaac, according to the *History of the Patriarchs*[308],

> addressed letters to the king of the Abyssinians (al–Habasha) and the king of the Nubians (al–Nuba), bidding them make peace together and praying that there might be no ill–will between them; and he wrote this on account of a dispute that there was between the two. Thereupon a certain intriguer seized the opportunity of slandering Abba Isaac before Abd al–Aziz [governor of Egypt 685–705], who was greatly incensed and sent his officers to bring him that he might put him to death. But the secretaries wrote letters different from the patriarch's letters, and gave them to the messengers whom he had sent to the Abyssinians, and took these first letters from them, in fear for the patriarch. This they only did lest evil should befall the church. And before the patriarch was brought before the Amir, they informed him that the messengers were there and the letters with them. So he sent in haste to seek them,

[307] Dictionary of Ethiopian Biography, pp. 157-8; there is a bibliography citing several versions of the 'Life'. See also G.W.B. HUNTINGFORD, *The Lives of Saint Takla Haymanot*, JES IV, 1966, pp. 35ff, for an account of the development of his legend.

[308] PO V, fasc. 1, p. 24.

and took the letters. And when he had perused them he found nothing in them of what had been told him. Thus his anger was pacified, and he sent at once, and bade the patriarch return to Alexandria, and did not cause him after this to come up southwards.

Evidently the Egyptian governor, conscious that the wrangles of the southern Christian kingdoms could only be profitable to his own country's security, would be indignant at the attempt by one of his own subjects to interfere in their internal affairs. Abd al–Aziz ibn Marwan was not ungenerous to the Copts[309] but obviously drew the line at any meddling in external political matters.

However, the question of the identity of the kings is more complex than the outline of the *History of the Patriarchs* reveals. The Coptic *Life of Isaac*[310], written by his contemporary Bishop Menas, enlarges;

> It occurred at that time, that the king of Makouria sent messengers to the Archbishop informing him of the way in which the bishops of his land had diminished because of the length of the road, and of the duration of the journey, since they were unable to pass, by command of the king of Maurotania, until he made peace with him. There were, then, two kings established in these lands; both were Christians but they were not at peace with each other. For one of them, the king of Maurotania, was at peace with the king of the Saracens, the other, of the great country of Makouria, was not at peace with the land of the Saracens. It happened that, when the Archbishop had read the letters of the king, he was very sad concerning the Churches; he wrote directly to the king of Maurotania, sending him advice and instruction, by the words of the Holy Scriptures, adding, further, "You are Christians, both of you". After having addressed to him many words to strengthen his soul in the Orthodox faith of the Son of God, he wrote afterwards that he might not prevent the people of the upper kingdom to pass through his land in coming for their bishop, to the end that the churches should not be deserted; he was ashamed on account of it before God. The enemies of our faith, having learnt this, slandered the Archbishop before the king, saying, We let you know, O king, that the king of Makouria has sent messengers with letters to Abba Isaac, the Archbishop, that he may set over them a bishop, whom they will take to their land. Not only that, but he has also sent a message to the king of Maurotania, advising him to make peace with the king of Makouria, our enemy. If this comes to pass, O king, they will have but one heart; they will rise in battle against us.

[309] LANE-POOLE, *op. cit.*, p. 26.

[310] PORCHER, ed., *op. cit.*, p. 377. E. AMÉLINEAU, *Histoire du patriarche copte Isaac*, Bulletin du Correspondance Africaine, Paris, 1890, and Bulletin de l'Institute Egyptien, 2e série, no. 6, 1885; QUATREMÈRE, Mémoires, Vol II, pp. 54-55.

The 'king' sent agents to Rakotis (Alexandria) to the *augustalis* there (the title is an anachronism from the Byzantine period) to have the patriarch duly arrested and sent to him.

This contemporary account would seem to be a clearer relation of the events that were later summarised in a less accurate form by the *History of the Patriarchs*. The latter may have used the *Life of Isaac* in its compilation, introducing the king of the Habash as a kind of gloss on what to the author seemed an error or confusion, the naming of two kingdoms in Nubia. By the time of the compilation of Severus there was only the kingdom of Makoria (*Maqurra, al-Nuba*), as a result of the union of the two kingdoms of Makoria and Nobatia at an uncertain date.[311] CONTI ROSSINI[312], taking Maurotania as Mauritania, the country of the Moors, was unable to envisage the likelihood of a clash between the Moors and Makouria, and thus assumed that the *History of the Patriarchs* provided the correcting gloss by the insertion of *al-Habasha* into the record.

John of Nikiu[313], writing in the later seventh century, at the same time as Bishop Menas wrote his *Life of Isaac,* used similar names when describing the conquest of "the barbarians of the provinces of Nubia and of Africa, called Mauritani and other barbarians called Marikos". MASPERO emended the text to read Libya for Nubia, but MONNERET DE VILLARD[314] held to the attribution of the word "Mauritani" to northern Nubia.

---

311 TRIMINGHAM, Sudan, p. 63, n. 2 made no attempt to date the union. He merely denied the suggestion of L.P. KIRWAN, *Notes on the Topography of the Christian Nubian Kingdoms,* JEA 21, pp. 57-62, that it was as a result of the Arab threat. JAKOBIELSKI, Faras III, p. 36, n. 6, quotes this and O. MEINARDUS, *The Christian kingdom of Nubia,* Cahiers d'Histoire Egyptienne X, Le Caire 1967, p. 143 as supporting LANE-POOLE's opinion that the union occurred as a result of the attack on Old Dongola in 652, when, Maqrizi says, there was one king ruling Nubia from the Egyptian frontier to 'Alwa. Though it is true that these writers support this theory, it is not expressed at all by LANE-POOLE in the reference supplied (History of Egypt, p. 22); LANE-POOLE simply quotes the Baqt treaty as noted by Maqrizi after Ibn Salim with no comment. MONNERET DE VILLARD, Storia, p. 81, followed by JAKOBIELSKI, Faras III, p. 45, n. 54, suggested 704 as the beginning of a new era; perhaps that of the uniting of the Nubian kingdoms or the commencement of monophysitism there? See also S.C. MUNRO-HAY, *Kings and Kingdoms of Ancient Nubia,* RSE XXIX, 1982-3, pp. 96ff.

312 C. CONTI ROSSINI, *Note Etiopiche I, Una guerra fra la Nubia e l'Etiopia nel secolo VII,* Giornale della Società Asiatica Italiana X, 1897, pp. 141-3.

313 John of Nikiu, ZOTENBERG, ed., p. 404.

314 MONNERET DE VILLARD, Storia, pp. 69-70.

However, he quotes the history of John of Nikiu as reading 'Mazikos' for the other people while ZOTENBERG chose to emend his reading 'Marikos' to Makoris (Makoria).[315] In 580 the *dux* and *augustalis* Aristomachus had defeated the Mazici, and in 583–4[316], apparently dealt with the Mauritani and the Marikos, or the Mazici again. If John of Nikiu does mean Nubia rather than Libya, it could be suggested that the Mauritani (Maurotania) were the Nobatae, the people of what was later called al–Maris.[317] It seems odd that there should have been friction at this time between the Roman government and Nubia, since 'Awarfiula', king of Nobatia, had so recently been pursuing a pro–Egyptian policy, and in 580 had written to Theodore of Alexandria (the patriarch elected by Longinus' party); but the incident may have been minor.[318]

It would seem that the affair in Patriarch Isaac's time, rather than having any connection with Ethiopia, entirely concerned the Nubian kingdoms. It occurred at the time of the king of Makoria who was probably the direct predecessor of Merkurius, crowned in 696/7. Merkurius is known to have been king of Dongola, capital of Makoria, from the *Life of Michael*.[319] King Merkurius was also able to erect churches at Faras (the Greek and Coptic foundation stelae of the cathedral are of his 11th year), and Tafa, both in Nobatia.[320] Thus the war between the two states seems to have been resolved in favour of Makoria. The truth of the statement of Eutychius and Maqrizi about the failure of the melkite succession and its consequences is borne out, since Merkurius' predecessor had to seek his bishops, in the end, from Isaac.

---

315 TEDESCHI, *Etiopia*, p. 240. n.3. TEDESCHI also provides a useful commentary on the whole story. He is undoubtedly right in correcting CONTI ROSSINI's identification as to which of the two kings was entitled 'Habasha' in the *History of the Patriarchs*, (Storia d'Etiopia, p. 266).

316 G. MASPERO, Histoire des patriarches d'Alexandrie depuis la morte de l'empereur Anastase jusqu'à la reconciliation des églises jacobites (518-616), Paris 1923, p. 285.

317 Unless any credit may be given to the idea of E. ZYHLARZ, *I reami della Nubia prima dell'Islam*, RSE III, 1943, p. 258, n. 2, identifying Sukkot region and Urrotan (Maurotania).

318 See the story in John of Ephesus; PAYNE-SMITH, *op. cit.*, p. 324.

319 Not from the Faras foundation stelae, as VANTINI, Faras, p. 186, states.

320 JAKOBIELSKI, Faras III, p.40, and ID., in: Rocznik Muzeum Narodowego w Warszawie X, 1966, pp. 99-106. The Tafa inscription was published by G. MASPERO, Le roi Mercure à Tâfah, ASAE X, 1909, p. 17. MONNERET DE VILLARD, Storia, p. 80.

A minor point of interest in the patriarchal relations with its southern foreign dependencies was the appointment of a Coptic bishop, Nabis or Barnabas, possibly around 700, to the port of 'Aydhab, to minister to seamen and merchants. It was recognised that there was not much need for a permanent bishop, so he sent priests and deacons occasionally there from Qift, his usual dwelling place; he remained bishop of 'Aydhab for forty years.[321] It is not inconceivable that the bishopric of Adulis, at least in the early days of Christianity when Moses was the incumbent (IIA: 9), might have been founded for similar reasons, and perhaps even administered in a similar way.

22. Patriarch Simon (693–700); the 'Indian' Priest

During the patriarchate of Simon, 693–700, a curious incident again caused trouble with the Muslim authorities.[322] Some 'Indians' not subject to the Muslims sent to request the consecration of a bishop for 'India', but the 'black Indian' priest who bore the request was refused by the patriarch until permission had been sought from Abd al–Aziz ibn Marwan, Caliph Abd el–Malik's governor of Egypt (685–705). The 'Indian' priest, on his way to the governor, met with some Gaianites, whose leader, Theodore 'the Phantasiast', had no such hesitation. He consecrated a man of Maryut as bishop for the 'Indians'. The priest and his assistants – and presumably the new bishop – being captured and questioned whilst travelling to 'India', the story became known. Patriarch Simon was summoned to account for the appointment. Upon his relating the truth of the matter, Theodore was punished. The patriarch and the 'Indian' priest were freed.

It is unclear from the text whether the priest was an Ethiopian or actually from the subcontinent of India.[323] Al–Makin, Ibn Rahib and Maqrizi merely repeat the same terminology. The latter reported that

---

[321] R. BASSET, ed., "Le Synaxaire Arabe Jacobite (Rédaction Copte)", PO III, fasc. 3, pp. 499ff; SERGEW, AMEH, p. 196; TRIMINGHAM, Sudan, p. 58, n. 5, for date of 700.

[322] PO V, fasc. I, pp. 36-42; T. ERPENIUS, ed., El-Makin, "Historia Saracenica", Leyden, 1625, p. 81; L. CHEIKHO, ed., Butrus ibn Muhaddib (Abu Shakir) called Ibn Rahib, "Chronicon Orientale", CSCO Scriptores arabici Ser. 3, T.I, p. 131; the dates are confused.

[323] See NEALE, *op. cit.*, II, p. 88, for a suggestion that Malabar is meant.

> In his days ambassadors came from the people of Hind to ask that a bishop be sent to them; but the patriarch declined, until he should have leave from the sultan to appoint another.[324]

TEDESCHI discussed this affair in detail,[325] and there is little need to add much more. His suggestion that the compiler of the *History of the Patriarchs*, Severus, refrained from "correcting" his source because he had already made an alteration before and feared to introduce new confusion, does not ring quite true. Nowhere else in his compilation does he let there be any doubt; always the references are to the *habasha*, and to the consecration of a *mutran*, metropolitan. It seems strange that he should let the anomaly stand, if anomaly it were. Another unusual factor is that the messenger, the 'Indian' priest, could allow a bishop from a rival sect to be consecrated for him; he must have known that the heretical Theodore and his sect were in conflict with the chief branch of the monophysites, as represented by the patriarch (but see below). Having seen the patriarch, and received from him an explanation how his actions were controlled, the priest would, one would think, at least wait until he heard the decision of the governor. It is possible that the system of acquiring the permission of the governor, as part of the policy of the Egyptian administration, was a new procedure and the envoy was in a hurry.

John of Ephesus mentions on two occasions the prevalence of the heresy of Julian of Halicarnassus, the Gaianite heresy, in Ethiopia – in his notes about Bishop Longinus, c. 580, and again in the account about the twenty–five year dispute with Justinian after 536 (IIB: 14). If the messenger had indeed come from Ethiopia, one might think that perhaps the sect had lasted there from that time, and that therefore the 'Indian' priest had no objection to receiving his bishop from the successor of Gaianus. There is no record of the heresy being carried to the Indian subcontinent, except in the very general comment of Michael the Syrian (I: 3). Perhaps to an 'Indian' priest, if he did come from those regions, the distinction between a Severan monophysite and a Gaianite was irrelevant. The identity of this priest remains insoluble for the present; even TEDESCHI's thorough study is not entirely convincing for the Ethiopian identity, though it certainly seems the most plausible explanation. As noted above (I: 5) LE QUIEN placed the 'Indian priest' among the bishops of Himyar, surely rather less likely as the place of origin of a 'black Indian' than either Ethiopia or India.

---

324 Maqrizi, ed., MALAN, p. 75.

325 TEDESCHI, *Etiopia*, pp. 243ff.

23a. Michael I (743–767) and the Invasion of Egypt by King Kyriakos

During the patriarchate of Michael I, the 46th patriarch of Alexandria, there occurred an incident which, like the events of Simon and Isaac's episcopates, has been presumed to have an Ethiopian connection. Certain aspects of this tale of invasion from Nubia in support of the patriarch led to its exploitation by the Christians of Egypt, vicariously enjoying the prestige of the military might of the neighbouring Christian kings subject to their patriarchate. They offered the tale, and expanded it, as a response, with an implicit threat, to the Muslim government's temporal control over the patriarchs. It served as a warning and, hopefully at least, a protection for the person of the patriarch. It is not known from Muslim sources whether the Egyptian rulers ever really took the incident seriously; but there were, on occasion, other military irruptions of the Nubians into Egypt in later times of weakness of the central authority. An awareness of Christian Nubia may have acted as some sort of check on arbitrary dealings by the Egyptian rulers towards the patriarchate.

In this instance, the *History of the Patriarchs,*[326] after supplying vital information about the monarchy in Nubia from the time of Merkurius to Kyriakos, continues

> Now letters had been sent to this king (Kyriakos) from Egypt, and had reached him while the father Abba Michael was in prison with us. And Abd al-Malik[327] heard of these communications, and therefore he seized the patriarch, and kept him in custody.

This was the second imprisonment of Michael; he had been imprisoned before, when he wrote to Kyriakos, and released so that he could tour the south to raise money to pay the impositions of the government.

> Then king Kyriakos marched forth from the land of the Nubians towards Egypt with a great army, including a hundred thousand horsemen and a hundred thousand camels; and when they approached Misr that they might capture the city, and had camped at the pool known to this day as the Pool of the Ethiopians, they plundered and slew and made prisoners of the Muslims.

[326] PO V, pp. 143ff.

[327] Last Umayyad governor of Egypt, Abd al-Malik b. Marwan b. Musa b. Nusayr al-Lakhmi, treasurer 749, governor 750; DE ZAMBOUR, *op. cit.*, from p. 101; LANE-POOLE, *op. cit.*, p. 49; EVETTS and BUTLER, *op. cit.*, p. 267 n. 2; Abu Salih actually refers to the Governor as Salah al-Din Yusuf, the Kurd, in error. TEDESCHI, *op. cit.*, p. 255, n. 2, mentions WIET's statement that Abd al-Malik was the grandson of Musa.

> And they had already treated the Muslims of Egypt in like manner. And the king, before he reached Misr, had sent an envoy, called the eparch, one of the great men of the kingdom, to Abd al–Malik, bidding him release the patriarch; but Abd al–Malik seized that envoy and imprisoned him with the patriarch. But when the Governor heard of the arrival of the king before Misr, not having any means of resisting him, and being greatly afraid of him, he released his envoy, the eparch, from prison. So the latter went forth to meet the king, having, previously, made an engagement to Abd al–Malik, and sworn to induce the king to return with his army to his own country, and not to let him approach his fortresses nor besiege him. Now the Muslims were in the habit of kidnapping the Nubians and selling them as slaves in Egypt. So the king, after carrying off much plunder from the Muslims, led back his army, because the eparch informed him that the patriarch had been released, and had been kindly treated by Abd al–Malik, and himself bade the Nubians to return home with his blessing.....Then Abd al–Malik sent to the patriarch, bidding him write to the king of the Nubians. So Abba Michael wrote letters of peace to Kyriakos, in which he prayed for him, and blessed him and his followers; and the king returned without fighting a battle. Now these events took place in the hundred and thirtieth year after the foundation of the empire of the Muslims (i.e. 747/8).

Ibn Rahib repeats the essentials of this, adding the date Anno Martyrum 461/745 AD.[328] Cyprianus, his name for the king, is a simple error. The Ethiopian translation of the *'Uyun al–Tawarikh* of al–Kutubi (d. 1362/3)[329], also supplies the same information, rendering the name Kiriakos. El–Makin, too, dates the event to year 461 of Diocletian, repeating much the same brief outline as his contemporary Ibn Rahib.[330]

The source of the tale, for Severus, was the narration of a friend and contemporary of Michael, the deacon John, who adds that Kyriakos was even then still ruling in Nubia; this, then, is the most credible version. Al–Maqrizi[331] merely mentions Abd al–Malik's demands for money and the efforts of the patriarch to meet them, but Abu Salih[332], though he confirms the incursion of Kyriakos, adds that the news of the patriarch's capture had reached also the king of Abyssinia, and another king subject to

---

[328] Ibn Rahib, ed. CHEIKHO, p. 134.

[329] MONNERET DE VILLARD, Storia, p. 98; For an Ethiopian version of Ibn Rahib from ms. d'Abbadie 211, "chronologie universelle d'Abu Shakir", see C. CONTI ROSSINI, *Notice sur les manuscrits Éthiopiens de la collection d'Abbadie*, Journal Asiatique, Ser. II, T.6, 1915, pp. 195-6. TEDESCHI, *Etiopia*, p. 255, n. 4. The date 461 of the era of Diocletian is printed as A.D. 945, presumably a misprint.

[330] El-Makin, ed. ERPENIUS, p. 99.

[331] Maqrizi, ed. MALAN, p. 78.

[332] Abu Salih, ed. EVETTS and BUTLER, Fol. 97a, p. 267.

the jurisdiction of the patriarch of Egypt (Alwa/Alodia would seem to be the only other possibility). The Ethiopian *Synaxarium*[333] contributes the information that the king of Ethiopia rose up in arms against the Egyptians, (Gebre Iyasus son of Muse son of Nasir being governor), to cause them to release Michael. The patriarch wrote to him when he had entered Egypt, at the behest of the 'king of Egypt', to return in peace since he, the patriarch, was now free. The final stage in the confusion of the invading kings is reached by the *Matshafa Tefut*[334], here the caliph is named correctly, Marwan al-Gadi, (called Merwal el-Gadin) 745–751, the last of the Umayyads. Michael being arrested, Sayfa Arad (1344–1372), king of Ethiopia, is said to have invaded Egypt and compelled the ruler to release Michael. Sayfa Arad having died, the patriarch was re-arrested, and so the Ethiopian king Dawit I (1382–1411) came down to Khartoum to commence the alteration of the waters of the Nile. Ahmad, son of Merwal el-Gadin, duly released the patriarch, and offered an indemnity; but the religious King Dawit preferred a fragment of the True Cross to the gold of Egypt. A mixture of two strands is here apparent; the expedition of Kyriakos to release Michael I, and an attack conducted by Sayfa Arad to release Patriarch Mark IV (1348–1363).

A similar incident is attributed to the reign of a King Dawit, in the *Gadla Marqoreuos*. The name of neither the patriarch nor of the 'tyrant of Egypt' are mentioned. The king's armies are said to have descended as far as Sinnar, when the terrified 'tyrant of Egypt' made peace with the patriarch. The patriarch sent emissaries, with the True Cross, and Dawit returned to Ethiopia.

The gradual development of this story is not hard to discern. The incident recalled by Michael's biographer had a powerful effect on the Christians, and the idea that the king of Ethiopia was involved doubtless had its origin in the curious wording of the rest of John the Deacon's description of Nubia under Kyriakos. John[335] declares that

> there were under the supremacy of Kyriakos, king of the Nubians, thirteen kings[336] ruling the country. He was the orthodox Ethiopian king of al-Muqurra (wakana malik al-Muqurra al-habashi al-urthuduksi) and he was the mighty king (al-malik al-'zim)[337], upon whom the crown descended from heaven,

[333] BUDGE, Synaxarium, Vol III, pp. 710-11

[334] A. CAQUOT, *Aperçue préliminaire sur le Mashafa Tefut de Gechen Amba*, AE I, pp. 89ff.

[335] POV, p.(399) 145.

[336] Not thirty as in MONNERET DE VILLARD, Storia, p. 99.

[337] MONNERET DE VILLARD, Storia, p. 172 says that John calls Kyriakos "al-malik al-kabir" confusing this with the phrase used by Abu Salih.

> and he governed as far as the extremities of the earth, for he is the Greek king, fourth of the kings of the earth, and none of the other kingdoms stands up against him, but their kings attend him when he passes through their territory. And he is under the jurisdiction of Mark the Evangelist, for the patriarch of the Jacobites in Egypt exercises authority over him, and over all the kings of the Abyssinians (muluk al–habash) and the Nubians (wa'l–Nuba).

John the Deacon seems to have been so eager to aggrandize the champion of his faith that he has produced a compilation of the kings of Nubia and Ethiopia in the person of Kyriakos. Apart from the reference to Daniel[338], the text also reminds one of the account in the Coptic *Kephalaia* of Mani, which names Aksum as third of the four kingdoms of the earth; a southern kingdom of the blacks usually appears in such geographical schemes.[339] This description of Kyriakos has been expanded into two by the time of the even more confused account of Abu Salih. When discussing Nubia, he mentions Kyriakos as supreme king over thirteen kings, calling him the great king (*al–malik al–kabir*). Under the heading of Abyssinia he places the king of al–Muqurra, with the titles of orthodox king, and great king, and fourth of the kings of the earth. Abu Salih, depending on the information of John and further confusing it by separating the attributes of Kyriakos, confirmed the error.

The date of 747–8/130 for the expedition must be preferred to 745, since both Abraham and Mark were kings of Nubia in the time of Michael, who came to the patriarchal throne in November 743.[340] Although Mark only reigned six months, there was a considerable amount of going to and fro between King Abraham and Patriarch Michael concerning the affair of Bishop Cyriacus, and the appointment of Bishop John, and this must have embraced a reasonable period of time. The situation of the patriarch, which is said to have encouraged the invasion, also took some time to develop. Finally, the governor mentioned, Abd al–Malik b. Marwan b. Musa, was only appointed, it seems, in 748/9.[341] Kyriakos is known from

---

[338] Daniel VII, 17ff; VIII, 2lff; X, 20; XI, 25ff.

[339] I. POLOTSKY, Mani, "Kephalaia", Stuttgart 1940, pp. 188-9. See also DE BLOIS in *The four great kingdoms in the Manichaean Kephalaia,* Orbis Aethiopicus, 1990, pp. 221-30.

[340] TEDESCHI, *Etiopia*, p. 254. PO V, pp. 141f.

[341] LANE-POOLE, *op. cit.*, p. 49, HASAN, *op. cit.*, p. 221, n. 50 quotes KINDI (p. 93) as giving the date Jumada II, 132, February 750, which differs a little from the date given in the *History of the Patriarchs.* However, he had been Treasurer before he became Governor, and it was primarily for failure to pay impositions that the patriarch was imprisoned the first time.

a document, which also mentions Paulos–Kolla, eparch of the land of Nobatia, perhaps the same eparch involved with Abd al–Malik.[342] Kyriakos was still living after 767, since he was alive when John was writing the *Life of Michael,* who died in that year.

Though according to the church historians the *casus belli* was the imprisonment of the patriarch, Kyriakos' invasion of Egypt occurred when the Umayyad empire was collapsing. In 747 the Abbasid revolt had begun, coupled with insurrections in Syria and Iraq. The Egyptian Christians had been suffering both religious persecution and fiscal oppression and were in a rebellious condition. Perhaps Kyriakos hoped to shake off the Nubian tribute, the *baqt* – if indeed this was more than an exchange treaty[343], and had become burdensome. The time must have seemed extremely favourable for an attack on Egypt. The reason given for the Nubian retreat seems rather feeble; perhaps there were reverses, not mentioned by the chroniclers, which led to their retirement from Egypt, or perhaps the attack was little more than a quick razzia, with plunder as the main incentive. By 758 the Egyptian governor Musa ibn Ka'b, representative of firm government again, was writing to the 'lord of Maqurra and Nubia' to demand the backlog of the *baqt*.[344] The letter, a magnificent example of a state document of the period, lacks the royal name, but can only refer to Kyriakos.

23b. The 'Aksumite' Presence

Of all the recent commentators on this invasion, only ZYHLARZ[345] and SERGEW HABLE SELLASSIE[346] assert an 'Aksumite' presence among the invading armies. Following, doubtless, the accounts of the *Synaxarium* and Abu Salih, the former conjectured that Kyriakos formed "un attiva unione di tutti gli Stati cristiani del Sudan" and with the Aksumites as well. He dated the attack to 735, adding that Kyriakos was reinforced, on top of his 200,000 troops, by Aksumite cavalry, and Beja camels. SERGEW

---

342 J. KRALL, *Beiträge zur Geschichte der Blemyer und Nubier*, Denkschrift der Kaiserlichen Akademie der Wissenschaften, (Phil-Hist. Classe), Wien 1900, Band XLVI, IV, pp. 16-17. MONNERET DE VILLARD, Storia, p. 172.

343 For the *baqt* and what it meant, see YUSUF. F. HASAN, *op. cit.*, pp. 20ff.

344 J.M. PLUMLEY, *An Eighth Century Letter to the King of Nubia*, JEA 61, 1975, pp. 241 f. and 60, 1974, pp. 237-8.

345 ZYHLARZ, *op. cit.*, p. 260.

346 SERGEW, AMEH, pp. 196-8.

HABLE SELLASSIE is more vague, merely stating that the "Aksumite Emperor" must have been included in the confusion of the description of Kyriakos by John. While this is probably true, it does not imply that the Ethiopian king (who was probably not at this time still ruling from Aksum) joined the military attack on Egypt. SERGEW HABLE SELLASSIE sees the war of the time of Patriarch Isaac as between "Mekuriah and Aksum" later settled by the victory of "the Jacobite faction". He suggests that these states allied for the push into Egypt. Only the later and corrupt chronicles offer the slightest evidence for this sort of interpretation, and the Ethiopian presence must be dismissed.[347] CONTI ROSSINI[348], noting the great weakness of the kingdom of Aksum at this time, is probably on somewhat safer ground. Ethiopian rulers may well have had enough to do at home, with the adjustments and realignments necessary in the period after the rise of Islam and the consequent loss of important overseas trading contacts. CONTI ROSSINI's stress on the "massimo indebolimento" of the Ethiopian state is perhaps going too far, since we know virtually nothing of the country's condition during this period. It is, however, notable that Arab writers like al–Ya'qubi and al–Mas'udi still represent the dominions of the *najashi* as constituting a rich and powerful state in the ninth and tenth centuries.

From 766–802, a certain Ignatios was bishop of Pachoras or Faras. On his funerary stele the writer of the text employed – together with three other dating systems – an Ethiopian era date (Year 794 from the Incarnation, 802 AD, computed from 7/8 AD as the birth of Christ), perhaps indicating some contemporary Ethiopian influence in the country.[349]

Beyond the brief remark in the biography[350] of Mark II, 799–819, that rebels robbed those travelling to Abyssinia and Nubia, there is no further evidence for contact between the patriarchate and Ethiopia until the time of Patriarch James (Ya'qub) 819–838.[351]

---

[347] TEDESCHI, *Etiopia*, p. 256 also rejects the Ethiopian participation.

[348] C. CONTI ROSSINI, *Pubblicazione etiopistiche dal 1936-1945*, RSE IV, 1944-5, p. 36.

[349] JAKOBIELSKI, Faras III, pp. 70-71.

[350] PO X, fasc. 5, pp. 427-8; TEDESCHI, *Etiopia*, pp. 258ff.

[351] PO X, fasc. 5, pp. 508ff.

24. Patriarchs James (819–831) and Joseph (831–849); the Metropolitan John

A passage in the biography of Joseph[352], indicates that Patriarch James (Ya'qub), predecessor of the short–lived Simon II (831), had consecrated a bishop for Abyssinia;

> There was at that time a bishop (usquf) named Yuhanna (John), whom the father, Abba James, had ordained for the land of Abyssinia. Now the king of the Abyssinians had gone forth to war. Then the people became disaffected and drove away that bishop, and appointed another of their own free choice, thus breaking the canon.[353] And the aforesaid bishop returned to Egypt and took up his abode at the Monastery of Baramus in Wadi Habib, because he had first become a monk there. But the Lord... did not allow that country and its inhabitants to remain in their disobedience, but he raised up against them the evangelical throne once more, that the Lord might show forth wonders, in the following manner. For he sent down upon them and upon their cattle a plague with great mortality, and caused their king to be defeated by all whom fought against him; and his followers were slain. So when he came back from the war, great sadness fell upon him. And he did not know what had been done to the bishop, nor how he had been banished from their city. For it was the queen who had caused this mischief, acting as Eudoxia did in her time against John (Chrysostom). As soon therefore as the king learnt this, he hastened and wrote a letter to the good shepherd, Abba Joseph, saying to him, "I prostrate myself before the evangelical throne, upon which thy Paternity has been accounted worthy to sit, and by the grace of which my royal authority is confirmed. Now the people of my country have strayed away from the light of the holy see, and have set their feet in a path full of thorns, by driving away their vicar. Therefore the Lord has sent down the punishment of that deed upon our heads, and has given us a taste of his full vengeance through the death of men and cattle, by the plague. Moreover he has forbidden heaven to rain upon us. But now, our holy father, overlook our folly and send us someone who will pray to God for us, and intercede for us, that we may be saved by their acceptable prayers". When the father had read this letter, he rejoiced over the king's faith, and quickly sent and summoned that bishop from the monastery of Baramus, and having encouraged him and consoled him, sent him back to the Abyssinians. And he despatched an escort of trustworthy men with him on account of the dangers of the road, and gave him sufficient provision for the journey. And he dis-

---

[352] See note 351 above. The story is also told by al-Kotobi, ms. d'Abbadie 211, C. CONTI ROSSINI, *Notice sur les manuscrits Éthiopiens de la collection d'Abbadie*, JA, Ser. II, T.6, 1915, pp. 196.

[353] The first of such attempts, according to SERGEW AMEH, p. 212, and AYELE TEKLAHAYMANOT, *Egyptian Metropolitans*, p. 25; but possibly it had happened in the time of Theodosius, see above, ASSEMANI.

> missed the party, giving them his blessing that God might make their path easy. And God heard him; for they safely reached the friendly king, who rejoiced over them with all the natives of the land. After this, Satan, the enemy of peace, suggested an idea to some of the people of that country. Accordingly they waited upon the king, and said to him "We request thy Majesty to command this bishop to be circumcised,[354] for all the inhabitants of our country are circumcised except him". And the working of Satan was so powerful that the king approved this proposal, namely, that the aged bishop should be taken and circumcised, or else that he should return to the place whence he had come. And when the bishop recollected the hardships of his journeys, both when he departed and when he returned, and then of what he would experience again, he dreaded the difficulties of the road both by land and water. So he said, "I will submit to this, for the salvation of these souls, of which the Lord has appointed me as shepherd, without any merit of mine. Yet now Paul the apostle enjoins us saying 'If any man is called without circumcision, let him not be circumcised'." So when he made this concession to them, God manifested a miracle in him, as he wrote to our father the patriarch, Abba Joseph; namely, that when they took him to circumcise him, and stripped him, they found the mark of circumcision in him, as if he had been circumcised on the eighth day after his birth. And he swore in his letter that he knew nothing of this before that day. Thus the king and the people of the country were satisfied, and rejoiced greatly over this wonder, and accepted the bishop with joy. When the letter containing an account of this matter reached the patriarch, he rejoiced greatly over the return of those erring ones to their shepherd, and over the miracle which had been manifested... And because this good shepherd took so much care of his sheep, and gave his life for them, he appointed many bishops, and sent them to all places under the see of Saint Mark the evangelist, which include Africa, and the Pentapolis and al–Kairawan and Tripoli and the land of Egypt and Abyssinia and Nubia. For he said "If the shepherds be not many to guard the flock, the sheep will perish..."

The story of John (Yuhanna), a bishop of Ethiopia who had been sent originally by Patriarch James, and was then later returned to Ethiopia after an absence by Patriarch Joseph, is repeated in the usual chronicles. Al–Makin[355]

---

[354] For this question of circumcision, see TEDESCHI, *Etiopia*, pp. 267ff; LE GRAND in LOBO, *op. cit.*, dissertation VIII, p. 281.

[355] El-Makin, ed., ERPENIUS, p. 183.

calls the bishop Ya'qub, but supplies exactly the same details; Ibn Rahib[356] also mentions him, but without name, merely stating that he was ordained by Patriarch Ya'qub (James). Both he and Maqrizi designate him *mutran*. In the Ethiopian version of Abu Shakir (Ibn Rahib) he is referred to as *pappas*, and his illegal replacement as *episqopos*. Al–Maqrizi adds that the patriarch (Joseph) "sent him with several bishops into Africa". The *Synaxarium* has taken parts of the account of the biography of Joseph almost word for word, adding nothing new.[357] These later versions, of course, are less to be relied upon than the contemporary account in the biography of Patriarch Joseph, written by one of his companions in prison. Evidently[358] Ya'qub and Yuhanna are the same metropolitan. But the claim, included in later texts, that other bishops were sent as well is not to be depended upon. TEDESCHI's reference to "una missione di ecclesiastici alessandrini" rests on very insubstantial evidence.[359]

The chronology of this period is uncertain, as far as Metropolitan John is concerned. The point was discussed by TEDESCHI[360] who suggested that CHAÎNE's date of c. 820 is too early, putting it nearer to 830 for various reasons. It is interesting to know that during that decade the king of Abyssinia is supposed to have suffered military defeats. This may have been one of the conflicts that resulted, in northern Abyssinia, in the establishment of a number of Beja 'kingdoms' – more or less defined tribal agglomerates. There is no indication about the identity of the enemy, but it is noteworthy that the 831 treaty of the Arabs with Kannun ibn Abd al–Aziz, 'king' of the Beja, seems to recognise his power as far south as Dahlak.[361] This may well indicate that some of the territory now under his control had been formerly part of the Ethiopian kingdom.

25. Nubia, the Baqt, and the Caliphate

The period of the episcopates of Mark II (799–819), James (819–831) and Joseph (831–849) was one of difficulties. For a summary

[356] Ibn Rahib, ed. CHEIKHO, p. 139. For an Ethiopian version see CONTI ROSSINI, JA, Ser. II, T. 6, p. 196.
[357] BUDGE, Synaxarium, Vol I, pp. 185-6.
[358] TEDESCHI, *Etiopia*, pp. 260-1
[359] *Ibid.*, p. 266.
[360] *Ibid.*, pp. 261-2; CHAINE, *op. cit.* (n. 124), p. 267.
[361] YUSUF F. HASAN, *op. cit.*, p. 39 for a translation of Maqrizi's text of the treaty.

of the rebellious state of the Abbasid realm after the death of Harun al–Rashid in 808, when the rivalry for the succession upset firm government and left the roads in a perilous state, the account of TEDESCHI is sufficient.[362] Egyptian affairs remained in disorder even after the re–establishment of al–Mamun in 813. In 831 a great rebellion of the Copts was crushed. Patriarch James, and Patriarch Dionysios of Antioch, played some part in the attempts to re–establish peace.[363] There was trouble, too, in Nubia and the Beja lands. In 831 al–Mu'tasim sent 'Abdallah b. al–Jahm [364] into the Beja territory, where he defeated the local ruler, Kannun. The Nubian *baqt* had, by 833, been held back for 14 years[365], and the caliph's demands for these arrears were the cause of the famous journey of George, the son of the Nubian king, Zacharias, to Baghdad. The difficulties of travel in these southern regions were not over, it seems, even after the treaty of 831 with the Beja. Later, between 832–854, troubles with the Beja under 'Ali Baba[366], as well as clashes between the Nubian kingdom and al–'Umari[367], must have continued to make things dangerous for communication between Egypt and the south. Patriarch Joseph's biography comments[368];

> ... he took thought for the affairs of Abyssinia and Nubia, and sent a letter to the people of those countries, and enquired after them and their churches. But he did not succesd in communicating with them on account of the hostility between their kings and the Muslim governors of Egypt. And he prayed to God that there might be peace between them, so that he might attain his object, which was to restore the buldings under the jurisdiction of the father Saint Mark the evangelist. And God heard his prayer, and answered his petition. Now this war had lasted fourteen years between them, until Ibrahim (i.e. al-Mu'tasim, 833-42)[369] brother of al-Mamun, began to reign. He set guards over the roads to Abyssinia and Nubia.

---

362 TEDESCHI, *Etiopia*, p. 258 f.

363 BUTCHER, *op. cit.*, vol I, p. 436; YUSUF F. HASAN, *op. cit.*, p. 35-6. H.A. MACMICHAEL, A History of the Arabs in the Sudan, Cambridge 1922, Vol. I, p. 163; "History of the Patriarchs", IV, pp. 492-495.

364 YUSUF F. HASAN, *op. cit.*, p. 38 and n. 101. QUATREMÈRE, Mémoires, pp. 145ff.

365 YUSUF F. HASAN, *op. cit.*, p. 26; the reference is from Severus, PO X, p. 282.

366 MACMICHAEL, *op. cit.*, p. 165; YUSUF F. HASAN, *op. cit.*, p. 51; VANTINI, Storia, p. 77 for the account of all this in Ibn Hawqal.

367 QUATREMÈRE, *op. cit.*, II, pp. 59ff. YUSUF F. HASAN, *op. cit.*, pp. 52ff.

368 PO X, p.503

369 TEDESCHI, *Etiopia*, p. 263, identifies Muhammed, who reigned as al-Mu'tasim, with this Ibrahim. Ibrahim is mentioned several times in the Life of Joseph PO X, IV. For example, it is noted (p. 495) that "there was in the suite of

The caliph wrote to King Zacharias, demanding the *baqt,* and the patriarch, learning of this, took the opportunity to write to the kings under his jurisdiction, encouraging the Nubian king to comply with the caliph's demand. The result was the embassy of Prince George.

26. Patriarch Joseph and the Abyssinian Pages

The final mention of Ethiopia in the biography of Joseph reports that it was the custom of certain kings to send young pages to the patriarch; these were "presented to the churches as gifts, and came from the king of the Abyssinians or from the Nubians or Romans".[370] Trouble arose when an interfering judge drew the notice of the Muslim authorities to Joseph's eight pages, who were being educated at the school in Alexandria. They were removed to be converted to Islam. TEDESCHI devotes some space to this account[371], which he seems to doubt. However, the biography is so specific about the places of origin of these pages that there seems little reason to question it, save perhaps as far as the Roman (i.e. from the Byzantine empire) pages are concerned, Byzantium always being linked with the melkite church in Egypt.

There are, however, circumstances which make the story of Roman pages rather more credible. There were two melkite patriarchs, Christopher (817–848) and Sophronius I (848–60), who were contempo-

al-Ma'mun his brother Ibrahim, who reigned after him". Ibrahim was enraged at Dionysius of Antioch because of the latter's comments about the rapacity of the tax collectors, who were "among his followers". The patriarch hastily left Egypt, and Ibrahim searched for him, but could not find him. "After the death of al-Ma'mun, and the enthronement of his brother Ibrahim" the patriarch Dionysius fled, until he had guarantees of safety from the new caliph. Next is noted Ibrahim, the brother of al-Ma'mun, whose reign began when the baqt had been held back for fourteen years in the time of king Zacharias; and after that (p. 519) we find mention of 'Ali b. Yahya, the Armenian (governor 841-3) acting on behalf of Abu Ishaq Ibrahim al-Mu'tasim, son of Harun al-Rashid, and brother of al-Ma'mun. Finally, p. 526-7, Harun al-Wathiq, son of Ibrahim, is mentioned; showing that al-Mu'tasim was the Ibrahim in question, who is generally called Muhammed. Perhaps the name was confused with that of the uncle of al-Ma'mun, Ibrahim b. al-Mahdi, elected in 816, and deposed in 818? See also VANTINI, OS, p. 317.

370 PO V, fasc., 5, pp. 528-9.

371 TEDESCHI, *Etiopia*, pp. 269ff.

raries of Joseph; and the latter was apparently a friend of his.[372] The pages might therefore have been obtained through his agency. However, even this suggestion seems unnecessary. The text itself indicates clearly enough that 'Roman' refers to those pages from Africa and the Pentapolis – "the Roman and Abyssinian pages of the patriarch, who had been sent as presents to him from Africa and the Five Cities and Abyssinia and Nubia". These regions called Africa and the Pentapolis, formerly part of the Roman empire, hence 'Roman', were at this time controlled by Muslims, but they remained under Coptic ecclesiastical jurisdiction. The question of Roman (i.e. Byzantine) pages does not arise.

27. The Melkite Patriarchate; Christopher and Sophronius

Ibn Khaldun commented that after al–Mu'tasim's expedition against the Beja in 833, the patriarchate of Alexandria was transferred to Rome (Byzantium), while

> at Alexandria remained only the Coptic patriarch to look after the faithful who live in those regions, and after the kings of Nubia and Abyssinia.[373]

This is an odd piece of information, since Patriarch Christopher held the melkite title from 817 until 848, followed by Sophronius I (see above) until 860, Michael I and II, Christodoulos and Eutychius until 940, then Eutychius' successors. Christopher is said to have been paralysed by a stroke shortly after his election[374], but he is briefly referred to in the biography of Patriarch James.[375] Sophronius too lived in Egypt, and is said to have frequently visited his monophysite contemporary Joseph (III: 26). Ibn Khaldun makes a further mention of the removal of the melkite patriarchate[376]; "We have omitted (Ibn al–'Amid's) statements on the Patriarchate since the conquest of Alexandria, because we thought we could dispense with them. Their great Patriarchate, which was in Alexandria, was moved

---

372 BUTCHER, *op. cit.*, Vol. 1, p. 444; the evidence for this is perhaps from the "History of the Patriarchs", PO X, fasc. IV, p. 547; "so that even their chief, the pseudo-patriarch, whose name was Sephronius, began to have faith and trust in our father, and paid several visits to him, and acted humbly towards him".

373 Ibn Khaldun, quoted in VANTINI, OS, p. 551, from the Beirut ed., Bk. II, p. 473.

374 BUTCHER, *op. cit.*, Vol. I, p. 436, n. 2.

375 PO X, fasc. IV, p. 450.

376 VANTINI, OS, p. 551, from the Beirut ed., II, p. 473.

to Ruma (i.e. Byzantium), and there it belongs to the Melkites (al–Malakiyya); they call him Pope (al–baba) which means "the Father of the Fathers".

BUTCHER suggested[377] that there was a gap of about a hundred years in the communication between the Egyptian and Ethiopian churches at this point. She assumed, as Abu Salih suggested, that the Abyssinian kings were able to fulfill the priestly functions themselves. This, apart from the manifest confusion of Abu Salih's account, is unlikely for several reasons. It is nowhere else recorded, apart from the case of Yimrehane Kristos (see below), that the kings could fulfill these functions. The kings themselves evidently did not feel able to fulfil the priestly needs of their country, and repeatedly made efforts to acquire new metropolitans. The kings' priestly functions – which would anyway only last for the lifetime of one ruler – could scarcely run to the consecration of bishops or even the ordination of priests, the essential reason for obtaining the services of a properly consecrated metropolitan.

In reality, this *argumentum ex silentio* does not indicate that there was no Ethiopian embassy to the patriarchate during this long period. The compilation by Severus of Ashmunein depended on the preserved records of earlier chroniclers; in addition he was evidently selective. Some of the Ethiopian embassies may well have passed unrecorded by previous biographers, or unnoted by Severus himself. The ensuing notice of the consecration of a new metropolitan by Kosmas III (III: 29) is not accompanied by the information that there were no bishops or priests, as must have been the case if there had really been a suspension of the metropolitanate of Ethiopia for a long period. Possibly the melkites too attempted, during the patriarchate of Eutychius, 933–939, to install a metropolitan, as the list later copied by Yusuf the Egyptian seems to indicate by its inclusion of al–Habasha (I: 5).

28. Patriarch Michael III (876–901?); the *ardh habash* and the Pool of the Ethiopians

Al–Maqrizi supplied the information that Michael III sold some of the land designated by the name 'Habash' outside Fustat Misr. This is the same district which Abu Salih[378] and others mention, adjacent to the Pool

[377] BUTCHER, *op. cit.*, Vol. I. p. 487; NEALE, *op. cit.*, Vol. II, p. 177, quoting Abu Salih, *op. cit.*, fol. 105b, p. 286.

[378] Abu Salih, *op. cit.*, Fol. 7b, n. 4, p. 16; Fol. 39b, p. 27; Fol. 41a, p. 130 for the lake and lands called "habash". The "Well of the Ethiopians", near the monastery of St. Victor, is mentioned in BUDGE, Synaxarium, Vol. II, p. 631.

of the Ethiopians *(birkat al–habash),* where there was a cemetery of the Jacobites and the bishops of Misr. The Copts referred to it as *niethush* and in it stood the church of Apa Victor of the Ethiopians *(apa biktor niethush).* In *ardh habash* was later buried Patriarch Zacharias, 1002–1032.[379]

Abu Salih reports that Patriarch Michael III sold part of it to the Jews to meet Ahmad ibn Tulun's demands[380]; part, however remained the property of the Jacobites. Yaqut adds[381] that the Pool was named after the gardens of *al–habash,* but Severus [382] implies that its name derived from Kyriakos of Nubia having camped there when he came to rescue Michael I (III: 23a). EVETTS and CONTI ROSSINI[383] however, suggest that the name is earlier than the Muslim conquest; it may imply original ownership of the land by an "Ethiopian" community. Much later, we are told by al–Maqrizi that Patriarch John VI, 1189–1216, too, was "buried in the plot of ground that belonged to the Abyssinians".[384]

29. Patriarch Kosmas III (923–934); the Metropolitan Peter; the Dispute over the Succession and the Impostor Minas

Whatever the situation between the 830s and 923, relations between Ethiopia and the patriarchate had certainly been restored during the episcopate of Kosmas III. However, during this patriarchate an incident occurred which severed the Egyptian church's relations with Ethiopia even more drastically than had happened during the patriarchate (535–567) of Theodosius I.[385] The break was caused essentially by the remoteness of the daughter church and the time it took for letters to pass to and fro between Ethiopia and Alexandria.

---

[379] Abu Salih, *op. cit.*, Fol. 43b, p. 135. NEALE *op. cit.*, Vol. II, p. 207: "History of the Patriarchs", II, II, p. 211 says that he was buried in the church of the Mistress at Bani Wayal, known as the Church of the Steps.

[380] Abu Salih, *op. cit.*, Fol. 44a, p. 136.

[381] F. WÜSTENFELD, Jacuts geographisches Wörterbuch, Leipzig 1866-1873, I, p. 591.

[382] PO V, fasc. I, p. 144.

[383] Abu Salih, *op. cit.*, p. 16, n. 4; see also C. CONTI ROSSINI, *Egitto ed Etiopia nei tempi antichi e nell'eta di mezzo,* Aegyptus III, 1922, p. 65, col. 2, p. 15, n. 1; TEDESCHI, *op. cit.*, pp. 256-7; CRUM, Coptic Dictionary, Oxford 1939, p. 65 col. 2 See also FIACCADORI, *op. cit.*, p. 360.

[384] Maqrizi, ed., MALAN, p. 95.

[385] ASSEMANI, *op. cit.*, Vol I, p. 384.

Briefly, the church historian and other sources[386] tell of the consecration by Patriarch Kosmas of a certain Peter as metropolitan *(mutran)* of Abyssinia, and of his welcome by the king there. The introduction to this text is of very great interest to Ethiopian historiography, since it includes what seems to be the earliest mention of the attribution of the queen of Sheba to Ethiopia; "al–Habasha... is a vast country, namely the kingdom of Saba from which the queen of the South came to Solomon, the son of David the king"; the next appearance of this legend is in the work of Abu Salih (see below, VI: 50). Kosmas' biography continues by stating that the Ethiopian king, on his death bed, granted the authority to the metropolitan to choose and appoint his successor from the two royal sons, since Peter was "the Vicar of the King Christ, the great God, by whose authority are all the kingdoms of the world". The king has been named Tabtahadj, Yabtahadj, or Babtahaj by translators of the Arabic text[387] – a name not identified in the Ethiopian king lists. In fact, there is no royal name; it is an erroneous reading for the Arabic expression *b–ibtihaj*, 'with joy'.[388]

Metropolitan Peter selected the younger of the brothers, whom he deemed the most suitable, to assume the throne, while the elder withdrew to a solitary place. However, two monks of Syrian origin, from the monastery of St. Anthony – who, the *Synaxarium* adds, had been driven out for their bad conduct – saw their opportunity in this situation. They entered Ethiopia and presented letters as if from Patriarch Kosmas to the elder brother, denouncing Peter as an impostor and his candidate for the throne as invalid. Naturally, the elder brother was delighted. He gathered the army about him, deposed both his brother and Peter, and appointed one of the monks, Minas, in Peter's place since the counterfeit letters confirmed him as the rightful metropolitan. Soon, however, the other monk, Victor, quarrelled with Minas and fled, taking much plunder with him.

---

386 "History of the Patriarchs", II, II, pp. 118-120; BUDGE, Synaxarium, Vol.III, pp. 666-668.

387 J. PERRUCHON, *Note pour l'histoire d'Ethiopie; Vie de Cosmas, patriarche d'Alexandrie, de 923 à 934*, Revue Sémitique, 1894, p. 84. BUDGE, History, Vol. I, p. 276, suggested that the kings were Degna Djan, then Dil Na'od and Anbessa Wudem; he also suggested that the new king, the eldest, was himself deposed. SERGEW, AMEH, p. 218 also suggested Dagnajan "whose reign probably dated from 939-950 A.D."

388 S. TEDESCHI, *La reine de Saba et le roi Tabtahadj*, AE XIV, 1987, pp. 171-2. E. GODET, *Tableaux chronologiques relatifs à la fin de l'époque axoumite et à la période des Zagwes*, in: Proceedings of the Ninth International Congress of Ethiopian Studies, Moscow, 26-29 August 1986, Moscow 1988, 6, p. 36.

Minas too did not last long, it seems. He was executed when the king (presumably the one who had been raised to the throne through Minas' own machinations, though this is not stated) learned in due course through new letters from Kosmas that he was an impostor. MEINARDUS writes that the patriarch himself "anathematized and excommunicated Abuna Mina and slew him"[389], a rather un–patriarchal proceeding. ISAAC, unfavourable as always to the Alexandrian patriarchate's dealings in Ethiopia, does not seem to credit the story of the imposture at all, asserting that "in retrospect Alexandria disavowed him".[390]

Kosmas now refused to consecrate a new bishop, even though the ex–metropolitan, Peter, had by this time died in exile. So the king of Ethiopia forced Peter's assistant – presumably an Egyptian? – to succeed him, despite his protests at the un–canonical position that he was compelled to adopt. The Ethiopian monarch refused to allow this new metropolitan to travel to Egypt for confirmation, so he continued in his illegal office throughout the episcopates of Macarius I, 934–953; Theophanes, 953–956; Minas II 956–974; Abraham, 975–978; on into the beginning of the episcopate of Philotheus, 979–1003. By this time he was very old, having been 'acting' bishop for at least forty–five years, and the kingdom of Ethiopia had decayed to a disastrous state.

389 MEINARDUS, *Abunate*, p. 44.
390 ISAAC, *Ethiopian Church*, p. 248.

CHAPTER FOUR

The Metropolitanate from the Mid–Tenth to the Mid–Eleventh Century

30. Patriarch Philotheus (979–1003); the Letter to George II of Nubia, and the Metropolitan Daniel

At this point other sources take up the story of the political troubles in the Ethiopian kingdom – generally still referred to in modern literature as 'Aksumite', though Aksum, as noted above, had probably already ceased to be the capital before the middle of the seventh century. Both the *Synaxarium* and the *History of the Patriarchs*[391] tell of a letter, sent to Nubia by an Ethiopian king.[392] The letter was transmitted to Egypt by the king of Nubia, George (Girgis) II.[393] This monarch is known to have been ruling in Nubia at the time of al–Aswani's embassy in 969[394], until at the latest 1002, when Abu Salih mentions a king named Raphael.[395] The letter sent to George is partly quoted and partly summarised by the patriarch's biographer as follows;

> In his (Philotheus') days, the king of Abyssinia sent to the king of Nubia, a youth whose name was George, and made known to him how the Lord had chastened him, he and the inhabitants of his land. It was that a woman, a queen of Bani al–Hamwiyah, had revolted against him and his country. She took captive from it many people and burned many cities and destroyed churches and drove him, (the king) from place to place. That which befell him was a retribution for what the king who (was) before him had done to the metropolitan in the days of the father Abba Cosmas, as we have explained earlier [see III: 29],

[391] "History of the Patriarchs", II, II, pp. 171-172; Budge, Synaxarium, Vol. I, pp. 233-234. George was presumably predecessor of Raphael, king in 1002 AD/ 392 AH, according to Abu Salih, *op. cit.*, p. 265.

[392] Identified as Sayfa Ar'ad (977-1005), by Ayele Teklahaymanot, presumably using information from one of the dated king-lists, (*Egyptian Metropolitans*, p. 26).

[393] S.C. Munro-Hay *Kings and Kingdoms of Ancient Nubia*, RSE XXIX, 1982-3, pp. 107ff.

[394] Quatremère, Mémoires, II, pp. 80-84. For other references, Monneret de Villard, Storia, p. 123.

[395] Raphael is only mentioned by Abu Salih, *op. cit.*, fol. 95b.

> through his falsification and his fraud. He (the king) said to him (George) in the letter which he sent to him: "I desire that thou shouldst help me and partake with me in the fatigue, for the sake of God and for the sake of the unity of the faith, and that thou shouldst write a letter on thy part to the father, the patriarch, in Misr, to beg him to absolve us, and to absolve our lands, and to pray for us, that God may remove from us and our country this trial, and may grant to us that he (the patriarch) may consecrate for us a metropolitan, as was the custom of our fathers and that he might pray for us, that God may remove his wrath from us. I have mentioned this to thee, O brother, for fear lest the Christian religion pass away and cease among us, for lo, six patriarchs have sat and have not paid attention to our lands, but they (the lands) are abandoned without a shepherd, and our bishops and our priests are dead, and the churches are ruined, and we have learned that this trial has come down upon us as a just judgement in return for what we did with the metropolitan".

King George received the letter sympathetically, and sent his own letters to the patriarch asking him to comply with this request, to which Philotheus agreed. He sent a monk of the monastery of Makarios, Daniel, as metropolitan, and the tale ends;

> They received him with joy, and God removed from them His wrath, and put an end to the affair of the woman, who had risen up against them.

This reference to six patriarchs includes Kosmas III, who refused to consecrate a successor to Metropolitan Peter, Macarius I, Theophanes, Menas II, Ephraim (Abraham), and Philotheus himself. The relation of this incident in the *Synaxarium* is almost the same, save that the mysterious queen is never mentioned, the text referring simply to 'enemies'.

31. The 'Queen of the Bani al–Hamwiyya' and Queen Gudit

The key question in the chronology of this period is the possible (almost certain) identification of the queen mentioned by the *History of the Patriarchs* (see also VI: 46) with one of the most famous figures in Ethiopian legend, Queen Gudit. The troubles that befell Ethiopia in the later tenth century through a queen are confirmed by Ibn Hawqal[396], and another Arabic reference (see below).[397] There are also numerous Ge'ez

396 J.H. KRAMERS and G. WIET, ed., La configuration du terre, Beyrouth and Paris, 1964, Vol. I, pp. 16, 22-23, 56, and 161.

397 M. EL-CHENNAFI, *Mention nouvelle d'une 'reine Éthiopienne' au IVe s. de l'Hegire / Xe s. ap. J-C.*, AE X, 1976, pp. 119-121.

chronicles which mention that a certain Gudit, generally referred to as a queen, caused havoc in the kingdom, destroying the cathedral of Aksum [398] and overthrowing the great stelae there. In spite of the temporary victory over their enemies mentioned in the biography of Philotheus, the 'Israelite' dynasty – as later chroniclers referred to it – was nearing its end in Ethiopia. The records grow increasingly obscure; traditional Ethiopian king lists record that Anbessa Wudem – perhaps the ruler who wrote to King Girgis of Nubia[399] – and Dil Na'od were the last of the dynasty.

The literary tradition of Ethiopia has preserved a magnificent series of chronicles, lists, hagiographies, and other works, some of them doubtless redactions of older texts, some of them the more recent products of oral traditions of various areas. However, rich though these sources are, they differ amongst themselves to an extraordinary degree. Any attempt to reconcile them is hampered by the almost total lack of any comparative historical evidence. Archaeology, as yet, has little to offer for this period. The inscriptional and numismatic material, so useful for the earlier Aksumite monarchy, has by this time come to an end. The late dates, even into the tenth century, formerly proposed for the end of the numismatic sequence can no longer be supported. As for the inscriptions, only those of the *hatsani* Dan'el have been credited to so late a date, though there is no actual evidence for the attribution.

A number of metropolitans occur in Ethiopian traditional history during this period, in which there are two main themes of interest. The first centres on the legends about the mysterious queen called Gudit (Yodit, Judith) – some documents record that she reigned in Tigray and that another woman, Esato, reigned in Amhara – and the kings of the end of the 'Israelite' dynasty. The second comprises the legends concerning the rise of the usurping Zagwé dynasty.

Some of the king lists[400] name Armah, Dagnajan, Dagajan also called Gidajan, Gudit and/or Esato, Anbessa Wudem, and Dil Na'od, in that order;

---

398 Unpublished *Chronicle of the Qese Gabaz Takla Haymanot of Aksum*, in SERGEW, AMEH, p. 226; also unpublished *Gadla Abreha and Asbeha*.

399 SERGEW, AMEH, p. 232.

400 C. CONTI ROSSINI, *Les listes des rois d'Aksoum*", JA, 1909; the names are subject to much variation in each list. The lists concerned are; A, which seems to have been in two recensions, the oldest without Esato, and with Anbessa Wudem as 37, and Dilna'od as 35, and the second with Esato, c. XVth century; this latter's independence of the *Synaxarium*, (and the "History of the Patriarchs") according to CONTI ROSSINI, pp. 312-3, is worth questioning; B,D,E,F, which gives Dilna'od as the last, but with different predecessors; G, and two unpublished lists, both dated, quoted by SERGEW, AMEH, pp. 202-3. See also G.W.B. HUNTINGFORD, *The Wealth of Kings' and the end of the Zague dynasty*, BSOAS 28, 1965, pp. 21-2 for further lists.

other lists, one should add, do not support this sequence. Dagnajan, according to certain chronicles, was the father of both Anbessa Wudem and Dil Na'od. He is said to have conducted a war against the Arabs to the west[401] and south.[402] He reigned nearly 20 years, or 12 years.[403] Dagajan or Gidajan is credited with either a ten month reign before the rise of Gudit, or a nine year reign.[404] Possibly, since one text bestows the name Gidajan on the son of Dagnajan who later ruled as Anbessa Wudem, the king doomed to spend his time constantly on the move to escape from Gudit[405], the period of ten months could reflect a short reign of Anbessa Wudem before the appearance of Gudit. Other lists include Ma'eday before Esato/Gudit, and name many other kings in completely different order .

Ibn Hawqal provides a much more reliable source, being a contemporary of these events. He noted that the queen reigning in Ethiopia in his time had already ruled for thirty years. She is said to have killed the previous king (perhaps either Dagnajan or Gidajan[406] if she is to be identified with Gudit). Ibn Hawqal's account of the current situation in Ethiopia is certainly reminiscent of that recounted by the chronicles, and of that depicted in the letter sent to George of Nubia.

By Ibn Hawqal's time Ethiopia had changed a good deal from the days of the Aksumite monarchy. The Graeco–Oriental veneer on Aksumite civilisation, together with the monetary economy, and a policy of expansion into South Arabia combined with the Red Sea trade based on Adulis, had long disappeared. Ethiopia had not, however, simply stagnated, but was expanding in other directions. Ibn Hawqal indicates that the kingdom still controlled a very extensive territory;

> Abyssinia extends beside the Red Sea, which is in reality the Persian Sea, and continues until the country of the Zanj; on one side it ends at the desert situated between Nubia and the Red Sea; and another frontier runs along beside the Beja and the impassable desert. The country of the Zanj is the longest of all the lands of the Blacks, and is bordered only by the Abyssinian empire. This last constitutes a well–defined region and a vast empire; many curious things are related about it.

---

401 SERGEW, AMEH, p. 203, n. 115.

402 TADDESSE TAMRAT, Church and State, p. 35, n. 1 and p. 36.

403 SERGEW, AMEH, p. 203; CONTI ROSSINI, list B, 12 years.

404 SERGEW, AMEH, p. 203; CONTI ROSSINI, list B.

405 In a ms. belonging to the *qese gabaz* Tekla Haymanot, see SERGEW, AMEH, p. 203.

406 For Dagnajan's death, see SERGEW, AMEH, p. 229, quoting a *Chronicle of Qese Gabaz Takla Haymanot.*

Dahlak would seem to have been under different rulers at this time, since the geographer continues;

> He (the Yemeni king) receives, following a treaty, presents from the ruler of the Dahlak islands...the queen of Abyssinia also sends him presents and good–will gifts....

The northern limit of Ethiopian influence may have been around Asmara, since the headwaters of the Baraka river rose in Abyssinia, watered the country of Bazin, and flowed on to the Beja lands. In declaring, however, that the port of ‘Aydhab is a town of Abyssinia, Ibn Hawqal must be using *habash* as a blanket term.

Ibn Hawqal repeats his information in another paragraph;

> The country of Abyssinia has been governed by a woman for many years; she killed the king of the Abyssinians, who was called Hadani [actually a title, the same as 'hatsani']. Until now she reigns completely independently over her country and the surrounding lands of the Hadani's territories, in the south of Abyssinia. It is a great country, without fixed frontiers, with wastes and deserts difficult to cross.

Precise dating for these passages is impossible. However, Ibn Hawqal seems to have written between c. 977[407] and 988, the latter date being suggested by KRAMERS and WIET for the "révision définitive, sinon de la composition de l'ouvrage".[408] The events of the queen's first years in Ethiopia appear, then, to have fallen somewhere between c. 947 and 958. After the king was killed, his successor, presumably, wrote to Girgis II of Nubia between 979, when Philotheus became patriarch, and 988 if that date can be accepted for Ibn Hawqal's final revision of his work.[409] There is a brief record that a "striped female donkey (zebra) coming from one of the districts of al–Habasha, over which reigns a queen" was among the presents sent by the Yemeni king , Abu'l–Jaysh Ishaq ibn Ibrahim Ibn Ziyad, to the Iraqi sovereign Bahliyar in 359/969–70.[410] This confirms the information from Ibn Hawqal.

Some of the dated Ge‘ez king–lists indicate that this queen's reign was approximately contemporary with the period of Anbessa Wudem, Gudit, and Dil–Na‘od; others place Gudit about a century later.

---

407 TADDESSE TAMRAT, Church and State, p. 40, n. 3.

408 KRAMERS and WEIT, *op. cit.*, p. XIII.

409 TADDESSE TAMRAT, Church and State, writes c. 980, on p. 41, n. 3.

410 M. EL-CHENNAFI, *Mention nouvelle d'une 'reine Éthiopienne' au IVe s. de l'Hegire / Xe s. ap. J-C.*, AE X, 1976, pp. 119-121.

The queen whom the Ge'ez chronicles call Gudit is still a shadowy figure. Her origins are obscure[411], but some of the Ge'ez chronicles accord her royal status, naming King Wudem Asfere as her grandfather in one instance, and Ayzour, who only ruled half a day, as her father in another[412]; in some, Ayzour was a predecessor of Wudem Asfere.[413] Gudit, sometimes referred to as a pagan, is said to have converted to Judaism, and motivated the first persecution in Ethiopia, as well as the destruction of the city of Aksum with the cathedral of Maryam Tseyon. She died after a 40 year reign. Thus – if we accept this nicely rounded figure of forty years, so familiar from the Ge'ez accounts of the reigns of the Zagwé kings – her death would fall in the period between c. 985–996 (assuming that the dating derived above from Ibn Hawqal's work is correct). She was succeeded by Anbessa Wudem, the length of whose reign, in the chronicles, is either 20 or 50 years. He, it seems, reigned until 905 AD.[414] SERGEW HABLE SELLASSIE suggests that these dates need to be advanced by 100 years, thus mending a discrepancy between alternatives for the chronology of Wudem Asfere; he is supposed to have lived for 150 years, and ruled for 30 of them (790–820 or 792–822 AD). Dil Na'od's reign is included variously as 10, 15, 4, or 40 years.[415]

These differing figures provide a good indication of the confusion of the Ge'ez records for the period. For further discussion about the complicated problem of the queen or queens who played so important a part in Ethiopian history at this stage, see VI: 46 below.

---

411 SERGEW HABLE SELLASSIE, *The Problem of Gudit*, JES X, I, 1972, pp. 113-124; repeated in SERGEW, AMEH, pp. 225ff; C. CONTI ROSSINI, *La caduta della dinastia Zague e la versione amarica del Be'ela Nagast*, RRAL, Vol. 31, Ser. IV, 1923, pp. 279-314. For a summary of the theories as to the meaning of "Bani al-Hamwiyya" see SERGEW HABLE SELLASSIE, AMEH, p. 230; and BELAYNASH MICHAEL in: Dictionary of Ethiopian Biography, pp. 35-36.

412 SERGEW, AMEH, p. 226 and n. 70.

413 CONTI ROSSINI, list B, nos. 61 and 64; list E, nos. 61 and 63; list F, nos 25 and 28; also SERGEW, AMEH, p. 203.

414 SERGEW, AMEH, p. 203: (885-905), p. 233 for a text from the *Chronicle of Qese Gabaz Takla Haymanot*, which says that Anbessa Wudem died in the "Year of Mercy 910" , having reigned 20 years. CONTI ROSSINI, list B (0) gives 50 years.

415 SERGEW, AMEH, p. 203 (905-915). p. 236 (910-925); CONTI ROSSINI, list B, 4 years; list E, 40 years. For the dates of Wudem Asfere, AMEH, pp. 203 & 226 n. 70.

32. The Metropolitans Michael and Salama Za–Azeb; Chronology

During the reigns of the last 'Israelite' kings of Ethiopia, two more metropolitans are mentioned. The texts that name them both add to the confusion of the chronology. The first of these metropolitans is recorded in a book of the Gospels kept in the rock–cut church of Mika'el Amba, Hulet Awila'ilo, Sira'e, Tigray;

> Abba Michael the sinner, son of St. Anthony of the monastery of El–Arebeh on the Red Sea Coast. ...consecrated by Abba Macarius, Archbishop of Alexandria, as bishop of Ethiopia during the reign of Anbessa Wudem, the king.[416] By the will of God I anointed seven kings, and inaugurated a hundred churches, and consecrated this monastery church [Michael Amba in Tigray] in the name of the Archangel Michael in year 866, Era of Martyrs.

Macarius II was patriarch from 1102–1129; Macarius I, 933–953, is disqualified, ignoring purely chronological questions, by his incumbency during the period when no metropolitans were consecrated until Daniel's arrival in the patriarchate of Philotheus, 979–1003.

The year 866, Era of Martyrs, is equivalent to 1150 AD. If this bishop was consecrated in the reign of Anbessa Wudem, a contemporary of Macarius II, and anointed seven kings, these must presumably have included Dil Na'od and the earlier Zagwé kings, unless the kings referred to were mere provincial kings under the authority of the *negusa nagast*. BUDGE's theory[417] that Metropolitan Peter, Kosmas III's (923–934) nominee for Ethiopia (III: 29), chose Dil Na'od in preference to his brother Anbessa Wudem would be discounted both by the date and by the evidence of this document.

The Metropolitan Michael who consecrated the church of Mika'el Amba can in fact be identified with a bishop who was appointed for Ethiopia in the episcopate of Patriarch Macarius II, 1102–1129, and survived until that of John V, 1146–1167. What is known of his life is discussed below (V: 43–4, VI: 45).

---

[416] SERGEW, AMEH, p. 203, n. 117. He appears to accept the note of Michael, consecrated somewhere between 1102-29, as well as the letter of George of Nubia in Philotheus' time (979-1003), p. 232, and the arrival of Salama II in the mid tenth century (p. 232, n. 106) as all occurring in the time of Anbessa Wudem.

[417] BUDGE, History, Vol. I, p. 276.

Gadla Iyasus Mo'a presents another metropolitan, difficult to identify in the historical sequence.[418] The text alludes to the arrival of a metropolitan called by Frumentius' title, Abba Salama, with the additional epithet Za–Azeb, 'He of the South'. He is mentioned as being "in the land of Adal". In due course he "re–entered his country", where King Dil Na'od was by then ruling. Later, in the seventh year of the king the royal seat is said to have been transferred from Aksum to the east, the king being accompanied also by this metropolitan. After the time of Dil Na'od, another king built a church dedicated to St. Stephen on an island in Lake Hayq, in the year 6362 (of the world), 862 AD.

The arrival of Salama Za–Azeb is said to have occurred in the year 618 after the arrival of Frumentius, Salama I, either in or just before the reign of Dil Na'od. Frumentius' own arrival date is rather uncertain; he was captured in the time of a king perhaps named Ella Amida, became an official of the Aksumite court, where he remained during the child–king's minority[419], before his consecration as the first bishop of Ethiopia early in the episcopate of Athanasius ("nam is nuper sacerdotium susceperat", after Rufinus). Athanasius was in office from 328–373; clearly, in terms of a retrospect of 45 years, the interpretation of what *nuper* might mean has some scope. The dating has been studied by DESANGES[420], who has suggested that the first evangelisation of Ethiopia occurred a little before 328, with Frumentius' consecration coming a little later. SERGEW HABLE SELLASSIE

---

[418] S. KUR, ed., CSCO, Vol. 259, Scriptores aethiopici, T. 49, "Actes de Iyasus Mo'a, abbé du couvent de St. Etienne de Hayq", Louvain, 1965, p. 111, p. 15, p. 39; "Ensuite, 618 ans après l'arrivée d'abba Salama, le métropolite, le revelateur de lumière, un autre métropolite vint, abba Salama Za-Azeb dans le pays d"Adal. ...Le métropolite rentra ensuite dans son pays et il raconta au roi Dil Na'ad. ...Plus tard, pendant la septième année de son regne, le roi vint avec ce métropolite, et le royaume passa d'Akuesem dans une province orientale. ...Après lui, en l'an 6362 (un autre roi) commenca à batir une église. ...Quand il eut fini sa construction, le métropolite versa sur elle du chrême et il l'oignit tout entière..." SERGEW, AMEH, p. 232; TADDESSE TAMRAT, Church and State, p. 36, n. 3. TADDESSE TAMRAT also adds a date from the chronicler of Ahmad Gragn, that is, 720 years from the foundation of the church of Dabra Hayq to its destruction by Gragn in 1531; i.e. 811 AD (see also TADDESSE TAMRAT, *The Abbots of Däbrä Hayq 1248-1535*, JES VIII, I, 1970, pp. 87-117, for a computation different from that of Basset, who errs in his Hegira dates etc.) This would be another date for Abba Salama II, since he founded the church with Dil Na'od. TADDESSE TAMRAT, however, considers that little credence should be paid to the names involved.

[419] Rufinus, "Historia Ecclesiastica", PL XXI, col. 478.

[420] DESANGES, *op. cit.*, p. 150, n. 1; CONTI ROSSINI, Storia, p. 147.

and PÉTRIDÈS accept 330 or 333, the *Evangelo d'Oro* indicates 333/4, while other scholars prefer a date even later, but within a decade or two.[421] Whether Frumentius' first arrival as a captive, or his second as bishop, is meant by the Iyasus Mo'a text, is also not clear. Further dates have been suggested for the conversion of Ethiopia (in Ethiopian terms, the arrival of Frumentius, but perhaps also sometimes referring to either an earlier influx of Christians, or to the 'second evangelisation' of the country by the *Tsadqan,* the Nine Saints, or other missionaries). For example, TADDESSE TAMRAT[422] notes 245 EC, equivalent to 252–3 AD, as a date for the establishment of the church in Ethiopia; KUR mentioned 350 AD[423]; the Ethiopic chronicle of Wolde Amid[424] has the date 434 EC/441–2 AD (see below); and the *Acta Marqorewos* suggests 430 EC/437–8 AD, though apparently attributing this date to Frumentius himself.[425] It is difficult to know what computation a particular chronicler might have chosen, since his reference works might have included both an 'historical' date for Frumentius arrival or consecration, and a selection of more or less legendary ones mentioning the arrival of Christianity in Ethiopia in one form or another. To compute the date of the arrival of Salama Za–Azeb using the dates noted above:

From 252–3 the date would be	870 –1 AD
From 328–30	946 –8 AD
From 350	968 AD
From 441–2	1059–60 AD.

Various attempts have been made to adjust the figures, as well as selecting different dates for the conversion. KUR, altering the date of the arrival of Salama Za–Azeb (Salama II) to 818, adds 350 to achieve a date of 1168. He approaches this date to the *Gadla Iyasus Mo'a* date (year of Creation 6362 (862 AD) by changing that also, to 6662/1167 – actually

---

421 J. DORESSE, Ethiopia, p. 62; "the Ge'ez tradition accepts the dating for the consecration of Frumentius as somewhere between 341 and 346". C. CONTI ROSSINI, *L'evangelo d'oro di Dabra Libanos,* RRAL, Ser. 5, Vol. 10, 1901, p. 193; SERGEW, AMEH, p. 103, for 330 AD, and p. 201 for 333 AD.

422 TADDESSE TAMRAT, *The Abbots,* p. 87; *Id.,* Church and State, p. 36.

423 KUR, ed., *op. cit.,* p. 111.

424 Ms. at Aksum, Fol. 39a. See SERGEW, AMEH, p. 240, n. 6.

425 C. CONTI ROSSINI, ed., CSCO, Script. Aeth. Ser II T. XXII, versio, Vitae Sanctorum Indigenorum, I. "Acta Marqorewos", p. 9. "Huius diebus Frumentius, qui est Abba Salama, lucis revelator, venit, iustorum Regem diebus, qui Abreha Asbeha sunt; religio Christiana a Christi ortu usque ad Aethiopiae conversionem annis CCCCXXX fuit", i.e. 437-8 AD.

1162. The alteration was undertaken to align the given date 6362, which refers to a successor of Dil Na'od, with one compatible with the short chronology for the Zagwé dynasty (commencing somewhere around the mid–twelfth century, suggestions ranging from c. 1137–1150 AD). KUR's results thus achieve a date for Salama's activities in Dil Na'od's reign, or before, in 1168; and a date later, in Dil Na'od's successor's reign (the Zagwé period?) of 1167 (1162). TADDESSE TAMRAT calculated 869–870 as the equivalent of the year of Creation 6362; he has perhaps added 7/8 years to compensate for the difference between the Ethiopian and Gregorian calendars.

It is of interest to note that Pseudo–Dionysios[426] dates the advent of Christianity in Ethiopia to the year 618 of Alexander (307AD). This date is probably ten years out, meaning 317, since the 323 war of Constantine and Licinius is dated to 313 AD, the year 624 of Alexander, instead of 634. Nevertheless it at least offers the possibility that there was a figure of 618 years of a certain era on the records for the arrival of Christianity in Ethiopia. There might have been a parallelism made; 618 from the inauguration of the Alexander Era in BC 311 to Salama I, then 618 years to the second Salama – and indeed Frumentius must have arrived in Ethiopia for the first time at some date not far removed from 317 AD. Could some such a mystic chronological balance have been in the mind of the author of the *Gadla Iyasus Mo'a*?

Some more dating suggestions can be made through study of the history of the Zagwé dynasty, which, according to Ethiopian tradition, usurped the throne from the 'Israelite' line (see V: 36). Suggestions for the possible identification of the bishop who was called Salama Za–Azeb with one or other of the bishops known from the historical record are discussed below (VI: 48).

33. Patriarch Zacharias (1004–1032); relations with Caliph al–Hakim

Under the Fatimid caliph al–'Aziz (975–996), the melkites' situation improved. The brothers of one of the caliph's wives, the Greek mother of the future Caliph al–Hakim, were elevated to high church office. One brother, Arsenius, became patriarch of the melkite church in Egypt, and another, Jeremias, patriarch of the melkites at Jerusalem.[427] However, dur-

[426] CHABOT, ed., *op. cit.*, p. 122.

[427] "History of the Patriarchs", II, II, pp. 170-1. Al-Makin, ed., ERPENIUS, Bk III, Ch 5, pp. 307-8; BUTCHER, *op. cit.*, Vol. II, p. 11, 18, 26.

ing the caliphate of al–Hakim (996–1021), violent persecutions broke out against the Christians, during which Jeremias was summoned to Egypt and beheaded, and Zacharias imprisoned. This unfavourable situation for the Christians lasted for about nine years. One result was that Christians, previously forbidden to emigrate, were in the end allowed to leave for other Christian countries. Abyssinia, Nubia and the Roman (Byzantine) empire are named.[428] Al–Hakim's signing of the decree to permit this exodus is mentioned in the life of Zacharias in the *History of the Patriarchs*.

Abu Salih[429] recalls that in the time of Patriarch Zacharias (who was buried in the *ardh habash* at Cairo) al–Hakim stopped the custom of the twice–yearly patriarchal letters to the kings of Abyssinia and Nubia. Abu Salih confirms that the practice was not revived, but adds;

> Nevertheless, when a letter comes from any of these kings to the Caliph at Misr or his vizir, he bids the patriarch write a reply to the letter, with all the respect and reverence due from Christians, and all the compliments which are customary among them. The patriarch charges the king of Abyssinia to avoid association with the Muslims who are under his government.

The biographer of Zacharias narrates[430] an interesting conversation with al–Hakim. The patriarch was brought before the caliph, who found him considerably less impressive than the bishops who surrounded him.

> He said to them, 'Is this the chief of you all?' They said to him, 'Yea O our master, may the Lord establish your kingdom!' He marvelled, and said to them 'Unto where does his judgement extend?' They said to him, 'His judgement is executed in the lands of Misr, Abyssinia, Nubia, the Pentapolis, Africa and other places:

The conversation continued, the caliph expressing amazement that this man could be obeyed without any troops or money, but merely by virtue of his office and the placing of the cross at the end of his letters; "They said to him 'All these tribes obey him by means of a single cross' ". This interview supposedly marked the cessation of the persecutions of the Copts by al–Hakim.

---

428 "History of the Patriarchs", II, II, p. 196. J.B. COULBEAUX, Histoire politique et religieuse de l'Abyssinie depuis les temps les plus reculés jusqu'à l'avènement de Ménelick II, Paris, 1929, p. 237, writes that c. 1080 the caliph began to favour the land and sea caravans to Ethiopia.

429 Abu Salih, *op. cit.*, p. 290.

430 "History of the Patriarchs", II, II, pp. 206-7.

34. Patriarch John of Antioch

Another account, interesting insofar as it reflects the monophysites' view of the role of the kings of Nubia and Ethiopia, even outside Egypt and Alexandria, as important exemplars of their faith, is preserved in the *History of the Patriarchs*.[431] SERGEW HABLE SELLASSIE[432] quotes it as an example of religious tolerance towards the Muslims. It is in fact an illustration of monophysite tolerance towards melkites.

The scene is set in Constantinople, and the actors are John (Yuhanna ibn 'Abdun), Jacobite patriarch of Antioch dwelling at Malatya, the 'Roman' emperor, probably Michael IV, and the melkite bishops. The emperor was trying to persuade John of Antioch to acknowledge the Council of Chalcedon, and in response John declared

> Thy authority has not the right to force anyone to forsake his religion, as we have two kings, namely, the king of Abyssinia (Habasha) and the king of Nubia (Nuba) and they do not force anyone of the people of your religion who is dwelling among them to change his faith.

The corrupt interpreter distorted this statement to "we have two kings greater than thou", for which John was exiled.

35. Patriarch Sinuthius II (1032–47) and Polygamy in Ethiopia

Abu Salih al–Armani[433], in a brief note, attributes to Patriarch Sinuthius II (Shenouda), the successor of Patriarch Zacharias, the final suppression of the practise of polygamy amongst the Ethiopians; they were to adopt "the mode of life existing among the Christians of Egypt and Syria". This attempt to alter the mores of the Ethiopians would rather appear to have been due to the labours of Metropolitan Severus, who was sent to Ethiopia by Patriarch Cyril II, 1078–92. That Abu Salih refers to Sinuthius II, 65th patriarch of Alexandria, as the 67th patriarch, actually the position of Cyril II in the sequence, probably indicates his error here. The history of Severus is related below (V: 40).

---

[431] "History of the Patriarchs", II, II, p. 218.

[432] SERGEW, AMEH, p. 248.

[433] Abu Salih, *op. cit.*, Fol. 106b, p. 290. LE QUIEN, *op. cit.*, p. 651. For the story of the metropolitan Severus, see the "History of the Patriarchs", II, II, pp. 327ff, and BUDGE, Synaxarium, Vol, IV, p. 995.

CHAPTER FIVE

Metropolitans attributed to Zagwé Times by the 'Long Chronology'

Introduction

The records of the patriarchate continue to provide the names of the metropolitans sent to Ethiopia, with some historical sketches, and Ge'ez documents supply similar material. However, the lack of an authoritative date for the beginning of the new Agaw dynasty of Lasta, commonly called the Zagwé dynasty, has caused some confusion. The Ethiopian records, gleaned from the *gadlan* or life–stories of local saints, are extremely muddled, growing more so as the events they relate become more distant. Accordingly, many modern scholars have concluded that the Zagwé dynasty came to power in about the middle of the eleventh century, instead of a century or so later. As a result, certain incidents involving pre–Zagwé metropolitans have been attributed to Zagwé times, involving attempts to fit them into the reigns of the known rulers of the dynasty. The following section (V: 36) therefore outlines briefly current and past theories about the dating of the appearance of the Zagwé. In this account the mid–twelfth century date is preferred. Relations between the patriarchate of Alexandria and the Zagwé kings are discussed in section VI below.

36. Zagwé Chronology

The Ge'ez chroniclers frequently record the total of the years of the duration of the Zagwé dynasty. The total figure varies considerably, the majority quoting 300 to 375 years, but some only 133 years. This latter figure has become the most widely accepted by modern scholarship. The longer chronologies tend to attribute to the most famous kings of the dynasty reigns of precisely forty years; such chronologies do not even balance with the Ge'ez sources' dates for the reigns of Anbessa Wudem and Dil Na'od.

Several interpretations of the evidence for the chronology of the inception of the Zagwé dynasty, and its duration, have been offered. A few, taken from a selection of chroniclers of the past and from some more recent writers, are as follows.

The Catholic patriarch, Alfonso Mendes[434], placed the commencement of the Zagwé dynasty in 960, lasting until 1300. The year 920 is suggested by TEKLA SADIK MEKURIA[435], the duration of the dynasty being 333 years, ending in 1253. SERGEW HABLE SELLASSIE[436] believed that the beginning of the dynasty was to be dated about 1030–1050, whilst HUNTINGFORD[437], using information from the *Be'ela Nagast,* dated it to 1033; the Zagwé are said to have reigned "133 years, 700 years from the bringing of the faith to Ethiopia". HUNTINGFORD selected 333 as the date of Ethiopia's conversion, to which is added the 700 years, giving the year 1033; the dynasty would then have lasted to 1166. CONTI ROSSINI[438], using a document from Debra Libanos of Shimezana that dates the Zagwé, also suggested that the dynasty only lasted for 133 years. The document gave the same account as that used by HUNTINGFORD, the transfer of power having taken place 700 years after the conversion of Ethiopia, that is, 1034 AD, and year 2034 from the reign of Menelik I.

DORESSE prefers the date 1135–7, but notes a chronicle giving 330 years as the duration of the dynasty. ULLENDORFF[439] and HEYER[440] also select 1137. An early seventeenth century manuscript copy of the history of Girgis Wolde Amid at Aksum preserves (fol.39) the note "Terda'a Gabaz had removed the kingdom to Zagwé, and they ruled 143 years, 700 years from the conversion of Ethiopia, and 1134 years from the birth of our Lord" [Terda'a Gabaz is an enigmatical figure, supposedly a princess of the 'Israelite' dynasty and instrumental in the transfer of power to the Zagwé; she may be identical with a similar figure called Masobe Warq in other texts].[441] This reference would appear to indicate that the author took 434 (presumably EC, which corresponds to 441–2 AD) as the date of the conversion (see also the note in *Acta Marqorewos* [442] which records that from

434 In LOBO, *op. cit.*, trans. S. JOHNSON, 1789, Diss. V, p. 251.

435 TEKLE SADIK MEKURIA, Ya Ityopya Tarik; Nubia, Aksum, Zagwiye, Addis Ababa 1951 EC, p. 356, quoted by SERGEW, AMEH, p. 240, n. 9.

436 SERGEW, AMEH, p. 240.

437 *The 'Wealth of Kings' and the End of the Zagwe Dynasty*, BSOAS 28, 1965, p. 1ff.

438 C. CONTI ROSSINI, *La caduta della dinastia Zague...*, RRAL, Vol. 31, Ser. 5. 1922, pp. 279-314.

439 J. DORESSE, Ethiopia, London, 1959, p. 93; E. ULLENDORFF, The Ethiopians, London 1960, p. 61.

440 F. HEYER, Die Kirche Äthiopiens, Berlin-New York 1971, p. 227.

441 SERGEW, AMEH, p. 240, n. 6; Dictionary of Ethiopian Biography, p. 161-26.

442 CSCO XXII, "Acta Marqorewos", p. 9. See note 363 above for a quotation of the passage.

Christ's birth – 7/8 AD by the Ethiopian calendar – to the conversion of Ethiopia was 430 years, i.e. 437–8). Using this figure, the date of the end of the Zagwé would be around 1277 EC, 1284–5). Applying this date 434 to the testimony of the *Be'ela Nagast,* the result is around 1267 EC; in fact 1268–70 AD appears fairly certain for the end of the dynasty. The discrepancies above could be due to orthographic errors – in several cases only one figure in the various combinations differs – or could even be a reflection of some continuation of Zagwé rule somewhere in the country.

Acta Marqorewos[443] attributes 303 years duration to the dynasty, which would therefore have seized power around 965–7 AD. For the duration of the dynasty in other chronicles, BUDGE[444] quoted a selection ranging from five to eleven kings and from 143 to 354 years.

SERGEW HABLE SELLASSIE notes CONTI ROSSINI's figures[445] from 133 years to 375 years, ending in 1268–70, and KUR[446], quoting the same source, comments that modern studies have fixed the date of the Zagwé around 1150. CONTI ROSSINI favoured the shorter period for the duration of the dynasty, largely because of the shorter king–lists; he attributed the longer ones to confusion about the succession, which seems to have resembled that of Nubia, uncle to nephew, or the Funj sultanate in the same area, brother to brother, rather than the usual patrilineal succession of the eldest son.[447] A figure of 137 years for the duration of the Zagwé dynasty is mentioned in a manuscript belonging to the *qese gabaz* Tekla Haymanot of Aksum, quoted by SERGEW HABLE SELLASSIE.[448] Though apparently incorrect, the longer period for the dynasty is the commoner in the Ge'ez sources.[449]

There has been some confusion in ascertaining the names of the Zagwé rulers themselves. TADDESSE TAMRAT, depending on some hitherto unpublished manuscript sources,[450] has been able to clarify this a little

443 *Ibid.*, p. 12.

444 BUDGE, History, Vol. 1, pp. 219-20. He quotes BM.Ms.Or.821, fol. 28b, eleven kings in 354 years; the *Tarik* of Debra Libanos (ed. CONTI ROSSINI), nine kings for 343 years; and Paris Ms.64, five kings, 1145/7 until 1268/70.

445 SERGEW, AMEH, p. 239, quoting CONTI ROSSINI, Storia, p. 303.

446 KUR, *op. cit.*, p.iii.

447 C. CONTI ROSSINI, *Il libro delle leggende, e tradizione abissine dell'Eccaghie Filpos*, RRAL, Ser. 5, vol. XXVI, 1917, p. 707. TADDESSE TAMRAT, Church and State, p. 55, n. 3.

448 SERGEW, AMEH, p. 203, n. 115.

449 TADDESSE TAMRAT, Church and State, p. 55, n. 3.

450 *Ibid.*, p. 54f.

and proposes the following order; Marara (Tekla Haymanot), Tantawidim, Yimrha–Kristos, Harbé, Lalibala, Na'akuto–La'ab, and Yitbarak. The table below is based on his suggestions; it will be noticed that it only comprises four generations, which could not possibly have occupied 333 years, even with the addition of Dilanda and the Zagwé council at the end of the period. TADDESSE TAMRAT concludes that "some lists include the princes who did not occupy the throne":

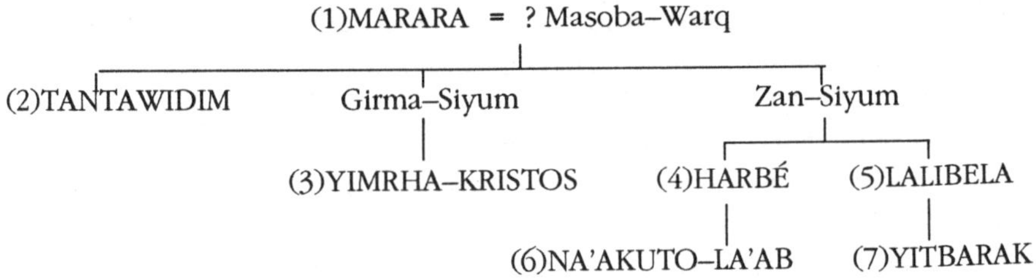

In fact, as CONTI ROSSINI had already surmised (see V: 44), a reference in the *History of the Patriarchs* to a usurpation of the Ethiopian monarchy in the mid–twelfth century seems to point clearly to the establishment of the Zagwé dynasty at that point. Further details are noted below (VI: 45).

37. Patriarch Christodoulos (1047–1077); the Removal of the Patriarchs from Alexandria

During this patriarchate, the seat of the Egyptian church government finally moved from Alexandria to Cairo. The event is recounted[451] as follows;

> The first sixty–four patriarchs resided at Alexandria, but Christians having dwindled to a very small number in that city, and most churches having been destroyed, Amba Christodulus, A.D. 1045, the sixty–sixth, removed his seat to Cairo where the patriarchs have sat ever since.

451 For those texts which deal with the removal of the patriarchate, see: C. BEZOLD, Kebra Nagast, Munich, 1905, p. 138; S.C. MALAN, trans., A Short History of the Copts and of their Churches, trans. from the Arabic of Taqi ed-Din El-Maqrizi, London 1873, p. 113; E.L. BUTCHER, The Story of the Church of Egypt, London 1897, I, pp. 386-7; ZAIS S. ATIYA *et al.*, "History of the Patriarchs", II, III, p. 267.

On the death of Patriarch John III in 686, 'Abd al-'Aziz had ordered that the election of the patriarchs should take place in Babylon (the great fortress now in Old Cairo, near the Arab foundation of Fustat, south of the later Fatimid city of Cairo). The actual consecration was still performed in Alexandria until the end of the eleventh century. The large patriarchal establishment at a place in the Egyptian Delta (al-Rif) called Damrua – sufficiently impressive to be dubbed the 'Second Constantinople' by a certain *qadi* in the days of Patriarch Christodoulos – was the seat of the patriarchs until the time of Christodoulos, when rebels devastated the Delta and captured and tortured the patriarch. There were seventeen churches there. It is mentioned in the life of Cyril, Christodoulos' successor, that he, too,

> used to live long in ar-Rif, but that he was not able (to do so) on account of the many messengers arriving from the lands of Habashah and an-Nubah, and returning to them, and the requirements of the Sultan that he (Cyril) should present himself to him at all times .

Thus we have a combination of reasons for the move; troubles in the Delta region, business affairs to attend to in the capital, the desire of the sultan to keep an eye on the church's activities, and not least the need to attend efficiently to the correspondence and other matters relating to the southern Christian kingdoms. Al-Mas'udi (d. 956) remarks that the monastery of Anba Makarios (Abba Maqara) was the seat of the patriarchs[452]; it was certainly one of the pre-eminent monasteries from which the patriarchs – and sometimes the metropolitans for Ethiopia, like Daniel (IV: 29) and George (V: 42) – were chosen, and a place to which they retired during times of persecution.

38. Patriarch Christodoulos and the Metropolitan Cyril 'Abdun

The affair of Cyril 'Abdun, the second usurping bishop of Ethiopia mentioned by the records, has been placed in a Zagwé context by the dating of the advent of the Zagwé dynasty to 1030–1050 AD.[453] Sergew Hable Sellassie suggests conflict between the new dynasty and the patriarchate as the reason for a long period without a metropolitan after the death of Metropolitan Daniel, who had arrived at some time in the late tenth century. We are, however, uncertain whether there really was such a gap between

452 Vantini, OS, p. 140.
453 Sergew, AMEH, p.243.

metropolitans. The letter to King Girgis II of Nubia, which caused Daniel's appointment, was sent, if we can credit the reference in the patriarchal biography of Philotheus, in the days when Girgis was a 'youth' – using an Arabic word generally applied to men of the ages between about 17–30. This presumably indicates that the event must be placed early in Philotheus' patriarchate, which ran from 979–1003, since Girgis had already reigned for at least ten years before 979. The destructive pagan queen had also maintained some sort of control over Ethiopia for at least ten years by 979, since she sent her zebra to the Yemeni ruler around 969/970. Daniel may have gone to Ethiopia at any time after the early 980s; the latest date possible is 1003, when Philotheus died, but an earlier date is much more likely. A successor of Daniel, Metropolitan Victor, died at some time in or before the period 1073–1077 (V: 39). There may well have been other metropolitans in between whose advent is not recorded in the available documents.

The problems in the Ethiopian church during the episcopate of Christodoulos[454] stemmed from the arrival in Ethiopia of a pretender to the metropolitanate, called Cyril or 'Abdun. His equivocal attitude towards Islam led to his being favourably contrasted before the *amir al-juyush,* Badr al-Jamali (1073–1092), with Victor of Nubia, another of the metropolitans under the jurisdiction of Christodoulos. Victor was accused of demolishing a mosque; as usual the Egyptian rulers arrested the patriarch in retaliation. He was released when the charge was proven false, a messenger having been sent to the king (perhaps King Solomon) in Nubia; Metropolitan Victor's accuser, a certain Ali al-Qifti, was put to death.

The patriarchal historian continues the story with Christodoulos' answer to the *amir* in council and a summary of previous events;

> Cyril who is called Abdun (is) a pretender to the priesthood, and he has taken by force the archiepiscopate (matranah), because I have not consecrated him, nor have I prayed over him, nor have I written to him a letter at all... It happened before this, that there had been arranged the journey of Abba Mercurius bishop of Wisim, to the lands of Abyssinia, with a letter from the patriarch and one of his vestments to clothe the aforesaid Cyril and to make him Metropolitan and the father, the patriarch, had wept when he was obliged (to do) this.

This gives the impression that the patriarch was forced to comply with Cyril's installation as metropolitan, though the patriarchal laying on of

---

454 "History of the Patriarchs", II, III, pp. 316ff.

hands at his consecration could not be performed. Later the text concludes;

> And when...the patriarch had spoken in the council meeting of the Amir al–Juyush...the affair of Cyril was cancelled.

The Ethiopian *Synaxarium*[455] also describes the affair, relating how Cyril had gone to Ethiopia pretending to be a bishop. He had sent a bribe to the 'King of Egypt' to persuade him to order the patriarch 'Abba Gebre Krestos' to appoint him officially. Accordingly the king summoned the patriarch to do this, but the latter said "This is undesirable, unless he cometh here". However, the point was pressed, and the patriarch had to obey. The Egyptian rulers doubtless favoured Cyril's candidature for other reasons than the mere hope of a substantial bribe; the *History of the Patriarchs* mentions his reputation; "he has respect for the Muslims, and loves them and honours them". The *Synaxarium* story continues with the comment that the patriarch and the bishops were unhappy over the matter. It then summarises the rest of the story – which happened some time later after the consecration of a new metropolitan, Severus (see below) – relating how eventually Cyril fled with much money from Ethiopia to Dahlak. There, the local ruler seized him and sent him to Egypt, where he was later executed.

SERGEW HABLE SELLASSIE[456] has confused two missions conducted by Mercurius of Wisim, asserting that Mercurius set out for Ethiopia with a special delegate of the amir, Kanz al–Dawla, who defected during the journey. The church historian refers to two entirely separate events. Mercurius of Wisim had been sent to Ethiopia as mentioned above. He had presumably performed the unwilling consecration and returned; though it is never properly confirmed that the consecration really took place. Mercurius of Wisim was then sent on another mission to the king of Nubia on behalf of the patriarch; with him went Sayf al–Dawla, to summon the rebel Kanz al–Dawla. The Nubian sovereign, probably at this time King Solomon, handed Kanz al–Dawla over to this messenger for punishment, just as King Raphael had handed over Abu Rakwah in about 1002. This mission had no connection with the Abyssinian ecclesiastical problem, but dealt simply with extradition questions between Egypt and Nubia.

455 BUDGE, Synaxarium, Vol. II, p. 379.
456 SERGEW, AMEH, p. 244.

BUTCHER and DORESSE mention a variant tale about Cyril 'Abdun, which seems to be based on that recorded by LE QUIEN.[457] LE QUIEN wrote that Cyril was accused to the *amir* of encouraging the Muslims of Abyssinia to drink wine when they dined with him, and Patriarch Christodoulos, questioned about this, said that he had not ordained 'Abdun nor had he sent him any letters that might make him metropolitan, but that he was about to send Mercurius of Wisim to invest him with patriarchal and monastic vestments. It seems that the patriarch considered that matters having reached such a stage, to avoid worse problems in the Ethiopian church he should be confirmed in his arrogated dignity.

39. Patriarch Cyril II (1078–1092) and the Metropolitans Victor, Cyril 'Abdun and Severus

Evidently "the affair of Cyril" was not really "cancelled" in Christodoulos' time, since the question of this metropolitan was taken up again during the patriarchate of his successor, Cyril II. Considerable correspondence

---

457 BUTCHER, *op. cit.*, Vol. II, pp. 58-9; DORESSE, L'Empire.., II, 12. This is from LE QUIEN, *op. cit.*, II, col. 651, who quotes RENAUDOT, *op. cit.*, p. 444. He reports that "apud Kouril sive Abdounem quotidie Mohammedanos comessari, vinumque potare. Quocirca Christodulus ad Viziri tribunal adductus negavit Abdounem a se ordinatum esse, vel litteras ei ullas a se datas, quibus metropolitam eum crearet: se autem quum multa de eo audivisset, Mercurium episcopum Wissim destinasse, qui Patriarchali & monastico habitu illum indueret. Satius namque fore, duxerat illius, qui metropolitae auctoritatem arripuisset, ad graviora mala evitanda, dignitatem confirmare: ut pote qui Aethiopibus acceptus esset, quam ut ea gens pastoribus iterum careret". RENAUDOT's text does not mention the question of drinking wine with Muslims; his text states; "Quantum ad res Aethiopiae, Christodulus as Viziri Tribunal adductus negavit Abdounem istum qui pro Metropolita se gereret, ordinatum a se fuisse, & manus impositionem vel autoritatem per literasd a se scriptas unquam accepisse. Verum cum de eo audivisset, destinasse Mercurium Episcopum Wissim qui in Aethipia proficisceretur, cum una ex vestibus Patriarchalibus, & Schemate seu habitu Monasitco, quibus Abdounem indfueret, simulque Metropolitam constitueret. Nempe quantum conjicere possumus, cum audiisset esse in Aethiopia, qui Metropolitae autoritatem usurparet, opportunius judicavit, ad majora mala fugienda, ut dignitatem illi, quasi apud populares accepto confirmaret, quam ut Aethiopes qui per multos annos ... sine Episcopis & Sacerdotibus fuerant, absque pastoribus relinqueret, cum periculo extinguendae in illis provinciis Christianae religionis. ... Jussit Vizirus proficisci in Aethiopiam Mercuriam Episcopum Wissim, ...

had evidently passed between the two countries – confirming, incidentally, a situation rather different from that represented by AYELE TEKLAHAYMANOT'S claim[458] that at this period the Egyptian church showed "little interest" in Ethiopia. It will be remembered, too, that the patriarchal historian includes[459] "the many messengers arriving from the lands of Abyssinia and Nubia" among the reasons for the patriarchate's move to Cairo.

Patriarch Cyril again took up the Abyssinian problem[460], consecrating a certain Severus, at the request of the *amir* Badr al–Jamali, as metropolitan. Presumably by now the *amir* had lost interest in supporting Cyril 'Abdun. Severus had promised the *amir* that he would send presents to him from Abyssinia and would also influence the king towards obedience to the *amir*, It would seem that he did not entirely understand the place of the church and its leader in the Ethiopian system – or at least that he rather overestimated the influence a metropolitan might have – though he was apparently the nephew of a previous metropolitan called Victor.

LE QUIEN, after RENAUDOT, and later MONNERET DE VILLARD[461], assumed that this Victor was identical with the metropolitan of Nubia mentioned above, appointed by Patriarch Christodoulos. Despite the unlikely–seeming coincidence of two contemporary metropolitans called Victor in Ethiopia and Nubia, neither of the texts involved seem to confirm this identification. It might be suggested that Victor 'of Nubia' was metropolitan of Ethiopia; the texts do not specifically name Nubia as the area of his jurisdiction, only stating that he had allegedly demolished a mosque there, and that the king of Nubia denied this. However, if this were the case – apart from the intrinsic improbability of such an action in a foreign country, the province of another metropolitan – it seems hardly likely that Cyril 'Abdun could have intruded in Ethiopia when there was already a living incumbent of the metropolitanate. AYELE TEKLAHAYMANOT[462] recognises a Metropolitan Victor of Ethiopia, stating that "following the death of Metropolitan Fiqtor towards

---

458 AYELE TEKLAHAYMANOT, *Egyptian Metropolitans*, p. 27.

459 "History of the Patriarchs", II, III, pp. 327-8.

460 *Ibid.*, pp. 329-330.

461 MONNERET DE VILLARD, Storia, p. 129. LE QUIEN, *op. cit.*, col. 651 quoting RENAUDOT, pp. 452 and 462; LE QUIEN writes "...Severum, Victoris Nubiae quondam metropolitae nepotem...", and RENAUDOT mentions "...Severum, nepotem Victoris, de quo supra dictum fuit in Christoduli vita, sed qui ordinatus fuerat Nubiae non Aethiopiae Metropolita: nam Mercurius Episcopus Wissim in Aethiopiae missus est, qui Abdoni, aliter Kourilo seu Cyrillo, vestem pontificalem deferret".

462 AYELE TEKLAHAYMANOT, *Egyptian Metropolitans*, p. 27.

1077, the See of the abunas of the Ethiopian Church was "vacant" again for a long time. A pseudo–abuna named Abdun or Cyril, taking advantage of the long "interregnum" succeeded in being recognised by the people as the true abuna". There is no evidence for this supposed interregnum; all we can say is that some time between 1073 and 1077 Christodoulos had been confronted with the problem of Cyril, and it may well have been immediately on the death of Metropolitan Victor of Ethiopia that this arose.

With regard to Victor, the patriarchal biography [463] merely states;

> The father Abba Cyril consecrated a metropolitan for Abyssinia. He was a learned young man whose name (was) Severus, the son of the sister of Victor, the deceased metropolitan. He had been brought up there with his aforesaid uncle.

The *Synaxarium*[464] account reports that "He was brother of the Bishop of Ethiopia and had been brought up in his house there"; to which BUDGE adds, in parentheses, "in Egypt". TADDESSE TAMRAT,[465] however, accepted that Severus knew Ethiopia well, having been brought up in that country. He suggested that Severus had established friendly relations with the court, which could have helped him in his later reforms of the matrimonial customs (V: 40).

On the arrival of Severus in Ethiopia he had to contend with Cyril 'Abdun, who was already installed there; the patriarchal biography declares that when Severus arrived in Abyssinia "Cyril (Kuril) whom we have mentioned before, opposed him". As we have suggested, it may have been on the death of Severus' uncle Metropolitan Victor that Cyril 'Abdun had seen his opportunity to get himself appointed to the metropolitanate. This Victor had perhaps succeeded Daniel during the patriarchates of Zacharias (1004–1032) or Sinuthius II (1032–1046). Cyril II's consecration of Severus might indicate that Cyril 'Abdun had never been legally consecrated. Though the *Synaxarium* does add that "during his period of office he (Patriarch Cyril) appointed a second bishop to the country of Ethiopia, whose name was Sawiros...", it does not seem very likely that Patriarch Cyril really intended that there should be two concurrent metropolitans, nor do the sources hint that Severus was only a subordinate bishop. Perhaps a loophole had been deliberately left; despite the sending of suitable vestments, and the acceptance of the *fait accom-*

---

463 "History of the Patriarchs", II, III, p. 329.

464 BUDGE, Synaxarium, Vol. IV, p. 995.

465 TADDESSE TAMRAT, Church and State, p. 48.

pli, the lack of the patriarchal laying–on of hands could have adduced as a reason for disregarding any proxy consecration that might have occurred. In the event, Severus' stronger legal position seems to be confirmed, since Cyril 'Abdun, who at first 'opposed' Severus, later fled to Dahlak. He took with him a considerable sum of money, which, however, was confiscated when he was arrested. He was transferred to Cairo by the ruler of Dahlak – perhaps the sultan Mubarak who died in 1093.[466] The *amir* had him brought before his council, then imprisoned him in the *khazanah al–bunud,* the Treasury of Flags. The text in the *History of the Patriarchs* mentions year 860 of the Martyrs as the year of the execution of Cyril by Badr al–Jamali, that is 1143–4, which is obviously far wrong. Perhaps 806, 1090, could be suggested; only a few pages further on, the historian mentions the date 802, and his tale is approximately chronological, the lines about Cyril's death being interpolated to finish the story. RENAUDOT, however, and after him LE QUIEN, indicate 1086, AM 802, perhaps taken from another manuscript of the patriarchal biography[467], as the date of Cyril's execution.

40. The Metropolitanate of Severus

The Ethiopic *Synaxarium* briefly describes the metropolitanate of Severus.[468] In the *History of the Patriarchs* Severus is said[469] to have written to Patriarch Cyril II, telling him that the land was in good order but for the problem of the polygamy practised by the king and others of his subjects. Severus apparently succeeded in getting the king's women reduced to "the mother of his children" and only one other. He exhorted the king to make this last sacrifice. The king replied that he had given up all his women, but that this one he could not give up on account of his great love for her. Severus was discreet enough not to push the matter any further and "dispensed him (the king) with regard to this, and he pretended to overlook it, for fear lest the affair might turn against him". Nevertheless he asked the patriarch to write with spiritual instruction. The patriarch wrote to the Ethiopians, as Severus requested, on this question, sending

---

466 Dictionary of Ethiopian Biography, pp. 120-121.

467 RENAUDOT, *op. cit.*, p. 453; LE QUIEN, *op. cit.*, p. 651. TADDESSE TAMRAT, *op. cit.*, p. 47, n. 3, for comments.

468 BUDGE, Synaxarium,,ol. IV, p. 995.

469 "History of the Patriarchs", II, III, p. 329.

his letter with the metropolitan's returning messengers. Thus far the *Synaxarium* 's laudatory phraseology is justified, but it ignores the later fall of Severus into disfavour.[470]

In the tax–year 478, or 804/5 of the Martyrs, 1088/9, the metropolitan's brother, Rijal, arrived in Egypt with a gift for Badr al–Jamali, which was evidently below his expectations. The patriarch was summoned; he arrived with ten bishops to find the metropolitan of Abyssinia's brother standing before the *amir*. The *amir* then complained about the paucity of the gift, and other matters, including the fact that no mosques had been built in Ethiopia. Abraham, bishop of Dibkua – detested by the bishops of Egypt for his influence over the patriarch — rather courageously commented that the metropolitan had been appointed only at the *amir* 's own command. The *amir* accused him and the patriarch of lying, and required that two bishops go to Ethiopia to settle the affair. He specified that they should see to the question of mosques, at the same time settling an arrangement of 'gifts' for the next fifty years. Also, he added, the waylaying of Muslim and other merchants had begun in those regions. This, the patriarch must forbid "otherwise I know what I shall do". The patriarch replied "O my lord, what have I to do with waylaying? Am I a watchman?"; at which the *amir* had them all ejected "in a most disgraceful manner" from the presence. He imprisoned Rijal, the metropolitan's brother, in the Treasury of Flags (an ominous precedent, since it was there that Cyril 'Abdun had been imprisoned before his execution). The patriarch and the ten bishops were kept under watch until they had decided to send bishops Mark of Wasim and Giza and Theodore of Singar to Ethiopia with letters.

However, the patriarch and the Christians were relieved from the rancour of the *amir* by the timely arrival of a substantial gift from Basil, king of Nubia. He had sent his cousin, son of the late king (probably to be identified as King George), to be consecrated as a bishop. Early in 1089 the *amir* summoned Cyril and the ten bishops. They came in trepidation, only to discover the *amir* in a courteous mood. A complaint against Rijal by a Muslim merchant being considered, he was brought in. The merchant testified that Rijal had taken his money in Abyssinia. He then revealed that, before he could gain redress from Severus, the metropolitan himself had been arrested. The *amir* asked "If the metropolitan was arrested, how was he able to give thee they rights? Nevertheless, the king is supreme lord in his lands". To Rijal he said "Thy brother accepted our conditions that he should build in the lands of Abyssinia four

470 "History of the Patriarchs" II, III, pp. 347ff.

mosques, and he has not done (so)". Rijal replied that seven mosques had been built, but the Abyssinians – not surprisingly – had demolished them and even threatened the life of the metropolitan. The Ethiopian king, learning of the affair, had gone so far as to imprison the metropolitan. The *amir* asked what the ecclesiastics had done in the affair, to which they replied that they had written letters in both Coptic and Arabic, offering that he have them interpreted to him. He expressed his trust, then asked who had been appointed to go with these letters and with the *amir's* own letter and messenger. They indicated the two selected bishops. No more is heard of the matter, save that a letter of the *amir* is quoted, which the patriarchal biographer says he had related to him by a good and trustworthy person. It threatened the king of Ethiopia that if he did not do certain things, the *amir* would demolish the churches of Egypt. The royal reply indicated that the king of Ethiopia remained unimpressed. It apparently read;

> If thou demolish a single stone of the churches, I shall carry to thee all the bricks and the stones of Mecca, and I shall deliver all of them to thee, and if a single brick of it is missing, I shall send to thee its weight in gold.

41. The Patriarchs Cyril II (1078–1092) and Michael IV (1092–1102); the Damming of the Nile

An incident involving the damming of the waters of the Nile is attributed to the patriarchate of Cyril II.[471] Similar occurrences are mentioned during the patriarchate of Michael IV by al–Maqrizi, and during that of Christodoulos (1047–1077) by BUDGE, while WIET too cited a number of references regarding current beliefs in such a possibility.[472]

A terrible famine in Egypt from 1066–1072 was apparently averted by an embassy from Caliph al–Mustansir to Ethiopia; famine is reported several times in the biography of Christodoulos. The incident attributed to the time of Cyril II occurs in the Ethiopian version of the chronicle of Giyorgis Wolde

---

[471] SERGEW, AMEH, p. 243.

[472] BUDGE, History, Vol. I, p. 279. The great famine is mentioned after the low Nile of 1065 by LANE-POOLE, *op. cit.*, pp. 146ff, and it lasted 1066-72. G. WIET, *Les relations Égypto-Abyssines sous les sultans mamlouks,* Bulletin de la Société d'Archéologie Copte, IV, 1936, pp. 115-140.

Amid, al–Makin.[473] The Arabic version of this, the *Tarikh al-Muslimin* – the *Historia Saracenica* of Erpenius – was the original used by al–Maqrizi. The Ethiopian version as paraphrased by SERGEW HABLE SELLASSIE indicates that a famine in Egypt was caused by the king of Ethiopia damming the Nile. The Fatimid caliph, al–Mustansir (1039–1094) ordered Patriarch Cyril to send an agent to try to have the dam broken through representations to the king; and this was successful. The metropolitan, it seems, had also protested at the plan, but, unable to gain any success, had withdrawn to a remote spot. In the other version, it is Patriarch Michael IV himself who was sent by al–Mustansir, bearing rich gifts to the king, who met him with reverence and enquired why he had come. After hearing the explanation, the king commanded certain works which restored the flow of the river. The patriarch, on returning to Egypt, was honoured by al–Mustansir.

The story, whose main theme recurs not infrequently, seems to be one exploited by the Copts to influence their treatment at the hands of the sometimes hostile authorities in Egypt. The Ethiopians themselves believed or pretended to believe that they could control the flow of the waters of the Nile, as related in the third *Dissertation* included with LE GRAND's translation of Jeronimo LOBO's account about Ethiopia.[474] This quotes the contents of a letter that King Tekla Haymanot I wrote in 1706 to the authorities in Cairo. The dispute arose because of impediments in the free transit of ambassadors to and from Ethiopia. The king threatened that

> The Nile might be made the instrument of our vengeance, God having placed in our hands its fountain, its passage, and its increase, and put it in our power to make it do good or harm.

LE GRAND[475] in his *Dissertation on the Nile*, denied the possibility of any such diversion, as did TELLES.[476] LUDOLF[477] discussed it at length, quoting the story from al–Makin; this also, it would seem, roused the interest of Athanasius KIRCHER.[478] Al–Qalqashandi,[479] too, referred to

---

473 The attribution to the time of Cyril occurs in the ms. of the Ethiopic version of Giorgis Wolde Amid (Al-Makin) in Addis Ababa, see SERGEW, AMEH, p. 248, n. 38. For the version mentioning Michael, see al-Makin, ed. ERPENIUS, pp. 358-9.

474 LOBO, trans. LE GRAND, Paris, 1738, p. 217. The letter is quoted on p. 173-5. It appears in the English translation by S. JOHNSON, on pp. 180-82, and in BRUCE's Travels in his section on the reign of Tekla Haymanot I.

475 *Ibid.*, pp. 216-9.

476 TELLES, *op. cit.*, pp. 19-20.

477 LUDOLF, *op. cit.*, pp. 40ff.

478 Quoted by LUDOLF, *op. cit.*, p. 42.

479 *Subh* V, 323.

Ibn al–Amid; he also did not credit the tale. In his earlier chapter on Egypt he produces some facts in contradiction. LE GRAND noted that the story was not mentioned in the patriarchal history, adding that there was no famine in Egypt in the one year in which both Michael IV and al–Mustansir held office contemporaneously, 1093.[480] In 1093–4 a tremendous and unprecedented abundance is recorded in the patriarchal biography[481]; perhaps this was the liberal flooding of the Nile that was attributed to either Cyril II or Michael IV, since it occurred just after the accession of the latter to the patriarchal throne. The legendary tone of these tales, however, is probably confirmed by the silence in the official history about what would have been so emphatic a propaganda feature for the patriarchate.

WANSLEBEN was one of those who did believe that the Ethiopians could influence the Nile. He first mentions the Copts' ideas about the river's annual increase;

> Ceux du Pays qui ignorent la veritable cause de cet accroissement, l'attribuent, mais sans fondement comme je pense, à une écluse, qu'ils disent estre en Ethiopie dans le Nil mesme, & que les Abyssins commencent à ouvrir le 12 de leur Juin, & continuent chaque jour de plus en plus en une certaine mesure jusqu'au quatorze de leur Septembre, qu'ils commencent á la fermer derechef, a proportion qu'ils l'auroient auparavant ouverte; mais c'est là philosopher à la Copte[482] ...Voyons maintenant si les Roys d'Etiopie peuvent détourner le cours du Nil de l'Egypte, et faire perir les Habitans par la faim, comme l'on se le persuade communément. Je suis de cette opinion, nonobstant les difficultez que le Père Telles apporte dans son Histoire d'Etiopie. Les raisons qui m'oblige à le croire sont; 1. Une lettre de David, Roy d'Etiopie, surnommé Constantin, écrite à Abu Seid Barcúk, Roy d'Egypte, l'année des Martyrs 1193... par laquelle il menace ce Roy d'Egypte...de détourner le cours du Nil...2. Qu'en effet, les Roys d'Etiopie ont empêché le cours du Nil en Egypte au temps de Mostansir...comme on peut voir dans l'Historie des Musulmans de George le Mekkin".[483]

480 Though al-Taghribirdi is said to report an exceptionally low Nile in 1093. Al-Taghribirdi reports, (see VANTINI, OS, p. 739) says that there was a Nile of most unusual meagreness in the year 1093; the level was a disastrous 13 cubits and 17 inches, instead of the usual c. 18 cubits. However, the date depends on the interpretation of the Hijra date, which is 489; not 1093, but 1096.

481 "History of the Patriarchs", II, III, p. 364.

482 WANSLEBEN, Relation, pp. 52-3.

483 *Ibid.*, p. 60. There is an English translation in: The Present State of Egypt, or, A new Relation of a late Voyage into that Kingdom performed in the Years 1672 and 1673, by F. Wansleb, R.D., London 1678, pp. 37-8.

The visit of a patriarch named Cyril to Ethiopia is noted in the *Gadla Yimrehane Kristos;*[484] and ALVARES[485] mentioned the tomb of a patriarch of Alexandria who visited that king. He apparently died and was buried in Ethiopia. SERGEW HABLE SELLASSIE,[486] who assumed that the Zagwé king, Yimrehane Kristos, was contemporary with the patriarchs Cyril II and Michael IV, commented that the Ethiopic version of Giyorgis Wolde Amid (al–Makin) does not report a personal visit by Cyril II, only that an envoy was sent. The shorter chronology of the Zagwé kings could not accommodate a visit by Cyril II at all. Even Cyril III 1235–43 could not have been a contemporary of Yimrehane Kristos, since, according to TADDESSE TAMRAT, he was the third king of the dynasty, and his second successor Lalibela (VI: 54) is mentioned in the *History of the Patriarchs* in connection with events in 1205 and 1210, under the patriarchate of John VI (1189–1216).

42. Patriarch Michael IV and the Metropolitan George

Michael IV was in office when both the caliph al–Mustansir and his great vizir Badr al–Jamali died. A marginal note in the *History of the Patriarchs*[487] reports that the caliph died seven months after Michael's enthronement; a note in the main text indicates that Michael was consecrated on Oct. 9th 1092, and that al–Mustansir died Dec. 29th 1094. Badr al–Jamali had a stroke in April 1094, and his son al–Afdal succeeded him in the vizirate. Eight months later al–Must'ali became caliph. In December 1101 he too died, and the six–year–old al–Mansur succeeded.

In that same year, a messenger came to al–Afdal[488] from the king of Abyssinia. Following the early dating of the Zagwé, SERGEW HABLE SELLASSIE identifies this king as Yimrehane Kristos;[489] AYELE TEKLAHAYMANOT[490] mentions the same king (even providing dates, 1072–1112). The message from

[484] In ms. mentioned by SERGEW, AMEH, p. 251 and n. 51.
[485] F. ALVARES, The Prester John of the Indies, ed. C.F. BECKINGHAM, and G.W.B., HUNTINGFORD, Hakluyt Society, London 1961, Vol. I, p. 204.
[486] SERGEW, AMEH, p. 248, n. 38.
[487] "History of the Patriarchs", II, III, p. 370.
[488] "History of the Patriarchs", II, III, p. 394.
[489] SERGEW, AMEH, p. 250.
[490] AYELE TEKLAHAYMANOT, *Egyptian Metropolitans*, p. 28.

Abyssinia was, as usual, to request a new metropolitan, who was to be sent to Ethiopia with the royal messenger on his return. The vizir summoned Patriarch Michael and told him of the affair, and Michael began to search for a suitable candidate. Eventually, he selected George, a monk from the monastery of Anba Makarios, consecrated him as metropolitan, and sent him off. George only stayed in Ethiopia for a short time. Apparently he acted in a disgraceful manner, which caused the king to arrest him, confiscate all his effects acquired in Ethiopia, and send him back to Egypt. He also sent a note to al–Afdal, complaining about George's behaviour. The vizir arrested George, imprisoning him in the Prison of the Guard in Cairo, where he remained for some years. Exactly what George did in Ethiopia is not specified; the patriarchal biographer merely noted "It is said concerning him that he transgressed there in infamous affairs and in vile deeds (which) did not become his rank". The sequel is not known, but doubtless the emissaries of the Ethiopian king took a new metropolitan back with them, perhaps early in the episcopate of Macarius II, 1102–1128.

SERGEW HABLE SELLASSIE, followed by GODET[491], employing the long Zagwé chronology, and supposing that these events occurred during the reign of Yimrehane Kristos, assumed that the Metropolitan Athanasius mentioned in that king's *gadla* succeeded Metropolitan George, preceding a certain Michael who was in Ethiopia in Patriarch Gabriel II's time, 1131–1145. It is known, however, from a retrospective remark in the biography of John V in the *History of the Patriarchs*, that a metropolitan called Michael (VI: 45) was consecrated for Ethiopia by Patriarch Macarius II.[492]

43. Patriarch Macarius II (1102–1128) and the Metropolitan Michael, Habib al–Atfihi

The name of a certain Michael, metropolitan of Ethiopia consecrated by "Abba Macarius, Archbishop of Alexandria during the reign of Anbessa Wudem", has already been mentioned (IV: 32), together with the reasons

[491] E. GODET, *Tableaux chronologiques relatifs à la fin de l'epoque axoumite et à la période des Zagwes*, in: Proceedings of the Ninth International Congress of Ethiopian Studies, Moscow, 26-29 August 1986, Moscow 1988, 61, p. 42; SERGEW, AMEH, p. 251 and n. 51.

[492] "History of the Patriarchs", III, I, pp. 90-91.

for attributing him to the time of Macarius II. He would, therefore – following the short chronology of the Zagwé, and leaving Metropolitan Athanasius, noted above from the *gadla* of King Yimrehane Kristos, for later discussion (VI: 49) – probably have been the successor of the deposed Metropolitan George. Michael, according to the Ge'ez text quoted above, was still alive in 1150 (866 AM) when he consecrated the monastery church of Mika'el Amba in Tigray, as recorded in a Gospel kept in the church. A Metropolitan Michael was indeed in office at this period. In the time of Patriarch Gabriel II, 1131–45, he became involved[493] in an interesting controversy about the appointment of bishops to Ethiopian sees.

44. Patriarch Gabriel II (1131–1145); a Tentative for Ethiopian Ecclesiastical Independence

The controversy arose when the reigning king of Ethiopia desired that Metropolitan Michael consecrate for him more bishops than the usual number allowed by ancient custom. The customary limit for Abyssinia and Nubia, as a marginal note adds, was seven. This was because ten bishops could constitute a synod capable of consecrating their own metropolitan in defiance of the patriarch of Alexandria, whose interests thus forbade any such increase in the number of bishops; "For if they complete ten, they would consecrate metropolitans (al–matarinah) and they will have no need for the Patriarch of Egypt (Misr)". Metropolitan Michael – formerly called Habib, adds the historian, conclusively identifying him with Michael Habib al–Atfihi, consecrated by Macarius II and still alive during the episcopate of John V, 1146–67, (VI: 45) – wisely referred the king to Patriarch Gabriel. Accordingly, the king sent letters to Gabriel and the ruler of Egypt , Caliph al–Hafiz (1130–1149). The caliph, persuaded doubtless by the king's letter, ordered the patriarch to comply. The latter, however, was concerned at the possibility of a diminution in the influence of the see of St. Mark. He employed the double–edged weapon of the patriarchs' purported influence over the Ethiopian monarchs by pointing out that if the Ethiopians thus became able to consecrate their own metropolitans, and Alexandrian influence was discarded, the kings would be able to attack Muslim lands with impunity, owing henceforward no obedience to the patriarchate. The caliph must have agreed, since the patriarch wrote warning the king. The

---

[493] "History of the Patriarchs", III, I, pp. 56-7; BUDGE, Synaxarium, Vol. III, pp. 800-801.

patriarchal messengers, returning to Egypt, told of great distress, pestilence and lack of rain in Ethiopia; fire had even descended from heaven and burned a part of the royal castle. The patriarch's letter convinced the king that he had erred. Now he wrote again to the caliph, asking him to intercede with the patriarch to obtain his blessing for the distressed land. Another patriarchal letter was accordingly sent to Ethiopia. In the hour of its arrival, rain fell, and the signs of the divine wrath were lifted.

The *Synaxarium* agrees with the story, save that it states that both Gabriel and the caliph had agreed to the consecration of more bishops, but that the nobles noticed the possibility of independence for the Ethiopian church, and thus discouraged the caliph.

MEINARDUS[494] attributes the events (see below, VI: 45) which happened in Michael's old age under John V (1146–1167) to Gabriel II's patriarchate.

SERGEW HABLE SELLASSIE believed that the Ethiopian king Harbé – as we have already noted[495], he identifies the kings of this period as Zagwé rulers – was deliberately trying to gain ecclesiastical autonomy. His aim would have been to avoid the consecration of metropolitans whose ignorance of the language and the affairs of the church in Ethiopia could only cause difficulties. He suggests that Harbé's reforms, meeting with great hostility, impelled the supporters of the old 'Israelite' dynasty to seek for a metropolitan of their own, hence the embassy sent to John V in 1152 (see below). CONTI ROSSINI[496], on the other hand, resting on the point that the king who sent this embassy was said to have been a usurper, decided that he was likely to have been the first of the Zagwé kings, thus dating their advent around 1150 (see below).

494 MEINARDUS, *Abunate*, pp. 47-8.

495 SERGEW, AMEH, p. 251. See also E. GODET, *Tableaux chronologiques relatifs à la fin de l'epoque axoumite et à la période des Zagwes*, in: Proceedings of the Ninth International Congress of Ethiopian Studies, Moscow, 26-29 August 1986, Moscow 1988, 61, pp. 42-3, and 54, where he suggests that the Anbessa Wudem mentioned in Michael's document is actually a Zagwé king (Harbé?).

496 CONTI ROSSINI, Storia, p. 303.

CHAPTER SIX

The Zagwé Kings and The Patriarchate of Alexandria from the Mid–Twelfth Century to 1270

Introduction

The uncertainty about the dating of the Zagwé dynasty has been discussed above (V: 36). In the present work, the mid–twelfth century date suggested by many recent writers, and CONTI ROSSINI's theory noted above, are both favoured.

The Zagwé dynasty, however dubiously its right to the throne may have been viewed by traditionalist Ethiopians, produced several kings whose saintly lives have been recorded by their biographers – some centuries after their time – with a wealth of detail. The overall consistency of these Zagwé biographies is striking; omissions or details puzzling today were probably taken for granted by contemporary writers or copyists. For the reign of Lalibela, too, the *History of the Patriarchs* at last steps out of the anonymity with which it had previously treated all the kings of Abyssinia, actually naming the contemporary sovereign. It thus supplies a linch–pin for the chronology of the rest of the dynasty. This applies also to the first king of the restored 'Solomonic' dynasty, Yekuno Amlak, whose land grants, preserved in copies, further assist with the dating; the large body of evidence available indicates that his reign began between 1268–1270.

45. Patriarch John V (1146–67) and the Metropolitan Michael

The story of the embassy to John V is preserved by the patriarchal historian as follows.[497] In 1152, when the vizir of the caliphate was al–Malik al–'Adil 'Ali ibn al–Sallar, a messenger of the king of Ethiopia arrived with a

[497] "History of the Patriarchs", III, I, pp. 90-91. For some additions of uncertain source, see SERGEW, AMEH, p. 253. John V can hardly have examined Michael before his consecration, since he had been consecrated by Macarius II. R. STROTHMANN, Die Koptische Kirche in der Neuzeit, Tubingen 1932, p. 145. He puts the incident in 1152 in the time of Gabriel II, the 70th patriarch.

letter to the vizir asking for a new metropolitan. The king already had a metropolitan, Michael, named Habib al–Atfihi, who had been consecrated by Macarius II (1102–1128), but he was now "old and advanced in age". The patriarchal biography mentions that the king and Michael had quarrelled, Michael rebuking the king because of his usurpation of the kingdom. Because of this the king sent for another metropolitan.

> ...And when he was old and advanced in age, the king sent to seek a metropolitan (mutran) other than him. And this Habib Abba Macarius the patriarch had consecrated. And when words occurred between him and the king, he (the king) changed towards him, and he wrote to seek another than him; and the reason for this (was) that the king had usurped the kingdom unjustly, and the metropolitan had rebuked him, and he (the king) had sent a letter to the Sultan...And he (the king) wrote also to the patriarch to seek a metropolitan other than him, while he (was) alive and not dead.

However, ecclesiastical law did not permit that Michael, having been consecrated metropolitan, be deprived of his office during his lifetime – though we know that this could be done in the case of some particular offence, as had occasionally happened, and was to happen again to other metropolitans. John V therefore refused to comply. He was thrown, fettered, into prison, whence the death of the vizir (who was assassinated in 1153) eventually released him. The cause of the favour shown by the *wazirs* to the requests of the Ethiopian kings, in opposition to the patriarchs, was very probably related to the promise of 'gifts'.

The report of this incident might well be the only record so far discovered in foreign sources which mentions the usurpation which founded the Zagwé monarchy. Though the date of 1152 seems rather late for the beginning of the dynasty if the (very confused) Ge'ez records are to be credited (see V: 36; VI: 48), it is not specifically stated in the record that the quarrel between the king and the old bishop was of very recent origin. It may be that the king had spent some time trying to persuade Michael to accept him before he decided to try to acquire a new metropolitan, or possibly the new Zagwé ruler had merely needed a certain amount of time to consolidate his hold on the country before turning his attention to church matters.

But more likely, it seems that this was simply the culmination of the previous affair in Patriarch Gabriel's time. If we may attempt a reconstruction of events, we might propose that the new king – and here the dating accords perfectly with the advent of the Zagwé around 1137 – had first of all made his attempt to free Ethiopia from Alexandrian ecclesiastical control. His action is easily imaginable as the inspiration of a new ruler, whose seat of power was centred yet further from Egypt, in Lasta. Such a new ruler might well wish to challenge certain decrees – particularly any so inconvenient and expensive as the tradition of Egyptian metropolitans – handed down by ancient tradition. But he met with resistance which we may presume soured relations with the incumbent Egyptian metropolitan, Michael; "he changed towards him". After the various letters had gone to and fro, and the idea of extra bishops had been quashed, resentments might have begun to accrue between the new Zagwé king and Metropolitan Michael, culminating a few years later in the embassy to Patriarch John V. Though by no means conclusive, Michael's reported protestations at the usurpation of the kingdom seem exceptionally appropriate in an early Zagwé context. Furthermore, as we have noted above (V: 36) it is precisely at this time that the Ge'ez texts now generally accepted as providing the most credible chronology would situate the advent of the new dynasty.

46. Chronology of the Tenth to Twelfth Century Metropolitans

Whilst it is difficult to resolve some of the chronological problems involving the metropolitans mentioned in the chronicles, the note of 'Michael the sinner' in the Mika'el Amba Gospels dating his consecration to the time of Patriarch Macarius (II), and his activity at Mika'el Amba to 866 AM/1150 AD is more helpful. It matches exactly with the details about the life of Metropolitan Michael as the *History of the Patriarchs* tells it, he having been consecrated by Macarius II and living at least until 1152 in John V's patriarchate. However, if his name and dates are correct, his statement that he was consecrated in the time of Anbessa Wudem, and that he anointed seven kings is more problematical.

If Anbessa Wudem reigned during and after the time of the queen mentioned in the letter to King Girgis II of Nubia and by Ibn Hawqal, presumably Metropolitan Daniel must have died, and later the king obtained Michael; but the patriarchal chronology (see below) would require a much longer interval than this for the episcopates between Philotheus and Macarius II. Unless there were two queens who invaded Ethiopia, the queen of the Bani al-Hamwiyya (IV: 31), and Queen Gudit, Anbessa Wudem would appear to have reigned contemporaneously with the patriarchates of both Philotheus (979–1003) and Macarius II (1102–1128), at least one hundred years apart.

The confusion in Ethiopia is reflected in the records and traditions as the government of the Ethiopian state changed. Power apparently passed from the control of the unnamed *hadani* to the queen of the Bani al–Hamwiyya, then to Anbessa Wudem and Dil Na'od (who are both still entirely unknown outside the Ge'ez texts), and finally to the Zagwé dynasty. One might accept that the queen's destructive rule was over by the end of the patriarchate of Philotheus, 1003, and that (despite difficulties with the dates of the chronicles if the queen is identified with Gudit) this was the period of the kings Anbessa Wudem and Dil Na'od and the metropolitans Daniel and then Michael. To accept the longer chronology of the Zagwé, beginning c. 1030–1050, would mean that some of the Zagwé kings were anointed by Michael. The shorter 133 year chronology leaves a gap between about 1030–50 and the advent of the new dynasty in c. 1137. Perhaps, at a venture, it could be suggested that the period was one of intermittent political unrest and upheaval – though Metropolitan Severus apparently reported that the land was in good order in the late eleventh century – details of which later became obscured in the rich cycle of stories about the last 'Aksumite' or 'Israelite' kings and the rise of the Zagwé monarchy?

Metropolitan Daniel took up his office after the incursion of the queen of the Bani al–Hamwiyya (Gudit?) in the late tenth century (before 1003). Later, (after a gap?) Metropolitan Victor was consecrated, then Severus to replace the uncanonical rule of Cyril 'Abdun between 1078 and 1089. Next came Metropolitan George, in 1101, then, a little later, Michael, Habib al–Atfihi. The Ge'ez chronicles would thus seem to have compressed a period of well over 100 years – containing the two vital events, of the queen's rule and the rise of the Zagwé – into the reigns of the two successive kings Anbessa Wudem and Dil Na'od; whilst only allowing them fairly brief reigns. Only if the highest, and most improbable, figures for these reigns are used can some sort of parallel be made with the years available; thus 50 years for Anbessa Wudem, and 40 for Dil Na'od.

But the chronology is not to be so easily resolved. Anbessa Wudem must either have been a contemporary of George II of Nubia, or his reign must be situated later, in the twelfth century, just before the Zagwé dynasty came to power around 1137 AD. It is certainly rather unlikely that there were two queens, one of the Bani al–Hamwiyya in the second half of the 10th century, and then Gudit in the later 11th or early 12th centuries, whose activities so closely matched each other; though it is interesting that some Ge'ez texts, as noted above (IV: 31) name Gudit and Esato as separate rulers in different regions, Tigray and Amhara. The only historical evidence for a queen–regnant in the Ethiopian region during the second of these periods is the record of the death in AH 455/1063 AD of Queen Badit bint Maya, almost certainly to be identified as the Muslim ruler of Haramaya, Tadin bint Mayalama, AH 431–455 / 1039–1063 AD.[498] However, none of the available documents mentioning the queen who conquered Ethiopia record that she was a Muslim. Curiously, her name and the name of her kingdom echo those of both Gudit and al–Hamwiyya; it is not difficult to imagine a transfer in writing or reporting from Badit to Gudit, or from Haramaya to Hamwiyya. Although Badit's dates are certainly too late for her to be identified with the queen noted by Ibn Hawqal, perhaps it is not impossible that one of the Egyptian chroniclers or copyists who knew of her included her name and title in a distorted fashion in the patriarchal history as the queen who had brought Ethiopia to its knees some one hundred years earlier. Severus' continuator Mawhub mentions that it was Michael, secretary to Patriarch Christodoulos, 1047–77 – and therefore a contemporary of Queen Badit of Haramaya – who wrote the biography of ten patriarchs including Philotheus.

To sum up, if we accept the long Zagwé chronology, commencing 1030–50, the information about Metropolitan Michael (consecrated by Macarius II in the time of Anbessa Wudem, and still living in the 1150's) could not be true. He would instead have been consecrated at some time after Daniel, presumably in Anbessa Wudem's reign. He would have anointed Dil Na'od and several Zagwé kings, and been himself succeeded by Victor, Cyril 'Abdun, Severus, George, Athanasius (after SERGEW HABLE SELLASSIE) and another Michael, Habib al–Atfihi, in the time of Harbé and Macarius II. Michael could not have been consecrated in the time of Anbessa Wudem by Macarius II, 1102–1129, if the Zagwé, his successors, were ruling by c. 1030–1050, or if the king of Metropolitan Daniel's time, before 1003, were Anbessa Wudem, as SERGEW HABLE SELLASSIE asserts.[499] If Michael had been consecrated by Macarius I, 933–953, he would have preceded Daniel, but his date of 1150 would be wrong, and he would have been appointed at the period when the sources declare that there

498 E. CERULLI, *Il sultanato dello Scoia nel secolo XIII*, RSE I, 1941, pp. 10, 21-2, 38; The Dictionary of Ethiopian Biography, eds., BELAYNESH MICHAEL, S. CHOJNACKI, and R.K.P. PANKHURST, Addis Ababa, 1975, p. 33.

499 SERGEW, AMEH, p. 232.

was no legitimate metropolitan in Ethiopia.[500] The short chronology would permit that Michael "the sinner" could be identified with the Michael of the Arabic texts, that his date of 1150 is correct, and that he was consecrated by Macarius II. It also indicates that Anbessa Wudem was a contemporary of Macarius, 1102–1128.

The most probable explanation is that unless Gudit was a later, closely similar, successor of the queen of the Bani al–Hamwiyya, the Ge'ez texts have become inextricably confused through copyists errors, deliberate suppression of certain episodes, or lack of reliable documentation, coalescing a longer period within the reigns of the two kings Anbessa Wudem and Dil Na'od. The end of this period saw the commencement of the Zagwé kingdom, which lasted only for four generations, with, perhaps, a brief period at the end under a regent and council – Dilanda –[501], the whole terminating between 1268–1270.

47. King Lalibela, Patriarch 'Michael' and the Metropolitan Justus

A further account mentioning the appointment of a metropolitan from Egypt is found in the *Zena Lalibela*.[502] In this chronicle, King Lalibela is said to have sent fifteen monks to Alexandria to ask the then patriarch, Michael, (the nearest Michael to Lalibela's time was Michael V, 1145–6) for a new metropolitan. They travelled through Nubia, returning with a metropolitan, Justus, and assistant bishops George and Cyril (Giyorgis and Gerilos – see VI:61). The name of the patriarch must be wrong; though there is proof for the communication of Lalibela with John VI (VI: 54–5).

---

500 SERGEW, AMEH, pp. 203, 232, 251, n. 51, 268-9, and index. SERGEW HABLE SELLASSIE evidently found the question of the bishops of this period a complex one. He ascribes to the time of King Anbessa Wudem three bishops, Michael (I), Selama II (Salama Za-Azeb) and Daniel, covering a span of at least one hundred years; Daniel was sent by Patriarch Philotheus, who died in 1003; Michael I was consecrated by Macarius II, 1102-1128; and there is another Michael, successor of Athanasius, mentioned in the time of Gabriel II, 1131-1135. SERGEW HABLE SELLASSIE's index names Michael "the sinner" as Michael I and Michael Mulabbas of Fuwa as Michael II, but there is no identification of the various Michaels with Habib al-Atfihi or with Anbessa Wudem's Michael.

501 CONTI ROSSINI, *L'evangelo d'Oro*, p. 193.

502 SERGEW, AMEH, p. 268, n. 22; there is a note about the *Zena Lalibela* ms., on p. 266.

The *Zena Lalibela* purports to be a contemporary account of the king, written between his year 39, 1207, and his death, 1212. The accession date of 1168 is still a considerable time after the death of Michael V, in 1146. According to one copy of a land–grant of Lalibela, the king was still reigning in 1225 (see VI: 57), though of course the date could be incorrect; in another document from the same source, the *Evangelo d'Oro* of Debra Libanos, the date in the (16th century?) copy of a land grant is written as Year of Mercy 1089.

48. The Identity of the Metropolitan Salama Za–Azeb

Salama Za–Azeb has already been introduced above (IV: 32). The name is rather a title, expressive of his comparison in the eyes of the Ethiopians with Frumentius, Salama I, the great founder of the national church. He was called Salama Za–Azeb, 'He of the South', perhaps to indicate that his main work was in the less well Christianised southern regions of Ethiopia, but his personal name is not mentioned. The compiler of *Gadla Iyasus Mo'a* evidently considered that he was still living in the years after the reign of King Dil Na'od, having arrived in Ethiopia either before or during the reign of Dil Na'od, 618 years after Frumentius' own arrival.

Salama II, in GUIDI's list II, no. 2, was the title of Metropolitan Minas, Frumentius' successor. In the same list, no 31 is Fiqtor, who is called Salama III in the London manuscript. The *Matshafa Tefut*[503] refers to Fiqtor as Salama II, adding that he lived at the time of King Dawit II, 1382–1411. This Salama is to be identified with the metropolitan nicknamed *matarguem,* the translator or interpreter, who was responsible for a renaissance in Ethiopian literature during his long episcopate (1348–88); in any event, he is set in a firm post–Zagwé context.

It seems that the Ethiopian traditional lists have not preserved Salama Za Azeb by that title. He could perhaps be identified with one of those metropolitans, Daniel or Michael, reported in the time of the last 'Israelite' kings.

Metropolitan Daniel arrived after the reign of the queen of the Bani al–Hamwiyya. His advent is supposed to have restored the kingdom from the ruinous state into which the queen's reign had plunged it. Since the legends about Gudit, so closely resembling this queen in her activities,

---

503 A. CAQUOT, *Aperçue préliminaire sur le 'Mashafa Tefut' de Gechen Amba*, AE I, 1955, p. 101.

assert that she was succeeded by Anbessa Wudem, whom she first drove about from place to place, Daniel could have arrived during his reign. Salama Za–Azeb is reported to have "arrived in the country of Adal", and later to have met Dil Na'od. He could conceivably have come, then, in Anbessa Wudem's time, and his identity with Daniel could be suggested. The conflicting dates are discussed below.

Michael, "the sinner", is another candidate for identification with Salama Za–Azeb. He is stated in the note in the Gospels of Mika'el Amba (see IV: 32) to have been consecrated bishop of Ethiopia in the time of Anbessa Wudem, at a date which must be later than 1102, in Macarius II's episcopate. He survived through the reigns of at least six other kings (unless some of these were sub–kings) to at least 1150. If the testimony of Michael's note is regarded, Michael must be identified with Salama Za–Azeb. Salama arrived, apparently in Adal, where he was for an unspecified period before he entered Ethiopia and met Dil Na'od (i.e. in Anbessa Wudem's reign?). Salama outlived Dil Na'od, while Michael is said to have anointed seven kings, presumably at least six after Anbessa Wudem himself. Even if it is considered that some of the kings he anointed were lesser kings, not always the *hadani* himself, his tremendous roll of baptisms and church dedications surely bespeaks a considerable time in office.

The question of the identity of Salama Za–Azeb resolves itself into the same fundamental problem; which of the two sets of events attributed to the reigns of Anbessa Wudem and Dil Na'od – the recovery of Ethiopia from the queen or the appearance of the Zagwé in the mid–twelfth century – actually belongs to those kings, and accordingly which set of dates may be accepted. The problem has, as its corollary, the further question as to which chronology of the Zagwé is correct. As already noted, the story of the queen of the late tenth century may not be the same story as that of Gudit, though their identity seems emphatically the most likely solution.

From other points of view the date of Michael's note and the nature of the events mentioned by the *History of the Patriarchs* for the life of Michael Habib al–Atfihi appear to accord with the general trend of modern studies, and the accounts of the Ge'ez legends. The attempt by a usurping king to replace Michael in 1152, has, as mentioned earlier (VI: 45), been set into several historical contexts. TADDESSE TAMRAT noted CONTI ROSSINI's proposal that the incident was the mark of the beginning of the Zagwé.[504] He comments extensively on the extremely unsettled course of the succession to the Zagwé throne;

[504] TADDESSE TAMRAT, Church and State, p. 55.

> Each of the princes of Bugna apparently claimed rights of succession to the crown and despite the hagiographical traditions of divine intervention, the problem was probably decided every time by force of arms. The trouble had already started in the reign of the second Zagwé king, Tantawidim,[505]

or again,

> The struggle for the succession is a common theme in the Zagwé royal traditions.[506]

Perhaps, then, we need not even look for an event of such significance as the change of a dynasty in or around 1152. The date of 1137 is already a high one to accommodate the traditions of long reigns in the dynasty, and to shrink the period to less than 120 years is going below even the most conservative of the Ethiopian traditions, especially as it is known from external sources that Lalibela, the fifth of the Zagwé kings, was already reigning by 1205. It might be suggested that we are dealing with the accession of the second Zagwé ruler? On the other hand, and perhaps more plausibly, the suggestions noted above associating the events of Patriarch Gabriel's time with those of 1152 (VI: 45) lend support to the date of 1137 or thereabouts as the beginning of the new dynasty.

49. King Yimrehane–Kristos and the Metropolitan Athanasius

The *gadla* of Yimrehane–Kristos, the third Zagwé king, notes[507] the arrival of a metropolitan called Athanasius (Atnatewos). Nothing is known about him, but it may be hazarded that it was he who finally replaced the aged Michael, Habib al–Atfihi, in the metropolitanate. As noted before (V: 42), some commentators, following the longer Zagwé chronology, include Athanasius as the successor of Metropolitan George, during the reign of the third Zagwé king, Yimrehane–Kristos, in the early twelfth century under the patriarchate of Macarius II (1102–28).

TADDESSE TAMRAT adds a note relevant to the reign of Yimrehane–Kristos. He suggests that the account of Abu Salih[508] about the kings who apparently

---

505 *Ibid.*, pp. 60-61.

506 *Ibid.*, p. 61.

507 SERGEW, AMEH, p. 251, n. 51; and in the Dictionary of Ethiopian Biography, p. 30.

508 EVETTS and BUTLER, *op. cit.*, p. 286, Fol. 105b. TADDESSE TAMRAT, *Church and State,* p. 58, n. 1.

acted as priests in Ethiopia could only properly apply to Yimrehane–Kristos, an ordained priest who continued as king to celebrate mass. Abu Salih may have known this. He must have been a contemporary of the Zagwé kings Yimrehane–Kristos and Lalibela, as he refers to events between the 1160s and 1208 as being in his own life–time.[509]

50. Abu Salih and Abyssinia

It has been noted above that Abu Salih al–Armani lived at the same time as the Zagwé kings Yimrehane–Kristos and Lalibela – at any rate, his contemporaneity with the last is absolutely certain. This author, among the fascinating hodge–podge of notes included in his description of the churches and monastic establishments of Egypt, adds details about Abyssinia (Habasha) and its church not even mentioned elsewhere. Much of what he records may be hearsay – though possibly some of it derived from Abyssinians who came to Egypt. In any event, Abu Salih's notes indicate something of the conception of remote Ethiopia retained by a reasonably informed Christian of apparently Armenian origin living in Egypt in the early thirteenth century – and one obviously very interested in ecclesiastical history and customs.

One particularly interesting detail concerns the coronation of the Ethiopian kings, with the participation of the metropolitan. Apparently the rulers (of the Zagwé period) were

> ...crowned with the royal crown in the church of the angel Michael, or the church of St. George, beneath their pictures. After that the king does not wear the crown, but the metropolitan blesses him, and lays his hand upon his head, and fastens a band over his head and beneath his chin, and clothes him in a robe of brocade.[510]

Ethiopian kings in (rather later) manuscript paintings are frequently depicted wearing a band round the head, often supporting some sort of jewel at the front, and with streamers at the back.

An intriguing feature of this note is the mention of the two churches. By now, neither Aksum nor Ku'bar appears to have been the capital; Arafah (Adafa after the *Gadla Yimrha–Kristos* – see VI: 56) is named as

---

[509] Evetts and Butler, *op. cit.*, pp. x and 8.

[510] Abu Salih, *op. cit.*, pp. 286-7. S. Tedeschi, *La reine de Saba et le roi Tabtabadj*, AE XIV, 1987, pp. 168ff.

"the royal city" of Lalibela by the *History of the Patriarchs* in 1210. Lalibela is reputed to have had the famous churches hewn from the living rock at the town he named Roha – possibly after al–Ruha or Edessa, lost to the Christian world in 1144 – now called Lalibela after him. Presumably Adafa – a name that does not seem to have survived – is more or less identical with Lalibela's Roha. The rock–cut monuments there include a church dedicated to Michael (or at least with one of its *tabotat* is so dedicated) next to the church of Golgotha, and one dedicated to St. George (apparently the last to be built). Could Roha, then, have been the coronation–place of the Zagwé kings about which Abu Salih had heard? Some of the edifices there, such as the churches of Mercurius and of the Archangels, might have been parts of the royal residence, later made into churches.

It has been noted earlier that the Aksumite style of architecture preserved in these churches might suggest an earlier date for (some of?) them than the reign of Lalibela; the information from Abu Salih might indicate that they were already in use during the reign of Lalibela, if not before. If there were two coronation churches, one at least must presumably have existed before the reign of Lalibela, Abu Salih's contemporary, unless Lalibela had them excavated – no brief process – before his own coronation, news of which was duly recorded by Abu Salih. That two churches are mentioned seems to imply at least two coronations. We cannot be sure as to the accuracy of all of Abu Salih's statements; but this information is, at the least, interesting given the prominence of the ecclesiastical structures at Lalibela. If Aksum were the site of the coronation church, we would expect St. Mary of Zion, Maryam Tseyon, to figure among those named. It seems not unlikely that the kings of a dynasty originating from Lasta would choose both to establish their capital, and to celebrate the great ceremonies of kingship there. Nevertheless, the *Book of Aksum* does record churches at the old capital called Mika'el 'Ofay and Beta Mika'el, while the name Beta Giyorgis is the modern name of the hill behind the town, where Ricci discovered the ruins of churches. One of these churches conceivably bore this dedication and gave its name to the hill.[511]

Abu Salih – who still employs the name al–Hind as an alternative to Abyssinia – had heard the legend (see above, III: 29) that Abyssinia was the same kingdom as Sheba.[512] He also knew that the Abyssinians were

---

[511] *Book of Aksum*, see U. Monneret de Villard, Aksum..., Rome, 1938, pp. 50-54; L. Ricci, R. Fattovich, *Scavi archeologici nella zona di Aksum. B. Bieta Giyorgis*, RSE XXXI, 1987, pp. 123-97.

[512] Abu Salih, *op. cit.*, p. 296; pp. 284-5.

supposed to possess the Ark of the Covenant.[513] He even describes it. The ark was overlaid with gold, with gold crosses on its lid, and five precious stones positioned at the corners and in the centre. The liturgy was celebrated on it in the royal palace four times annually. When it was carried from its own church to the palace church a canopy was spread over it. This sounds exactly like the sort of processions still seen regularly at church festivals in Ethiopia today, when the *tabot* or altar tablet is carried out from a church. Abu Salih's comment about the royal palace may indicate that the Ark – whatever precisely this was – was lodged at Adafa or Roha during the Zagwé period. Ethiopian tradition asserts that it now reposes at Aksum. The 'Abyssinian' king of al–Muqurra, according to Abu Salih, possessed the Ark of Noah.[514]

Abu Salih commented that in Abyssinia the eucharistic loaves were "discs of unleavened bread, without stamp", doubtless contrasting them with the stamps impressed on those used in Egypt. He also noted that the Abyssinians used, by ancient custom, only water, though sometimes mixed with vinegar, instead of communion wine.[515] Among the royal treasures was the throne of David, which, like the Ark, was covered with crosses of gold.[516]

An interesting note concerns the rite of consecration to be used for churches.[517] It seems that one of the patriarchs (apparently Sinuthius II or Cyril II; the text is not quite clear about this) conceded to the Ethiopians the right to follow a traditional practice of their own – the sacrifice of animals at the completion of the building of a church. Accordingly, the metropolitan was directed to organise the sacrifice of twelve animals (oxen, sheep and goats) "as a gift to God", and to distribute the flesh.

Confession over a censer is another custom attributed by Abu Salih to the Ethiopians.[518] A handful of the incense usually burned in the sanctuary (consisting of frankincense, sandarach, styrax, ladanum, mastic, aloes and cassia) was taken, the sin was confessed over it, then the incense was thrown into the censer with dried rose–leaves. This custom led to the belief that the incense wafted the guilt away. The idea had apparently died out before the Jesuits arrived in Ethiopia.

[513] abu Salih, *op. cit.*, pp. 287-8.
[514] *Ibid.*, p. 286
[515] *Ibid.*, pp. 288-9
[516] *Ibid.*, p. 290.
[517] *Ibid.*, p. 291.
[518] *Ibid.*, pp. 21, 286.

51. The Letter to al–'Adid

Maqrizi[519] preserves the account of an Ethiopian mission that seems, unusually, to have had no connection with the church. Nevertheless, considering the precedents, it could possibly have included a request for a new metropolitan. A letter and gifts of great value were sent to the last caliph of the Fatimids, al–'Adid (1160–71). These only arrived in 1172–3/567, by which time the Ayyubid Saladin had proclaimed the Abbasid caliphate and become *wazir* of Egypt as a prelude to declaring its independence in 1174. TADDESSE TAMRAT[520] suggests that this could be paralleled with the letter of King Yimrehane–Kristos to the "king of Egypt" asking for a certain wooden door.

It has been suggested that a Zagwé king may have tried to enter into relations with Rome around this time.[521] Pope Alexander III wrote in 1177 to a ruler whom he addressed as "John, the illustrious and magnificent king of the Indians", alluding to the fact that he had heard of this king through a certain Philip, his physician. The king was apparently seeking to submit to Rome, and to receive a church there, and an altar at the Church of the Holy Sepulchre in Jerusalem. It seems that this mysterious ruler, whose envoys Philip had apparently encountered in the east, might have been a Zagwé king, possibly still exploring ways of reforming his church after the failure with Patriarch John V. The Pope – who agreed with the proposals, but whose reply probably never reached its destination – evidently assumed that the king whose envoys Philip had met was the same 'Prester John' whose letter to Emperor Manuel Comnenus (1143–80) was then circulating. Interestingly, a few years later arrangements for the Ethiopians were appar-

---

519 *Suluk*, ed., AZIZ S. ATIYA, II, II, S. 113-4 for the first message in 1172/3. See also S.Y. LABIB, Handelsgeschichte Ägyptens im Spätmittelalter (1171-1517), Wiesbaden 1965, p. 48. Maqrizi, quoted by CONTI ROSSINI, Storia, p. 306; "Macrizi informa che nel luglio del 1173 il sultano Salah ad-Din riceve un'ambasciata dal re d'Abissinia, apportatrice di doni e d'una lettera, indirizzata al suo predecessore, il califfo al-'Adid; i doni sono graditi, la lettera è letta. Quale l'oggetto dell'ambascieria, lo storico egiziano non dice. Ma una fonte greca (this is T.P. THELEMIS, Les Grecs aux Lieux Saints, Jerusalem 1921, p. 68, quoting P. KERAMEUS, Analecta Bollandiana, p. 409) narra che intorno al 1187 Saladino, su domanda del re d'Abissinia, fa fare agli Abissini importanti concessioni; due stanze in Gerusalemme... per loro dimora, e la chiesa della Invenzione della Croce pel servizio divino; a Betlemme, un posto divino, ... e, per stanza, una parte del narthex"...

520 TADDESSE TAMRAT, Church and State, p. 58.

521 A.H.M. JONES and E. MONROE, A History of Abyssinia, Oxford, 1935, pp. 52-3.

ently granted by Saladin after his conquest of Jerusalem in October 1187. Perhaps the king had successfully transferred the attention of his envoys from the outgoing Latins to the new Muslim power in Jerusalem (see VI: 53).

52. The Letter to Patriarch Mark III (1166–1189)

The general situation of the church at this period, as far as its jurisdiction over foreign countries is concerned, is happily confirmed by a contemporary Coptic letter. This remains unpublished, but is briefly noted by PLUMLEY.[522] Found at Qasr Ibrim in 1974, the letter is from the Nubian ruler (or rulers; the name is written in different documents as George Moses, Moses George, Moses, George, or, in the Greek subscript of the letter itself, as Moses and George) to Patriarch Mark III. The subscript of the letter, which is dated to year 902 of the Martyrs, 1186/7, presents the king's name and titles as;

> Γ
> ΜωΥCΗC Κ(ΑΙ) ΓΕωΡ ΒΛC ... ΚΑΙ ΠΑΝΤωΝ ΤWΝ ΒΑΡΒΑΡωΝ
>
> Δ Τ
> ΒΛC ΗΜωΝ ΑΡΟΥΑ Κ(ΑΙ) ΜΑΚΟΥ Κ(ΑΙ) ΝΟΒΑΔΙΟΝ (ΚΑΙ)
>
> Τ
> ΔΑΜΑΛ (ΚΑΙ) ΑΞΙωΜΑ...

that is, claiming rule over Alodia, Makouria, Nobatia, Ptolemais (the port of Barqa, standing for the Pentapolis, the Five Cities of Libya), and Aksum or Ethiopia. The king's improbable titulary seems to simply be copied from the patriarchal protocol; though conceivably he held a high kingship over all the Nubian kingdoms – the previously unknown kingdom called Dotawo in Nubian documents is first heard of in this reign. He was certainly a contemporary of Abu Salih the Armenian, having ruled from at least 1155, and his claims perhaps encouraged Abu Salih's adoption of the extravagant description of the Nubian ruler after John the Deacon (III: 23a), "Great King among the kings of his country ... fourth of the kings of the earth ". However, as far as 'Aksiőma' is concerned, highland Ethiopia was by this time firmly under the control of the Zagwé kings. Claims to authority over 'Aksum' are unlikely to have had much to substantiate

---

[522] J.M. PLUMLEY, *Qasr Ibrim 1974*, JEA 61, 1975, p. 7. ID., *New Light on the Kingdom of Dotawo*, Études Nubiennes, Chantilly, 2-6 juillet 1975, Le Caire 1978, pp. 230-241.

them; though, possibly, the political troubles in Ethiopia, and the collapse of the old dynasty ruling from Ku'bar, had lost some western border districts to Alodia, partly justifying the claims of Moses George. The special interest of the letter from the point of view of Nubian ecclesiastical organisation is that it shows the king apparently asking the patriarch for a specific person (Iesu?) to be appointed to a Nubian bishopric. At the time of writing, no more information about this letter was available.

In WIET's additions and corrections to MASPERO's *Histoire des Patriarches d'Alexandrie*[523] there is the following note;

> In a treaty concluded between Saladin and Hildebrand, ambassador of Pisa, the titles of patriarch Mark II can be read. The Arabic text is lost; here they are in a contemporary Latin translation: "Et de hoc fuit testis Marcus patriarcha de Alexandria et de Babylonia et de Nubia et de Saba". If the document was not dated 25 September 1173, several months before the conquest of the Yemen by Saladin's brother, one would have thought of this country, following the interpretation of Amari. It is very tempting to suppose that the original Arabic read 'al–Habasha', Abyssinia.

This proposed alteration would seem in every respect probable if it was not known that Abu Salih (VI: 50) only a few years later identified Sheba with Abyssinia. Possibly the writer of these titles did indeed really mean 'Habasha' but wrote 'Saba' (Sheba) as a synonym.

53. Saladin and al–'Adil

It is recorded that in 1194 a delegation from Ethiopia arrived in Palestine to seek a new metropolitan and to discuss the Ethiopian concessions in Jerusalem.[524] Saladin apparently responded favourably to the request. Saladin, however, died in 1193, on 3 March, and his brother al–'Adil must be meant, the embassy being in fact that noted by 'Abd al–Latif[525] in AH 596/1200 AD;

---

523 G. MASPERO, Histoire des patriarches d'Alexandrie, Paris 1923, p. 382; WIET cites AMARI, I diplomi arabi del R. archivo Fiorentino, pp. 261 and 459.

524 SERGEW, AMEH, p. 262, quoting S.Y. LABIB, *op. cit.*, p. 48; O. MEINARDUS, *The Ethiopians in Jerusalem*, Zeitschrift für Kirchengeschichte, Vierte Folge 14, 1965, pp. 117-147, 217-232; E. CERULLI, Etiopi in Palestina; Storia della comunità etiopica in Gerusalemme, Rome 1943-7, Vol. 1, pp. 31ff, discusses the reality of Ethiopian ecclesiastical connexions with Saladin and Jerusalem.

525 Abd al-Latif, "Relation de l'Egypte, ed. and trans. A.I. SILVESTRE DE SACY, Paris 1810, p. 334; J. WHITE, Abdollatiphi *Historiae Aegypti Compendium*, arabicè et latinè, Oxford 1800; quoted in EVETTS and BUTLER, *op. cit.*, p. 285, n. 3.

> In the month of Shawwal [which began on July 16th 1200] an ambassador of the king of Abyssinia arrived, bearing a letter by which that prince notified that the metropolitan of the Abyssinians had died, and asked that he be sent another in his stead. He noted in this letter that the rains had been meagre that year in Abyssinia...

This embassy could possibly have resulted in the despatch of Metropolitan Michael of Fuwa (see below, VI: 54–5).

BUTCHER[526] comments that many Egyptians, skilled workmen particularly, emigrated to Ethiopia as persecutions broke out at the time of the great famine of 1200–1201, early in al–'Adil's reign. Such men may have assisted King Lalibela in his vast project to recreate the churches of the heavenly Jerusalem at Roha in the province of Lasta, or at least those which really date to his reign (see VI: 50 and IIC). However, if this was the case, their influence must have been more on techniques and decorative elements than on architectural forms, since the churches of Lalibela clearly announce a strong inspiration from Aksumite architecture. Whatever the truth about this, it does seem that many foreigners went to Ethiopia at this time and that it was later believed by the Ethiopians that some of these foreigners built or cut the rock churches.[526]

It is also said[527] that in 1203, at Lalibela's request, the sultan of Egypt intervened on behalf of the Ethiopians in the Holy Land; the sultans had been in control over Jerusalem since it had fallen to Saladin late in the year 1187. Saladin is said to have granted many sites in Jerusalem to the Ethiopians; possibly it was knowledge of certain connections between Saladin and Zagwé Ethiopia that encouraged Patriarch John VI's biographer to include Ethiopia (al–Habasha) among the "nations and kings" that obeyed Saladin – " his order was executed in the lands of Ethiopia, Nubia, Baga (Beja) and the Yemen and Hijaz..."

The fascinating sideline to Ethiopian ecclesiastical history, the story of the Ethiopians in Jerusalem, is largely outside the theme of this book. It

---

526 BUTCHER, *op. cit.*, Vol. II, p.119; COULBEAUX, *op. cit.*, p. 266; MEINARDUS, *op. cit.*, p. 49.

526 TADDESSE TAMRAT, Church and State, p. 58, n. 2.

527 R. SAUTER, in: Dictionary of Ethiopian Biography, p. 102. The claim that Saladin reserved the Chapel of the Invention of the Cross in the Church of the Holy Sepulchre, as well as an altar in the Church of the Nativity at Bethlehem, for the Abyssinians, rests on an unconfirmed statement of Neophyte of Cyprus, c. 1844; see J.S. TRIMINGHAM, Islam in Ethiopia, p. 56, n. 4.

has been told in some detail by CERULLI.[528] Here it may be worth noting one addition to CERULLI's study; some material evidence for very early Ethiopian connections with Jerusalem and the Holy Land has lately been provided by a few Aksumite coin finds, dateable from the late fourth century, from Jerusalem itself, Caesarea, and Beth Shan.[529]

54. King Lalibela and Patriarch John VI (1189–1216); the Metropolitan Michael of Fuwa

The patriarchate of John VI is of exceptional interest for the study of the Zagwé period in Ethiopia. The chronicle of the patriarchate of John VI (who was buried in the *ardh habash* in Cairo) is very rich in detailed information about the king of Ethiopia and the contemporary metropolitans.[530] It relates that, during the reign of the Ayyubid al–'Adil (1192–1216(?), ruler of Egypt from 1199), the king of Ethiopia and Nubia (*sic* – more traces of Moses George and his 1186/7 titulary?) sent messengers to the sultan asking that he lay the question of a new metropolitan before Patriarch John VI. The custom, the chronicle specifies, was that a letter, accompanied by splendid gifts, would arrive at the sultan's court, requesting that the sultan approach the patriarch for the consecration of the new metropolitan. They would generally stay about three months, while the patriarch sent out to the monasteries in Scetis (Wadi Habib) and other places, and considered potential candidates from Misr (Old Cairo) and Cairo.

Patriarch John received the request, and began a search, but could find no–one suitable in Cairo or the monasteries. He perceived, however, that the messengers, "impatient from the length of their stay" – presumably, therefore, far exceeding the usual three months' delay – were preparing to complain to the sultan. So he turned to the bishops in his

---

[528] E. CERULLI, Etiopi in Palestina, I, 1943, pp. 33-7.

[529] S.C.H. MUNRO-HAY, Aksum, EUP, 1991, Ch. 9.

[530] "History of the Patriarchs", III, III, pp. 184ff. J. PERRUCHON, *Notes pour l'histoire d'Ethiopie; Extrait de la vie d'Abba Jean, 74e patriarche d'Alexandrie, relatif àl'Abyssinie*, Revue Sémitique VI, 1898, pp. 267-71, Arabic text pp. 366-72. See also J. DORESSE, L'Empire..., p. 56. The period of office of this patriarch is dated by SERGEW HABLE SELLASSIE, AMEH, p. 264, to 1171-1193, but later in the same work he notes the dates 1200-1218 after MALAN; the dates here follow the list in BUDGE, Synaxarium. CHAINE, *op. cit*, also prefers 1189-1216.

search, a proceeding strictly out of order, since the Coptic church did not permit episcopal translations. However, the pressing need, and the agreement of the rulers and ecclesiastics concerned – and perhaps the fact that Fuwa, near Rosetta, was sacked by a Crusader fleet in 1204 – settled the metropolitanate on Kiil (Michael) ibn al–Malbas, of Tukh Muthur in the province of al–Gharbiah, bishop of Fuwa.

He and the messengers departed southwards. The account goes on to describe the rich reception accorded to the new metropolitan by the ruler of Ethiopia. The king (Lalibela) himself came three days distance out of the capital to greet Michael, accompanied by priests and bishops. On arrival at the royal city, Michael entered it under an umbrella of gold–woven cloth with a jewelled top. The first celebration of the liturgy was accompanied by the panoply of wealth, gold being "scattered over him" and the censers filled with aloe–wood and ambergris. At the residence of Michael, the House of the Metropolitanate, ten priests served him and guarded the wealth of the church; meanwhile, horses, mules and male and female slaves were delivered. As in the days of Metropolitan Daniel, and of the arrival of the letter of blessing of Gabriel II, the rains fell again. The metropolitan, much respected, was favoured by royal visits; "the king used to ride at all times to his house".

55. Patriarch John VI, the Deposition of Metropolitan Michael and the Appointment of Isaac

However, this state of affairs only lasted for four years. In the fifth year the patriarch learned that Michael was on his way back to Egypt. The reason for his return, as he later related, was that the queen had forced him to consecrate her brother, Khairun or Hirun as bishop of the capital. On this being achieved, the new bishop began to go about under the umbrella of state, usurping the prerogatives of Michael, whilst also scheming against him, and in the end plotting to kill him. MEINARDUS[531] states that Michael alleged that "the city of Aksum had become unsafe for him"; but it is not likely that Aksum was the city in question.

According to his story, this persecution was the cause for Michael's flight. He began his journey with a large concourse of people, most of whom he sent back. Even so, about a hundred persons continued with

---

531 MEINARDUS, *Abunate*, p. 48. The name of the queen's brother is given as: Gebron or Gabron after PERRUCHON and DORESSE; Hetron after MEINARDUS; Gobrom after Abba AYELE TEKLAHAYMANOT.

him on the way to Egypt, most of whom perished through the exigencies of climate and terrain and the hostility and greed of the local rulers. Michael arrived in Egypt with a female slave, two male slaves, and (a realistic touch) a civet–cat. The patriarch appointed a residence for him. He then wrote to the Ethiopian king, by the agency of the priest Musa and one of his own attendants. A year later the reply arrived. Michael, wrote the king, had killed a priest, the chief of the ten guarding the church treasure, by having his slaves beat him to death on a charge of theft of a gold bar. Michael had not allowed the priests to question him on this, and the relatives of the priest had been those who tried to kill the metropolitan in revenge. Khairun had died two months after the departure of Michael. Also, it was added, there had been no rain again, and another metropolitan was required. The extravagance of Michael was cited, how he had built a vast house in the royal capital, with trees and water–systems, called 'the Castle'. It was whitewashed, and contained long corridors, so that "He who enters them becomes weary before he reaches their lowest part and their highest part". Michael went out only on Sundays, in high state, with five hundred retainers, plus priests, seated on a mule with the umbrella over him. He entered the sanctuary robed in garments woven with gold and studded with precious stones. (These extravagances were attributed by Doresse to 'Gabron', instead of to Michael).

Thus read the king's report. With it arrived his messengers to formally request a new metropolitan, carrying with them the customary offerings. These consisted of a gold crown for the patriarch, and for the sultan gifts including an elephant, a lion, a giraffe and an onager (or zebra). The difficulties of conveying these to Cairo can only be imagined.

The embassy returning from Ethiopia with the priest Musa arrived in 1209–1210 (606 AH/926 AM as specified in the text), which enables the date of the earlier mission to collect Michael to be approximately calculated as follows. The messengers first came to al–'Adil with gifts; then the patriarch was contacted, and they were delayed at least three months before the patriarch even began to consider consecrating Michael; indeed this might not have happened until 1204 when his see was devastated by the Crusaders. Michael then journeyed to Ethiopia, where he stayed four years, leaving some time in the course of the fifth year. After his return, the priest Musa took a year to go with messages to the king and return, so we may suppose that Michael took a similar time on his journeys, going in state and returning with difficulty through inimical territory. (The account of Michael's return makes it evident that it was difficult, travelling "among the infidel kings". This is a decade after the last known date for Moses

George, king of Dotawo, and almost nothing is known about Nubian history at this time. But if Michael went by the sea route, he could well have encountered some of the Muslim rulers of the coast. Sultan Abdullah of Shewa ruled from 1193 to the 1230s, and there may have been other states between Shewa and the sea coast). Before the despatch of Musa some time doubtless elapsed while Michael was being examined. All this could well add up to some eight to ten years.

CHAÎNE[532] dated Michael 'vers 1190'. This seems exaggerated; indeed so early a date is precluded by the arrival of Ethiopian messengers in July/August 1200 (VI: 53). If Michael was in office from 1190 until his deposition in 1209–10, this mission need not have been sent. On the other hand, the *Dictionary of Ethiopian Biography* arrives at c. 1205 for Michael's elevation, following strictly the statement that when Michael left Ethiopia it was his fifth year in office. This date of 1205 for Michael's consecration – which may well be correct – does not take into account the long journey involved, nor the other delays noted above, before the selection of the new prelate. It seems very probable that the 1200 mission was the one that eventually resulted in Michael's consecration.

It may have been at this time, or perhaps in 1210, that a certain David of Fayyum was rejected by Patriarch John VI as a possible successor to the metropolitanate of Ethiopia. Later, on the death of Patriarch John in 1216, David of Fayyum was a candidate for the patriarchate itself, and this rejection was remembered against him.

Continuing the story of Michael of Fuwa, the *History of the Patriarchs* records that the patriarch took all the Ethiopian gifts to al–Kamil, al–'Adil's son, since the sultan was then absent. Al–Kamil greatly admired the crown; he had not known there were any among the Ethiopians who could make such things. The messenger who had brought it then said that it was well known that the patriarch's modesty would not allow him to wear it; had the king thought he would have worn it, jewels worth the tax of all Egypt would have been added. On enquiries being made about the king and the state of his troops and wars, the messenger handed over the royal letter to the sultan, which requested a metropolitan

---

532 CHAINE, *op. cit.*, p. 268. For the story of David of Fayyum, see NEALE, *op. cit.*, II, pp. 282-3. He recounts that at the death of patriarch John VI in 1216 a certain David of Fayyum was among those who hoped to be elected patriarch. But it was alleged that he had already been a candidate for the metropolitanate of Ethiopia and has been "refused with indignation" by the late patriarch (NEALE pp. 282-3.)

other than Michael. Al–Kamil suggested that this be immediately implemented. Further exaggerated praise of the Ethiopian king's might followed, at which al–Kamil smiled. Then the patriarch, after some polite wrangling, was persuaded to take away his gifts, and departed to arrange the new consecration.

The ceremony caused a great stir. Innumerable people wanted to go to al–Mu'allaqah church to view it, and the price for the hire of donkeys at the Zuwailah Gate to go up to Old Cairo increased to three dirhams. The proceedings began with the deposition – and excommunication – of the old metropolitan "on account of the misuse of his stewardship". He "descended from the church of al–Mu'allaqah with great shame, and he was shrieking and putting dust on his head". Then a monk selected by the patriarch, called Isaac, was consecrated metropolitan (one manuscript reads, patriarch). He, and his elder brother Joseph, who was to go with him as a priest, came from the monastery of St. Anthony, whence also had come Michael, "the sinner" and the ill–famed Victor and Minas. This new consecration occurred on the 11th Baramhat 926 AM/9th Ramadan 606 AH; 7th March 1210 AD.

A possibility, no more, of a further trace of Michael is the inscription on a rock near Ibrim[533], which is reported as reading ΕΓϢ ΧΑΗΛ ... ΚΟΛΛΟΥ ΕΠΙΣΚϢΠΟΥ ΜΗΤΡΟΠΟΥΛ ΠΑΧϢΜΙΟΥ. The designation "metropolis" is interesting; there were only a few of these with any relationship to the Ibrim region. Of these, Pachoras or Aksum come to mind from the form of the name as recorded. A simple misreading of a worn rock inscription may conceal one of the Khaels of Pachoras/Faras, or even, conceivably, a Michael, metropolitan of Aksum, travelling via Ibrim in transit to or from Ethiopia.

56. King Lalibela

Much useful information is supplied by the historian[534] about the contemporary Ethiopian king and his kingdom.

Metropolitan Isaac had been consecrated for "'Arafah, the royal city... and over all Ethiopia (al–Habashat)". Presumably, then, the metropolitan's episcopal seat was by now at the Zagwé capital in Lasta, also

[533] CABRAL and LECLERCQ, *op. cit.*, col. 623, after BARTH.

[534] See also CONTI ROSSINI, *L'evangelo d'Oro*, p. 188 for a note on *puppus* Mika'el between 1205 and 1210, and for Lalibela's titulary. For Adafa, see TADDESSE TAMRAT, Church and State, p. 59, n. 5.

known from the *Gadla Yimrha–Kristos* as Adafa, rather than at Aksum or another successor capital. The text further specifies that the king caused the metropolitan to reside in the city of ‘Arafah.

The Arabic text reveals that the king's name was Lalibalah ibn Shanuda, meaning 'the Lion', of the tribe of Al–Nakbah. His wife was called Masghal Kabra, 'Great is the Cross'. The province from which the dynasty originated was al–Bakna (Bugna). Interestingly, CONTI ROSSINI also quotes from a (probably 16th century) Ge'ez text including Lalibela's protocol, showing it to be a derivative of old Aksumite usages and similar in detail to some of the patriarchal biographer's account; "Be'osi 'Uzal [the mighty man] who is not conquered by the enemy, by the might of the Cross of Jesus Christ, son of Marara, son of Zan Seyum, son of Ased (the Lion)".

The king's eldest son was called Yabarak (Yitbarak); the name of the younger whose name is written without diacritical points, poses some difficulties. PERRUCHON (whose *"Extrait de la vie d'Abba Jean, 74e patriarche d'Alexandrie"* contains another version of this text) reads it 'Aytab, ('Inab or 'Itab). TADDESSE TAMRAT [535] plausibly thought that the name could be read La'ab, that is, short for Na'akuto–La'ab. However, it seems that this future Zagwé ruler is more likely to have been the son of King Harbé, the brother and predecessor of Lalibela, and probably, in the system of succession, the legal heir, being the eldest son of the elder brother. Yitbarak was perhaps the most prominent at the court at the time, and the messengers of the patriarch perhaps did not realise that the other royal youth was not the king's own son.

SERGEW HABLE SELLASSIE[536] implies that Metropolitan Isaac died in the reign of Lalibela's successor Na'akuto La'ab, adding that then the Mamluk sultans refused to allow the ordination of a new metropolitan, thus forcing the illegal temporary elevation of *abuna* Tekla–Haymanot. He adds that "less reliable sources" – not quoted – state that Isaac lived until the reign of Yekuno Amlak. The political involvement of Tekla–Haymanot apparently belongs to the later redactions of his legend, when he is raised to the rank of *abun,* and, moreover, assumes an important part in the change of dynasty (VII: 66).

---

535 TADDESSE TAMRAT, Church and State, p. 62 and n. 2.

536 SERGEW, AMEH, p. 282.

57. The Metropolitan Giyorgis

In a 16th century copy of a land–grant dated to 1225[537], a certain Bishop Giyorgis is mentioned; the land–grant was purportedly made during the reign of Lalibela and is recorded in the *Evangelo d'Oro* or Golden Gospel of Debra Libanos of Shimezana. In Giyorgis' retinue were Abet, the *qala–pappas*; Za–Adonaya, the *qas–hatsani,* and Harayo, with the title *episqopos,* bishop (see VI: 60).

Further, it is said that the *Kebra Nagast* was first rendered from the Coptic to Arabic in Ethiopia in the Year of Mercy 409, at the time of Lalibela Gebre Masqal and Giyorgis.[538] The date is the 409th year of the second 532 year cycle of the Era of Martyrs, corresponding to 1225 AD. The colophon reads:

> In the Arabic text it is said: "We have turned (this book) into Arabic from a Coptic manuscript ... in the four hundred and ninth year of mercy in the country of Ethiopia, in the days of Gabra Maskal the king, who is called Lalibela, in the days of Abba George, the good bishop.

58. Late – Post Zagwé Metropolitans; Cyril and John

Two more metropolitans are mentioned in the *gadlan.*[539] The first, Cyril, the *pappas* Gerilos or Qerelos of the *Gadla Tekla–Haymanot, Gadla Samuel of Debra Wagag, Gadla Qawistos,* and *Gadla Zena Marqos,* was active at the time of Tekla–Haymanot. A *liqa–pappasat* named Qerelos also appears in a land–grant of Yekuno Amlak dated to 1269/70 preserved in the *Evangelo d'Oro* of Debra Libanos of Shimezana (see VI: 59 below).

Another metropolitan, John (Yohannis), is mentioned as residing at Aksum – a return to old customs – by the *Gadla Qawistos*. Qawistos was a relation and contemporary of Tekla Haymanot, and his *gadla* was written in the reign of King Dawit I (1382–1411). A metropolitan called Yohannis

---

537 CONTI ROSSINI, *L'evangelo d'Oro*, p. 190.

538 CHAINE, *op. cit*., p. 268. E.A.W. BUDGE, The Queen of Sheba and her Only Son Menyelek, London 1932, p. 228; The Dictionary of Ethiopian Biography, pp. 74-5.

539 For references to these *gadlan*, see TADDESSE TAMRAT, church and State, p. 7-, n. 1; SERGEW, AMEH, p. 282, n. 10 S. KUR, trans.,"Gadla Samuel of Dabra Wagag", CSCO, Scriptores aethiopici, T. 50, Louvain 1968.

(see also VII: 67) is also mentioned in the *Gadla Basalota–Mika'el.*[540] He was the predecessor of the active propagator of monasticism and evangelisation, Metropolitan Jacob (Ya'iqob), who arrived c. 1337. This Yohannis, who was arraigned by Basalota–Mika'el for simony, is perhaps the same as the one mentioned in the *Gadla Qawistos*.

59. The Ordination of St. Tekla–Haymanot; Benjamin and Cyril

A metropolitan named Cyril or Qerelos has already been noted (III: 20) as the *pappas* who, during the Zagwé interlude, in the country of Amhara, ordained Tekla–Haymanot deacon supposedly "in the days of Abba Benjamin, Archbishop of Alexandria". This is not possible, the dates of the Alexandrian patriarchs called Benjamin being; Benjamin I, 622–661; Benjamin II, 1327–1339. St. Tekla–Haymanot lived from about 1215 until 1313, though there are a number of different estimates of his life–span in the different accounts of his life.

If the problem is not caused by a simple error in the name of the patriarch, the solution may be proposed that the hagiographer transposed the names of metropolitan and patriarch (unlikely though this seems). The saint would then have been ordained by a Metropolitan Benjamin in the days of Patriarch Cyril III (1235–43). Perhaps CHAÎNE had this possibility in mind too, when he noted in his list beside the name of Takla Haymanot , "Il vivait du temps du patriarche Cyrille III", selecting only the brief patriarchate of Cyril for mention out of the seven patriarchs who sat during his long life. Only Thomas, ordained illegally in 1237 by Patriarch Ignatius II of Antioch (VI:62), is known as metropolitan of Ethiopia for the patriarchate of Cyril III. His consecration may imply that there was a vacancy in the metropolitanate during the time of Cyril.

The identification of Metropolitan Benjamin is a little more difficult; but there is mention of a metropolitan (?) called Benyam in the *Gadla Iyasus Mo'a.*[541] At some unknown date after Salama Za–Azeb, this Benyam conferred a blessing on the monastery of Debra Naguadguad in Lake Hayq;

> There have been seven blessings on this convent [St. Stephen of Hayq]; the first among them....Abba Salama II, Za Azeb....the second time it was blessed by the hand of Abba Benyam, *pappas,* who arrived after him....

---

540 TAMRAT, Church and State, pp. 114, 117.

541 KUR, ed., A*ctes de Iyasus Mo'a*, pp. 49 of text, and 40 of trans.

If, however, Qerelos' name is correctly cited as the *pappas* who ordained Tekla–Haymanot (see III: 20 above), he could perhaps have been one of the assistant bishops who came in the time of Lalibela with Justus the metropolitan (VI: 47), or perhaps the *liqa–pappasat* Qerelos who appears in a land–grant dated to 1269/70.[542] AYELE TEKLAHAYMANOT[543] mentions a note in a manuscript containing a list of metropolitans, stating that a certain Ya'qob (II), the 44th in the list, had ordained Tekla–Haymanot.

60. Church Dignitaries under the Zagwé Dynasty

It is clear from later evidence that there were holders of the title of bishop or *episqopos* in Ethiopia, clearly differentiated from the metropolitan or *pappas* (I: 6). Several holders of this title are named in the land grants attributed to the reign of King Lalibela. Similar Ethiopian bishops, as aside from metropolitans, are mentioned at times in the other sources, as we have already seen (eg. III; 19: V: 44).

In one copy of a land–grant[544] of Lalibela, apparently issued originally in the time of *pappas* Abba Mika'el (doubtless the ex–bishop of Fuwa), there were at least three persons bearing the title *episqopos;* Ezra, Yerda'e Mika'el and Samuel. Other dignitaries of the church at the time were the *qas–hatsani,* the royal confessor or chaplain, Zakarayas, and Endreyas the *qala–pappas,* the interpreter for the *pappas,* an essential functionary considering the foreign origin of the metropolitan or *pappas.* In fact, he is named first in the list, before the metropolitan and the three *episqoposat.*

No internal evidence is available for the time of Metropolitan Isaac (Yeshaq), 1210–? Contemporary with Metropolitan Giyorgis, in the land–grant of King Lalibela dated to 1225 preserved in a later copy in the *Evangelo d'Oro* of Debra Libanos of Shimezana, were the *episqopos* Harayo, the *qas–hatsani* Za–Adonaya, and Abet the *qala–pappas.*

542 *Dictionary of Ethiopian Biography,* p. 135 for other references.

543 AYELE TEKLAHAYMANOT, *Egyptian Metropolitans,* p. 31, n. 43 (Conti Rossini Collection, Accademia dei Lincei, Rome, no. 7)

544 CONTI ROSSINI, *op. cit.,* pp. 187-191. For all these dignitaries, see Dictionary of Ethiopian Biography, Vol. I, under the appropriate name.

61. Thirteenth Century Metropolitans and Assistant Bishops

The order of the metropolitans of Ethiopia during this period may be tentatively listed as follows;

Michael of Fuwa 1200–1210;
Isaac 1210 – (?);
Justus (?);
Giyorgis –1225 – (?);
(Benjamin (??) in the time of Cyril III (1225–43));
Thomas, appointed by Ignatius of Antioch 1237;
Qerelos in 1269/70.

Metropolitan Christodoulos, said to have been killed with the last Zagwé king, Yitbarak, and buried beside him at Daga Qirqos in Gaynt, Begmeder, appears to be unknown from any other sources. Nevertheless, there is ample room for him in the late Zagwé period,[545] and GUIDI's list I seems to confirm the name by citing among the *pappasat za–Ityopya* a certain 'Abba Gebre Krestos' who was buried at Beguena with three other metropolitans whose names were no longer known when the list was compiled. Beguena (Bugna) being Zagwé territory *par excellence,* this seems to reflect the tradition of a Zagwé metropolitan of that name, though with a different burial site. At the Enseta Debra Qirqos burial site – on the opposite side of Lasta from Bugna – the tombs are marked by the remains of pillars.

This tentative list, together with further evidence from the first reigns of the Solomonic dynasty (see below), suggests that there were indeed metropolitans in Ethiopia in the later thirteenth century, in contrast to AYELE TEKLAHAYMANOT's assertion that "from 1250 to the end of the reign of Yekunno–Amlak (1270–1285), the seat of the metropolitan of Ethiopia was vacant".[546] It is certain that there were metropolitans in the country, albeit apparently Syrian, during Yekuno Amlak's reign (see VII below), since King Yigba Tseyon specifically mentions that his father protected them.

The details about Benjamin (VI: 59) remain uncertain. The two names Giyorgis and Qerelos recall the names of the 'assistant bishops'

---

[545] SERGEW, AMEH, p. 284. See also Eric GODET's useful *Tableaux chronologiques relatifs à la fin de l'epoque axoumite et à la période des Zagwes*, in Proceedings of the Ninth International Congress of Ethiopian Studies, Moscow, 26-29 August 1986, Moscow 1988, 61, p. 48, where he notes suggestions for the identity of Christodoulos with metropolitans of this name in some of the lists.

[546] AYELE TEKLAHAYMANOT, *Egyptian Metropolitans*, p. 30.

who came with Metropolitan Justus, as noted in the *Zena Lalibela* (VI: 47), assigned tentatively to the later part of the reign of Lalibela. It would be tempting to regard these two 'assistant bishops', as coadjutors consecrated by the patriarch, empowered to take over the functions of the metropolitan by right of succession. Such a succession was arranged for Ethiopia by the Roman church during the pontificate of Julius, in a similar situation where great distances were involved. TELLES reported[547]

> It is to be observed, that the two Bishops [Andrew de Oviedo, bishop of Hierapolis and Melchior Carneyro, bishop of Nicaea] were appointed coadjutors to the Patriarch [Don J. Nuñez Barreto] and to succeed him, one after the other in the said dignity, with full power to Consecrate other Bishops, ordain Priests, and use all Patriarchal and Episcopal Jurisdiction.

There is no record of this sort of arrangement among the Egyptian bishops sent to Ethiopia during the period covered by this study. Later it was evidently possible, as is reported in the account of the two 'Abimas' who came in the time of King Eskender (see I: 4 above). However, there was often anxiety about the succession of the metropolitans, so vital to ensure the continuation of church offices. Consecration of successive bishops would have been a wise move towards ecclesiastical continuity. Although the Coptic church may not normally have employed this stratagem – certainly there is no hint of it in all the previous long succession of metropolitans until the *abuna* Mark sent in Eskender's reign – there were occasionally special arrangements made for Ethiopia; for example the animal sacrifices (VI : 50), and the translation of a bishop (VI: 54). It may be that the arrangement in King Eskender's reign was not the first time the succession had been ensured in this way.

62. Patriarch Cyril III (1235–1243); Ignatius of Antioch and the Appointment of the Metropolitan Thomas

A very unusual episode in the history of the Ethiopian church began during the patriarchate of Cyril III. The results were, it seems, still being felt fifty years later (VII: 63–4). The documentation of the incident records the appointment for the first time of a Syrian metropolitan for Ethiopia.

Gregory Abu'l Faraj or Barhebraeus[548] relates that in view of the large

---

[547] TELLES, *op. cit.*, p. 133.

[548] CERULLI, *op. cit.*, Vol. I, pp. 71ff.

number of Copts in Jerusalem, Patriarch Cyril III of Alexandria (probably in 1235 or 1236) consecrated a metropolitan for them. This was a trespass on the rights of the patriarch of Antioch, under whose jurisdiction came the city of Jerusalem and Palestine; the border between the two patriarchates was at al–Arish. In 1237 the Antiochene patriarch, Ignatius (1222–53), arrived at Jerusalem, where he was approached by an Abyssinian nobleman, called Thomas, who desired to be made metropolitan of his country. Ignatius perhaps saw the opportunity for a just and exact revenge; and he too irregularly ordained a metropolitan in the territory of his brother patriarch. Barhebraeus noted that the wish of Thomas to be made metropolitan was doubly irregular, first because Ethiopia was under Alexandrian jurisdiction, second because since the time of the conversion of the country, none of their own people, but only an Egyptian could hold the office.

CERULLI commented on the political aspects of this affair *vis à vis* the Latins, who were against the patriarch of Antioch's consecration of the Ethiopian Thomas, but who supported the Coptic bishop of Jerusalem. The result of the affair, which is similarly recounted by RENAUDOT[549] – save that no mention is made of the metropolitan of Ethiopia – is unknown; though MEINARDUS[550] avers that a compromise was made, both

---

549 RENAUDOT, *op. cit.*, p. 579; NEALE, *op. cit.*, II, p.301.

550 MEINARDUS, *Abunate*, p. 49, quoting RENAUDOT, p. 579. This latter (pp. 579-80) reads as follows; Deinde Metropolitam Hierosolymorum ordinavit, multis reclamantibus; neque enim licere dicebant, ut in territorio alieno, quod ad sedem Antiochenam spectabat, Alexandrinae conjunctissimam, Episcopum ordinaret; esseque id non minus contra veterum consuetudinem, quam contra Canones, qui Dioceseon limites definaverant. Verum ille rationes illas insuper habens, novem illum Metropolitam misit Hierosolymam, attributa illi in omnem provinciae autoritate. Cumque instaret Paschalis solenitas, advenerunt in eam urbem Ignatius Patriarcha Syrianorum, hoc est Jacobitarum, Antiochenus, & Patriarcha Armenorum. Ut adventum Syrianorum Patriarchae Cyrillus audiit, munera ex Aegypto ad eum misit per Episcopum Khandekae, & unum ex Misrae Sacerdotibus. Illi ad Metropolitam a Cyrillo ordinatum diverterunt; & postea Patriarcham Syrianorum salutatum iverunt; muneraque obtulerunt, quae laetus accepit, monens, tamen Alexandrino Patriarchae nihil juris esse suis in Diocesibus; tum illos ut apud se hospitarentur invitavit. Cum venueret Episcopus negaretque posse se id facere absque Metropolita licentia Syrianorum Patriarcha, munera Cyrilli ad illum remisit: Metropolitamque excommuneraverit, nec Episcopum postea in conspectum suum admisit. Metropolita auxilium a Francis petiit, quorum autoritate confirmatus dignitatem retinuit, & in Coptitas eorumque Ecclesias plenam jurisdictionem obtinuit. Vulgo ferebatur eum subscriptione sua testatum ipsis fuisse, quod eamdem fidem, eamdem doctrinam quam illi, profiteretur. "Ea enim", inquit Autor "ipsorum consuetudo est, ut neminem prorsus sibi adjungant, nisi postquam id fecerit". De hoc nove Metropolita superius dictum est; videturque quantum colligere ex variis

patriarchs recognising the illegally consecrated prelates. One would assume that the Latin opposition had sufficed to stop further proceedings, were it not for letters which imply the contrary. These, preserved in the *Life of Qala'un*, date from the time of the Ethiopian kings Yekuno–Amlak (c. 1268/70–1285) and Yigba–Tseyon (1285–1294). They again mention 'Syrian metropolitans' in Ethiopia (VII: 63–4).

VANTINI[551] notes Barhebraeus' comment that

> Patriarch Ignatius II of Antioch ordained an Ethiopian by name of Thomas metropolitan for Ethiopia, thus violating the Synod.

In addition to observing that appointing the metropolitans of Ethiopia was an Alexandrian prerogative, Barhebraeus adds that Ignatius' action was also illegal

> ...because the Abyssinians, since they were instructed (in the faith), had no metropolitan ordained from among them – whereas it was necessary that someone from Egypt be placed at their head, to whom they gave their obedience.

Barhebraeus, himself later a *maphrian* of the Syrian church, compared the situation in Ethiopia with the Syrian custom;

> And this custom is somewhat similar to the one (observed) among us in the east, in that the Easterners do not permit the maphran to be consecrated but by the West. Still, (the maphran) shares both the spoken and the written language with the people of his own diocese, while the Egyptian (metropolitan) who goes to the Abyssinians is skilled in neither their spoken nor their written language.

VANTINI introduced a further question based on his interpretation of Barhebraeus' comments. He suggested that ;

> According to Barhebraeus, the ordination of Thomas was unlawful....because Thomas al–habashi did not know the local language (of Habasha). CERULLI raised doubts whether Thomas was ordained for Ethiopia proper, or for Nubia. It must also be noted that the ignorance of the local language was never accounted for a lawful impediment to the ordination, because the Egyptian–born metropolitans of Ethiopia could not be expected to know the Ethiopian language.

Itinerariis antiquis & recentioribus possumus, hinc originem habuisse nova illa & olim inaudita apud Jacobitas Aegyptos Hierosolymorum Metropolis. Nam ab illius institutione quae tentata olim, tunc vero consummata existimanda est, originem habuere Antistites, qui Coptitis ad hanc usque diem in urbe sancta praesuerunt. O. MEINARDUS, *The Ethiopians in Jerusalem*, Zeitschrift für Kirchengeschichte, Vierte Folge, 14, 1965, p. 118.

551 VANTINI, OS, p. 424.

552 CERULLI, *op. cit.*, Vol I, p. 65.

This comment is based on a misunderstanding. CERULLI[552] was of the opinion that Barhebraeus' report was better adapted to the situation in Abyssinia. There the well–known proviso in the pseudo–canon of Nicaea excluded Ethiopians from the metropolitanate, while in Nubia as explicit a prohibition was never, as far as is known, in force, and native Nubians were duly consecrated to high ecclesiastical office. CERULLI emphasised that the attribution to Ethiopia and an Ethiopian was more likely in every respect than to Nubia. Nor does Barhebraeus' text indicate that the lack of knowledge of the local language was anything to do with the legality of the appointment; indeed, since Thomas was an Abyssinian himself, "quem nobili inter Abyssinos genere oriundum esse dicebant", he was perhaps the first metropolitan destined for Ethiopia who did know the local language.

CHAPTER SEVEN

The Metropolitanate at the Time of The 'Solomonic Restoration'

A passage from Marco Polo, relevant to Ethiopian ecclesiastical history, was quoted by GEDDES[553], but was mis–dated by him to 1258. It is cited below (VII: 64) under its correct date of 1288.

63. The Letter of Yekuno–Amlak and the Reply of Sultan Baybars

Problems about the ecclesiastical situation in Ethiopia seem to have arisen not long after *pappas* Qerelos' appearance in a land–grant of 1269/70 (VI: 58–9). If Qerelos were indeed one of the assistant bishops who had come with Metropolitan Justus he would certainly have been very old by the time of the accession of Yekuno–Amlak. This succession may not be very likely, for why then would Thomas have made his attempt to be elevated to the metropolitanate if there were already an Egyptian incumbent? Just possibly, Giyorgis had succeeded by 1225, and died around 1237, and news of this had inspired Thomas to make his request of Patriarch Ignatius, while at the same time Qerelos had automatically succeeded in Ethiopia. Whatever the case, Metropolitan Qerelos seems to have died four or five years after the fall of the Zagwé, since al–Nuwayri (d. 1332), al–Mufaddal (d. 1358), al–Qalqashandi (d. 1418), and al–Maqrizi (1364–1442), all record[554] a letter

---

553 GEDDES, *op. cit.*, p. 19.

554 QUATREMÈRE, Mémoires, Vol. II, p. 267, from Maqrizi's "Kitab al-Suluk", also translated in: Histoire des sultans mamlouks de l'Egypte, by E. QUATREMÈRE, I, Pt. II, 1840, p. 122 (n. 151 gives Nuwayri's version and the reply to it from ms. d'Ascelin, fol. 53 verso, 54 recto. Maqrizi, *Kitab al-Suluk*, ed. M. ZIADA, Cairo, 1934-9; See also VANTINI, OS, pp. 679-80. Mufaddal from the *Life of Qala'un*; Mufazzal Ibn Abil-Fazail, "Histoire des sultans mamluks," ed. and trad., E. BLOCHET, PO XIV, 1919-20, p. 383. ABDUL AZIZ AL-KHOWAYTER, A Critical Edition of an Unknown Source of the Life of ...Baibars, Ph.D thesis, London Univ., 1960, ii, pp. 315-6 (not, unfortunately, included in the published version: Baibars the First, his endeavours and achievements, London 1978). For a general account of the Mamluk-Abyssinian relations see also G. WIET, *Les relations Egypto-Abyssins sous les sultans mamlouks*, Bulletin de la Société d'Achéologie Copte IV, 1936, pp. 115-140.

from the *haty*, king of Abyssinia, Yekuno–Amlak (1270–85) to Sultan al–Malik al–Zahir Rukn al–Din Baybars al–Bunduqdari in 673/1274–5, asking for a new bishop.

A copy of Yekuno–Amlak's letter was later enclosed with another that was sent by his successor King Yigba Tseyon (1285–94) to Sultan al–Mansur Qala'un in 1289 (VII: 64). Yigba–Tseyon's letter enclosed under the covering a sheet of paper on which was written "I append the letter which my father received from the sultan". This Egyptian letter, written, according to al–Nuwayri and al–Mufaddal in 672/1273, and according to al–Maqrizi on the first day of the month *raby al–akhir* 673 (26th June 1275), in the name of Baybars, was to the late king, Yekuno Amlak, in reply to the one from him.

Al–Qalqashandi[555], quoting the only letter from Abyssinia that he could find in the archives, transcribed the following version. It was addressed by the Abyssinian king to Sultan al–Malik al–Zahir Baybars, through the Yemeni sultan, al–Malik al–Muzaffar. Al–Qalqashandi adds [556]

> It was written by qadi Muhiy al–din ibn 'Abd al–Zahir (and is found) in the treatise dealing with the letters despatched by the court of the sultan to the infidels of the southern lands. But the contents of the said letter do not agree with his claims of grandeur. In fact, were he (the king of the Habasha) not so dependent (on Egypt), so that he accepts the archbishop sent him by the patriarch of Egypt, his pride would have exalted him to the stars, in his letter; but this may have happened in the past.

Both al–Nuwayri and al–Mufaddal also quote Ibn 'Abd al–Zahir (author of biographies of several sultans of Egypt; Baybars, Qala'un and al–Ashraf), as the origin of this letter (which he evidently copied from the original). He was the secretary who was ordered by Baybars to write the reply.[557] The letter, as preserved in this version, read;

> The humblest slave, Mahar–Amlak, kisses the ground, and informs al–Malik al–Zahir, whose power may God make permanent, that an envoy has reached me from the governor of Qus, concerning the monk (rahib) who has arrived here, but we have not had come to us the metropolitan (mitran) from

555 Al-Qalqashandi, quoted in M. GAUDEFROY-DEMOMBYNES, ed. and trad., Ibn Fadl Allah al-'Omari, "Masalik el-Absar fi Mamalik al-Amsar", p. 38, App.III. See also Al-Qalqashandi, *La Syrie sous les Mamlouks*, ed. M. GAUDEFROY-DEMOMBYNES, 1923, t. VIII, p. 119.

556 VANTINI, OS, p. 580, quoted from the Cairo ed. of 1913-19, Vol. VIII, pp. 119-20.

557 Mufaddal, ed. BLOCHET, PO XIV, p. 383ff. See VANTINI, OS, pp. 494-5.

> our lord the sultan, whose slaves we are. Let our lord the sultan command the patriarch to send us a metropolitan who should be a man wise and good, having no care to amass gold and silver, and let him send him to the town of 'Awan.[558] The least of slaves addresses this, which is urgent, to the agent of our master, al–Malik al–Muzaffar, sultan of the Yemen, who will convey it to the agents of our lord the sultan. Circumstances have delayed the presence of ambassadors before our lord the sultan; I was at Sukar (?) when king David died and was succeeded by his son. I have, in my army, 100,000 Muslim horsemen; as for the Christians, they are innumerable; all are your servants, at your orders. The 'great bishop' prays for you, and the faithful reply, Amen. Every Muslim who shall come into our country, we shall be the least of slaves for him; we shall protect him, we shall let him travel as he wills, according to his requirements. The envoy whom we have sent is ill; because our country is unhealthy. When one among us is ill, no–one should go near him, for whosoever breathes in his breath falls ill and dies. We shall protect all those who come from the Muslim lands. Send us a metropolitan; he also will protect them.

A variant translation of the line mentioning King David reads

> The ambassadors have been delayed on their return journey to the court of the sultan only because I was engaged on a campaign (bikar). King Dawwud died and his son succeeded him in the kingdom.

Yekuno–Amlak's letter was written as part of the process necessary to procure a new metropolitan. It seems possible that there had already been correspondence on the same subject, as the letter mentions a messenger from the governor of Qus about a certain monk who had come to Ethiopia. The governors of Qus were always those who were in charge of the Egyptian relations with 'Aydhab and its region; perhaps the monk may even have been a messenger from the patriarch?

The date of the letter is either AH 672 or 673, the former being the most likely, since it was taken directly from the record of the Chancery Secretary himself.[559]

Yekuno Amlak may have found it more convenient to send his messengers by way of the Yemen, through the good offices of Sultan al–Muzaffar, in view of the constant trouble in Nubia, where claimant

558 "... 'Aswan, (an ancient sea-port between Massawa and Assab"), VANTINI, OS, p. 495, n. 3. Al-Mufaddal later notes (BLOCHET, PO XIV, p. 387) that "celui qui veut se rendre dans l'Amhara part de la ville de 'Avan ('Awan) qui se trouve sur la côte du pays des Abyssins".

559 S.C. MUNRO-HAY, *Kings and Kingdoms of Ancient Nubia*", RSE XXIX, 1982-3, p. 118 and n. 110. VANTINI, OS, p. 494, puts the date at 671/1272-3.

after claimant was enthroned at Dongola; one of these, David or Dawwud, caused considerable trouble by attacking 'Aydhab and Aswan in 671/1272.[560] Even in the north of his own country there were problems, as Mufaddal notes: "This sovereign had sent an ambassador to sultan al–Malik az–Zahir, with gifts and presents, among them lions black as night. The ambassador arrived in the land of Sahart [near Antalo, southern Tigray], where the ruler rebelled against the king of Abyssinia, arresting the ambassador, with the things he had with him".

Perhaps the long delays on the part of the Yemeni ruler, and at the ports, together with increasing anti–Muslim feeling, encouraged the Ethiopian king eventually to seek a Syrian nominee for Ethiopia (see below). The crusaders may have lost Jerusalem and Palestine, but areas of Syria, particularly the principality of Antioch, and some coastal parts of the Holy Land remained in their hands. It may have been possible that some sort of contact with them or with the eastern Christians under their rule permitted such a solution, based on the precedent noted above by Barhebraeus. Conceivably, too, the process might have been easier and cheaper, as one might imagine that the Syrians and the Latin Christians, eager to increase their area of influence in a Christian region south of Egypt, would not have demanded the usual fees.

However, before any such necessity arose, Sultan Baybars seems to have been well–enough disposed to the Christian king's demands, to judge from his reply to Yekuno Amlak's letter. He had previously appointed, at the request of Michael Palaeologus, the Byzantine emperor, a certain Rashid the oculist to the melkite patriarchate in Alexandria in 661/1262. His reply to Ethiopia read as follows[561];

---

[560] For the accounts of the incidents in Nubia at this time, see MUNRO-HAY, *op. cit.*, pp. 117-18; QUATREMÈRE, Mémoires, vol. II, p. 96ff. MACMICHAEL, *op. cit.*, pp. 179ff; YUSUF F. HASAN, *op. cit.*, pp. 106ff. The Arab sources sometimes vary in their accounts; Ibn 'Abd al-Zahir, in "Rawd al-Zahir", III, 1145, and "Tashrif"(quoted in VANTINI, OS, p. 427); Al-Nuwayri, "Nihayat al-Arab fi funun al-adab", quoted in VANTINI, OS, pp. 470ff. Al-Mufaddal, in his continuation of al-'Amid's history, ed. BLOCHET, as "Histoire des Sultans Mamlouks", PO, XII, 3, XIV, 3 and XX, l, quoted in VANTINI, OS, pp. 494ff. Ibn al-Furat, in his *Ta'rikh,* quoted in VANTINI, OS, pp. 530ff. Ibn Khaldun, in the "Kitab al-'Ibar", quoted in VANTINI, OS, pp. 558ff.

[561] Preserved by al-Mufaddal, quoting Ibn 'Abd al-Zahir, who wrote it himself; For Mufaddal see BLOCHET, *op. cit.*, pp. 385-6 and VANTINI, OS, p. 496.

> We have received the letter of the most exalted king, the magnificent prince who reigns with justice and equity over all his empire, the sovereign (*hati*) of the kingdom of Amhara, the greatest of all the kings of the Hubshan, who exercises the supreme authority over all the lands under his dominion, the najashi of his epoch, the most precious ornament of his kingdom, as long as he rules, the sword of the Christians, and support of the states which follow the Christian faith, the friend of all kings and sultans, the sultan of Amhara – God guard his life and build his foundations on prosperity! We have acquainted ourselves with this letter, and have understood all that was written therein.
>
> As for the request for a bishop, which you have submitted, nobody ever came to our court on behalf of the king to talk to us about this matter, so that we, too, do not know at all what you expect from us. As for the letter of sultan al-Malik al-Muzaffar, we have received it. It informed us that he had received from the king a letter and a messenger, whom he kept in his house until he would send back a reply through him, to that king.
>
> As for what he mentioned about the multitude of his soldiers and the one hundred thousand Muslim horsemen, God has put a greater number on the side of the Muslims; and about the miasmas of his country, it belongs to God to put an end to life, for nobody dies except by his permission, and after he has completed his course.

QUATREMÈRE also translated this letter.[562]

64. The Letter of Yigba–Tseyon to Sultan Qala'un; the Syrian Metropolitan

It seems that no Egyptian metropolitan ever arrived in Ethiopia during the reign of Yekuno–Amlak. Perhaps, as Yekuno–Amlak consolidated his power, and began to harry the Muslim territory of Ifat, Baybars began to think less kindly of the request, and saw to it that nothing was done. This would be the decade when, somehow, the Syrians moved in. In 689

[562] QUATREMÈRE, Mémoires, Vol. II, pp. 269-70. He gives the date as *rabi al-akhir* I, 673. WIET, in *Les relations Egypto-Abyssines sous les sultans mamlouks*, p. 119, after QUATREMÈRE, notes that the metropolitan may not have been sent owing to a fault in the required etiquette. He adds that Sultan Baybars' letter said "Your letter speaks of the request for a metropolitan; but you have not sent an ambassador in whose presence the choice might be made. Nevertheless, you want the prelate to be one known for his complete disinterest; but a man of this character can only be chosen in the presence of your ambassador".

(1289/90), Yekuno–Amlak's son King Yigba–Tseyon wrote to Sultan Qala'un, according to Ibn 'Abd al–Zahir's *Life of Qala'un*.[563] At the same time the king sent gifts to the then patriarch of Alexandria (John VII, in his second period as patriarch) and to the Abyssinian monks in Jerusalem. To reassure Sultan Qala'un, Yigba Tseyon affirmed that he was a protector of the Muslims in his kingdom; he proposed that mutual embassies be sent. He mentioned that he was sending an emissary to greet the sultan, and to carry a carpet made in Abyssinia, with a hundred candles to be lit in the churches, to Jerusalem. He then put the request for another metropolitan, to bring peace to his land. His letter, as quoted by QUATREMÈRE, continued

> I am not like my father; I protect the Muslims throughout my kingdom; and I desire that the sultan our lord does the same for the Christians in his lands, so that an unchanging friendship might reign between us, cemented by mutual embassies. As for the slaves of both sexes, the gold and the other gifts, which by custom must be delivered in return for a metropolitan, they will arrive with the ambassador, but I had to delay because of the Syrian metropolitan who upset the country in the reign of my father [Yekuno Amlak]. I ask that the new metropolitan be sent accompanied by an ambassador of the sultan and by my messenger. If the sultan, as I trust, will accede to this request, his response will calm the troubles in Abyssinia and make peace between the Muslims and the Christians.

The troubles, seemingly Christian–Muslim relations, appear to have been exacerbated by the Syrian metropolitan. The king added that directly the new metropolitan and the two ambassadors returned, he would satisfy the sultan. Meanwhile he asked him to notify the patriarch.

Another letter arrived at the same time (in AH 689) from al–Malik al–Muzaffar (1250–95), who had stopped an ambassador of the king of Ethiopia in his country, on his way to seek a metropolitan. The Yemeni ruler wished to enquire about the sultan's wishes in the matter. Then a further letter[564] came from Saleh ibn Yasin, nephew of the Abyssinian ambassador (Yusuf) Abderrahman. He stated that having reached 'Aydhab on his way from Mecca, he learned that his uncle the ambassador had died there – TADDESSE TAMRAT takes this remark to mean that the ambassador had died in Cairo.[565] In due course the suite of the dead man arrived, with another Abyssinian ambassador. He bore an Arabic missive from Daud ibn Azz, 'vizir' of King Yigba Tseyon, who sent a eunuch as a

---

[563] QUATREMÈRE, Mémoires, Vol. II, pp. 267ff.
[564] *Ibid.*, pp. 270-1.
[565] TADDESSE TAMRAT, Church and State, p. 129.

gift, with excuses for the modesty of the present. He, too, complained about the Syrian metropolitan. He further assured the sultan that on the arrival of the new metropolitan, the usual presents would be despatched. With this came a letter[566] in Ethiopic destined for the patriarch, John VII (1262–93) – Gabriel, the legitimate patriarch, was only able to occupy the patriarchal throne in 1269–71 in Baybars' absence, and after his death John was left undisturbed.

The letter, from King Solomon Yigba Tseyon to the patriarch, read as follows

> I address my request to the patriarch. Send me a virtuous metropolitan, who will teach me all sorts of good and useful things. These Syrian metropolitans who live in Abyssinia have earned our hatred. Loyal only to the Egyptian patriarch, we have not allowed these strangers to exercise their episcopal functions any longer, and have expelled them from their sees, where they would not have been supported except by the protection of my father, who had no bishop of your choice near him. Now do not command the ruin of a kingdom submissive to you; send us a metropolitan. Select a metropolitan for us, if the matter depends on you; if not, ask the sultan's permission. Do not allow these Syrians to remain longer in our land. If you decree their expulsion, they will be expelled; if you command that we keep them, we will obey your order. You have disapproved our conduct with respect to them, but deign to pardon us our fault.

The covering note for this letter, addressed to the sultan, read

> O Mansur, [al–Malik al–Mansur Qala'un 1279–90], greetings. Listen, sultan of Egypt, may God protect you in all circumstances! Grant to the patriarch the necessary authorisation that he may send us a metropolitan, for, from the time of St. Mark until the present we have not ceased to profess the same faith as he. If you acquiesce to our request, we shall not fail to send the gifts due to you in such cases.

Then, finally, another letter[567], written in Ethiopic, "From the ruler of Abyssinia to the city of Jerusalem, and to the tomb of the Messiah, my Lord. Greetings, O monks of Abyssinia, who have persevered until now in the exercise of the religious life, and have tolerated with constancy the inconveniences of cold and heat. I send you a veil of red silk, and 100 candles accompanied by my royal sash. I wish that you wear it during the mass, not on every day of the year, but only on festivals, and that it be used only by the priest who offers the sacrifice. Receive these presents from me, and write to me when they reach you. Remember me in your prayers, and never forget me".

---

566 QUATREMÈRE, Mémoires, Vol. II, pp. 271-2.
567 *Ibid.*, p. 273.

'It would seem that the Syrian metropolitans, first instituted by Ignatius II of Antioch in the 1230s, had either been present in parallel to Egyptian ones, or had even, in the time of Yekuno–Amlak, come to exercise complete ecclesiastical authority in Ethiopia. There is no indication whether Thomas really took up his appointment in the time of Lalibela's successors from c. 1237, but if not the precedent his appointment created seems to have been revived by the restored Solomonic dynasty. Metropolitan Qerelos was apparently already in office in the year of inception of the new dynasty, 1269–70. He would, therefore, appear rather more likely to have been inherited from Yekuno–Amlak's predecessor than to be a newly arrived metropolitan (ignoring the question of the mysterious Christodoulos supposedly killed with the last Zagwé king Yitbarak). There would scarcely seem to have been time to arrange this, and no such previous application is mentioned in the exchange of letters with Egypt four or five years later. Qerelos does not appear to have been the Syrian metropolitan protected by Yekuno Amlak, successor to Thomas.

Butcher and Wiet[568] suggested that melkite (Greek) metropolitans were in question. However, it seems more probable, since we know the story of Thomas' elevation, that these Syrians were monophysites under the jurisdiction of the patriarchate of Antioch. Yekuno–Amlak's letter shows that he made some effort to get a metropolitan from Baybars (1260–1277) and John VII, but failing, had evidently turned to this other source. Only Maqrizi declares the outcome of Yekuno–Amlak's request to have been successful.[569] It would seem, from Yigba–Tseyon's remark, that the Coptic patriarch disapproved strongly of the Syrians and this may have made for added difficulties. There is no evidence that an Egyptian metropolitan arrived in Yigba–Tseyon's time either, though it is of course possible. After him, from 1294 to 1299, a succession struggle developed in Ethiopia; only with the accession of King Widim Ra'ad (1299–1314), were the purely dynastic troubles settled.

568 Butcher, *op. cit.*, Vol. II, p. 167. Wiet, L*es relations Egypto-Abyssines sous les sultans mamlouks*, p. 120.

569 Vantini, OS, pp. 679-80 quotes from Vol. I, pp. 615-6 of Ziada's edition; "A letter was received (at Cairo) from the king of Habasha, by name al-Hatti - which means "the Successor" (al-khalifa). He put his request to the Sultan in these words, "the least of the slaves prostrates himself, kissing the earth at its lowest" and asked that a bishop (mitran) be sent to him by the patriarch (batraq). His request was granted". 673H, 1274/5. Similarly, in Quatremère, Historie des sultans mamlouks, I, pt. II, p. 122. Wiet, *Les relations Egypto-Abyssines sous les sultans mamlouks*, p. 119, notes that Maqrizi was doubtless mistaken in this statement.

However, even if there were no (Egyptian) metropolitan, there do seem to have been bishops in Ethiopia during the reign of Yigba–Tseyon. It was during this reign that the incident mentioned by Marco Polo and dated to 1288 occurred. It is quoted here in GEDDES' pleasantly archaic English version (see note 475);

> an Habassin king having been hindered by his Councellors from going in person to Jerusalem, did send a Bishop thither, with rich Offerings, who was not only robbed of all that he had as he passed through the Kingdom of Aden, but upon his refusal to turn Mahometan, was sent home with a mark of infamy upon his Body; at which barbarous Treatment the Habessin was so much incensed, that having got together a great Army, he marched against that Sarasen Tyrant; and having beat him in a pitched Battel, and made great Desolations in his countrey for some Weeks, he returned home laden with Spoils and Honours.

SALT[570] suggested that the context compels one to read Adel for Aden, and indeed the kings of Ifat were often referred to as the 'king of Adal' by the Ethiopians. 'Umar Walasma had increased the power of Ifat by the annexation in 1285 of the sultanate of Shewa, but during the reign of Yigba–Tseyon, the Muslim and Christian states seem to have recognised the status quo, and no invasion of the magnitude envisaged seems to have occurred. It seems unlikely that any incident of the sort could have involved Aden either, but it is known from the letters of Yekuno–Amlak that the Yemeni sultan was not very helpful to the Abyssinians, delaying the king's messengers in transit to Egypt. Most interesting of all, we know that in 1289/90 Yigba–Tseyon did send to Jerusalem[571]; and possibly this message was accompanied by the unfortunate bishop, who did not have the privilege of miraculous circumcision granted to his distant predecessor Metropolitan John (III: 24). The Ethiopian kingdom had its Syrian metropolitan at the time and there must have been assistant bishops too; perhaps the bishop in question was an Ethiopian *episqopos* consecrated by one of the Syrian metropolitans. Though the military conquest of Aden adds an improbable aspect to the story, the facts are confirmed by the letters of Yigba–Tseyon; an Ethiopian bishop in transit to or from Jerusalem through the territories then ruled by al–Malik al–Muzaffar fits perfectly within the context of the letters of Yigba–Tseyon.

---

570 GEDDES, *op. cit.*, p. 19. H. SALT, A Voyage to Abyssinia, London 1814, App. V, pp. lxvii-lxviii; SALT's reference is Lib. iii in G.B. RAMUSIO, Della navigazione e viaggi, Venice 1540, p. 59, c. 38.

571 See the letter in QUATREMÈRE, Mémoires, p. 273, already quoted.

65. Diplomatic Contacts between Ethiopia and Egypt

Some interesting details concerning the protocol observed by the patriarchate and the Mamluk chancery in their diplomatic dealings with Ethiopia emerge from the records of al–'Umari, who was himself employed in preparing the official correspondence of Sultan al–Malik al–Nasir Nasir al–Din Muhammad. Al–'Umari reports[572];

> in spite of the extent of their country and the great number of the inhabitants and the soldiers, the Abyssinians have need of the protection of the ruler of Egypt, since the metropolitan, who is the supreme head of the law in all the Christian regions of their land, must be chosen from among the Jacobite Copts of Egypt, and the royal command comes from Cairo to the patriarch of the Jacobite Christians to send them a metropolitan. This decision is preceded by a request despatched by the king of Abyssinia, whom they call in their language Hati, and borne by an embassy, which tenders gifts.

This was written when "the name of the king reigning over them today is 'Amda–Siyon ".[573] He ruled Ethiopia from 1314–1344.
Al–'Umari mentioned this matter again in his *Ta'rif*[574];

> since the doctrine of Christians of the Jacobite sect is, that the sacrament of baptism is not valid unless it originate from the patriarch, and since his seat is a church of Alexandria, the king of Abyssinia must ask him to appoint each successive metropolitan. This correspondence is a blow to his pride, but he is compelled to it. The commands of the patriarch are treated by him with the respect due to religion itself. When the patriarch writes a letter, and it arrives at the frontier of the Abyssinian dominion, a high official of that province comes, sets the letter at the top of a standard, holding this in his hand until it leaves the province; while the ecclesiastics, such as priests and deacons, accompany on foot with censers. At the provincial frontier, they find the dignitaries of the neighbouring province, and the same ceremony continues until Amhara is reached. The sovereign in person comes forth, and continues to watch it, save that it is the metropolitan who carries the letter, because of his high rank, and not because the king disdains to do so. The king promulgates no decree, great or small, of execution or defence, until the arrival of the letter has been proclaimed and an assembly has been held on the Sunday in the church; the letter being read, the king stands, and he holds no audience until he has fulfilled the command of the patriarch.

---

572 GAUDEFROY-DEMOMBYNES, *op. cit.*, p. 30.

573 *Ibid.*, p. 24.

574 *Ibid.*, pp. 32-33, in Appendice I, which is a complete translation of the appropriate chapter.

The rules of conduct laid down by the court of the sultan for relations between the government and the patriarchs, melkite and Jacobite, under the Egyptian jurisdiction are most interesting. The Chancery Secretary, al–Qalqashandi, was naturally well informed on these matters. He comments that the Secretary, when corresponding with certain office–holders, should add orders appropriate to each post.[575] As far as the melkite patriarch was concerned, he was particularly enjoined not to give shelter to foreigners, and not to pass on information he may have heard from the sultan to any foreigner. Letters from any king must be shown to the sultan, nor should the patriarch reply to them. He must keep away from the sea, and from anything coming from overseas, which might be the cause of suspicion. The main stricture on the Jacobite patriarch was that he must be warned to avoid anything coming secretly from the Ethiopians. The degree to which the link with Ethiopia was held to be dangerous is illustrated by al–Qalqashandi;

> If the order is addressed to the Patriarch of the Jacobites,...; the words "Let him avoid the sea" should be replaced by the following: "Let him avoid what may cause him trouble, and beware what may come to him secretly from the side of al–Habasha; if possible, he should even avoid breathing the breeze of the south. Let him know well that that matter, though (apparently) safe, is dangerous (literally, though plentiful, is short), and that he should not rely upon the power of the Blacks (su'dud al–sudan) because Allah created the sign of the night to be dark and the sign of the day to be bright.

WIET[576] adds some comments about the situation. He notes that the sultans attempted to prevent any actual communication in secret between the patriarch and the southern Christian kings of Ethiopia. He quotes a rather later incident (20 Jumada I 852/22 July 1448) to show that this preoccupation grew yet stronger, doubtless in response to reports about King Zara–Ya'qob's increasing power. At a council in the presence of the then ruler of Egypt and four *qadis*, the patriarch of Alexandria, John XI (1428–53), appeared. He was enjoined to write out a promise that he would have no correspondence with the *negus* of Abyssinia, nor send any ecclesiastic, without the sultan's permission. If he did, the sentence was death.

66. St. Tekla–Haymanot and the Ethiopian Metropolitanate

It has already been noted that it may have been because of the absence of a metropolitan of Egyptian origin, leaving a hiatus in the succession, that

---

575 Al-Qalqashandi, from the *Subh*..., quoted by VANTINI, OS, pp. 580ff.
576 WIET, *op. cit.*, p. 122.

the legend of the vital position of St. Tekla–Haymanot in the foundation of the new dynasty, the 'Solomonic Restoration', emerged. TADDESSE TAMRAT[577] established that Tekla–Haymanot was probably still only in the early stages of his monastic career in 1270; he is hardly likely to have been acting–metropolitan, the administrator of the handing over of the Zagwé power, as the later hagiographers assert. However, that there were powerful and highly favoured native ecclesiastics active at exactly this time is well known. The story of the support given to Yekuno Amlak by Iyasus Mo'a, founder and abbot of the monastery of St. Stephen at Debra Hayq in Wallo province from about 1248–1292, may have been gradually transferred to the legend of his spiritual son, Tekla–Haymanot[578], for prestige reasons as Tekla–Haymanot's own foundation, the monastery of Debra Libanos in Shewa, grew more influential.

Iyasus Mo'a is supposed to have materially aided Yekuno–Amlak in reaching the throne. As a reward one–third of the land in the kingdom was apparently bestowed on the church by the new king.

Tekla–Haymanot, after staying ten years with Iyasus Mo'a, and then residing at Debra Damo, eventually settled with the disciples who followed him at Debra Libanos in Shewa, not yet Christianised at this time. In due course this monastery became a prominent centre, as Tekla–Haymanot's work was expanded by his disciples and successors. Eventually, after the fifteenth century, Debra Libanos became powerful in Ethiopian politico–religious spheres. It is after this time that TADDESSE TAMRAT envisages the expansion of Tekla–Haymanot's legend to magnify him to an important figure in the political affairs of the Solomonic restoration.

ISAAC disagrees with the idea that Tekla–Haymanot was only

> drawn into the field of power politics after the 17th century, or that the part really or allegedly played by Iyasus Mo'a was later transferred to Täkle–Haymanot.

He believes (I: 3a) that the saint was *abun* or metropolitan bishop of Ethiopia, and that it was his influence which really established the Coptic abunate there, accompanied by such propaganda instruments for the new

577 TADDESSE TAMRAT, Church and State, p. 162, n.2. Essentially the same conclusions were drawn by G.W.B. HUNTINGFORD, *The Lives of Saint Takla Haymanot*, JES IV, 1966, no. 2, with regard to the later development of the political myth of Tekla Haymanot, pp. 35ff.

578 TADDESSE TAMRAT, *The Abbots*, pp. 89-90. See also TADDESSE TAMRAT, Church and State, p. 67, n. 3, and C. CONTI ROSSINI, *Appunti ed osservazioni sui re Zague e Takla Haymanot*, RRAL, ser. 5, Vol. IV, 1895, pp. 444-468.

dynasty as the *Kebra Nagast*. He even suggests that Tekla–Haymanot could perhaps be "the second Abba Salama".[579]

In the version of the *Life and Miracles of Tekla Haymanot* published by BUDGE, there is a special claim for the saint's position in the statement that a voice from heaven declared to him; "Thou art not like other Bishops whom Archbishops appoint because I Myself appointed thee with Mine own mouth". It is later noted that he was blessed by the patriarch of Alexandria, adding an earthly legitimacy to this heavenly grant.

The *Life* also relates that the saint met a Patriarch Michael of Alexandria in the Holy Land, when both were travelling to Jerusalem. Michael V's brief episcopate 1145–6 is far too early, and that of Michael VI, 1475–81, too late, to fit in with this part of the tale.[580]

67. The Metropolitanate under King 'Amda Tseyon; the Metropolitan Yohannes

The successive abbots of the monastery of Iyasus Mo'a, St. Stephen at Debra Hayq, bearing the high rank of *'aqabe–sa'at*, 'Guardian of the Hours' were in very close contact with the kings of the restored dynasty. In a land grant[581] of 'Amda–Tseyon, who succeeded Widim Ra'ad the year after the death of Tekla–Haymanot, we read,

> And I also granted this land which had already been granted in the days of Yikuno–'Amlak; and I, king Amda–Siyon, whose regnal name is Gabra–Masqal, restored and granted this land to Stephen of Hayq while the Aqqabe–Sa'at was my Father Kristos Tasfana son of Iyasus–Mo'a; and while the bishop (pappas) was Abba Yohannes....

This Yohannes must be the metropolitan who eventually arrived from Egypt, in or after the reign of Yigba–Tseyon. The document continues with a list of officials, and the placing of Yohannes next to the abbot and *'aqabe–sa'at* in a document of that prelate's own monastery clearly indicates his place at the head of the hierarchy. The *'aqabe–sa'at* is especially favoured here, since the *pappas* or *liqa–pappasat* is usually named first. TADDESSE TAMRAT notes, however, that "since this rather unusual protocol is not always similarly extended to other abbots of Däbrä Hayq, it

579 ISAAC, *Ethiopian Church*, pp. 249-252.

580 E.A.W. BUDGE, The Life and Miracles of Takla Haymanot, London, 1906, pp. 134, 184.

581 TADDESSE TAMRAT, *The Abbots*, pp. 96-7.

cannot be argued that this mention of the Aqqabé–Sä'at before the Egyptian bishop, in such an important royal grant, represented an Ethiopian spirit of independence *vis a vis* the patriarchate of Alexandria". The grant adds a few more ecclesiastic titles to the list. Isayiyas was the *afa 'aqabe–sa'at,* a title denoting the assistant of the abbot at St. Stephen of Debra Hayq; the *qese gabaz*, a priest responsible for administrative and routine church work, was Fiqitor; and the *qas–hatsani* was Birhana–Hiré.

Metropolitan Yohannes was accused by the eager reformer Basalota–Mika'el of ordaining priests for money. The charge of simony was eventually set before the king, as had happened so long before in the days of Metropolitan Eleyas (IIB: 16); and just as then King Za–Gabaza Aksum had exiled Abba Libanos, so 'Amda–Tseyon punished Basalota–Mika'el, exiling him to Tigray.[582]

It is not known which patriarch of Alexandria consecrated Yohannes. The earliest Egyptian contact known for 'Amda–Tseyon was in 726/1325–6, in the third reign of Sultan al–Nasir Muhammad b. Qala'un, and in the episcopate of John IX of Alexandria (1320–1327). An account is preserved by al–Maqrizi.[583] Envoys of the Abyssinian king arrived, bearing the king's letter, which declared that the sultan should rebuild the churches which had been demolished (in 724/1324[584]), and that the Christians should be well treated. Failing this, he threatened to destroy the mosques in his kingdom, and to tamper with the flow of the Nile. The sultan merely laughed at this and dismissed the embassy. Metropolitan Yohannes died during the reign of 'Amda–Tseyon, and was replaced by Jacob (Ya'iqob), in whose time lived Ewostatewos, founder of the 'Eustathian' order of monks.

Interestingly enough, there is an account[585] by Niccolo da Poggibonsi, in his *Libro d'Oltremare*, which relates his visit to the Holy Land in 1347, which mentions some details about the Ethiopians there at that time. His chapter CCLVII reads as follows;

> Of the same faith [i.e. as the Jacobites of Egypt] are those of India and Ethiopia, but the Christians of India are very few; but those of Ethiopia are a big generation and are all black. This generation loves us Christian Franks more than any other generation, and willingly would unite with us Latins; [this seems to be rather wish-

---

582 C. Conti Rossini, ed. and trans., "Acta S. Basalota Mika'el et S. Anorewos", CSCO, Scriptores aethiopici T. XX, 1905, pp. 22-3.

583 Quatremère, Mémoires, Vol. II, p. 275; Gaudefroy-Demombynes, *op. cit.*, p. 30, n. 1.

584 Gaudefroy-Demombynes; or Quatremère, p. 227, 721/1321.

585 Quoted in Vantini, OS, p. 135. Fra Niccolo of Poggibonsi, A Voyage beyond the Seas (1346-1350), trans., by T. Bellorini, and E. Hoade, Jerusalem 1945.

ful thinking; though there had been occasional messages sent to the rulers of the west or the papacy by kings of Ethiopia at this time] but the Sultan of Babylon never allows a Latin to them, lest they negotiate war against him. But those of Ethiopia pass into Egypt and into the Land of Promise without paying tribute to the Sultan and they can carry the cross uncovered through all Saracen lands, and also they enter the Holy Sepulchre without paying tribute; and no nation, save Ethiopia, enjoys this grace; and this is granted by the Sultan; and I heard he does this from fear, for the Lord of Ethiopia is the greatest Lord of the World...

This may indicate that the Egyptian attitude had changed, perhaps in view of the tremendous speed with which 'Amda–Tseyon had dealt with his enemies in regions close at hand. Though Muslim, these far regions had no contact with the Egyptian Chancery, as Ibn Fadl Allah al–'Umari observed in his *Ta'rif*[586]; there was therefore no recorded protocol for addressing them. The open display of the Ethiopians seems hard to credit considering the current harsh decrees against the Christians, the revival of the sumptuary laws (1301), the riots, and the church demolitions[587], but there may have been special privileges granted to the foreign pilgrims. Arnold VON HARFF, between 1496 and 1499, observed[588] the same thing, adding the old explanation; "no injury must be done them, lest the river Nile should be stopped".

The history of the metropolitan episcopacy of Ethiopia from the arrival of Ya'iqob until the twentieth century is rather better documented than the earlier period we have dealt with here. A considerable amount of information about the lives of subsequent metropolitans is available in royal chronicles and other Ge'ez works. In later centuries there are even useful foreign sources. Together these may one day furnish material for a volume on the later course of the Ethiopian metropolitanate. For the first thousand years of its existence the story of the metropolitanate, played out against a very shadowy historical background, shows how determined the Ethiopians were to maintain the existence of their national church. Even the immense difficulties forced on them by their having to seek the metropolitan always from Alexandria, with the concomitant problems of relations with Egypt and intervening lands, were unable to discourage them from this purpose. Ethiopia's maintenance of the link with the Alexandrian patriarchate for so many centuries remains a truly remarkable achievement.

---

586 GAUDEFROY-DEMOMBYNES, *op. cit.*, p. 33.

587 LANE-POOLE, *op. cit.*, pp. 310-311; QUATREMÈRE, Mémoires, Vol. II, pp. 222-266.

588 MEINARDUS, *The Ethiopians in Jerusalem*, p. 120.

VIII BIBLIOGRAPHY

ABD AL-LATIF, Relation de l'Egypte, tr. A. I. SILVESTRE DE SACY, Paris 1810; see also J. WHITE.

ABU SALIH: see B.T.A. EVETTS & A.J. BUTLER (eds.)

ADAMS, W. Y., *Architectural Evolution of the Nubian Church*, JARCE IV, 1965.

D'ALMEIDA, *Historia Aethiopiae*, in: C. BECCARI, Rerum Aethiopicarum Scriptores Occidentales Inediti, V, Roma 1907.

ALTHEIM, F., and STIEHL, R., *Die Datierung des Königs 'Ezana von Aksum*, Klio XXXIX, 1961, pp. 234-248.

ALVARES, F, The Prester John of the Indies, the translation of Lord STANLEY OF ALDERLEY (1881) revised and ed. by F.C. BECKINGHAM, and C.W.B. HUNTINGFORD, Hakluyt Society, Cambridge 1961.

AMÉLINEAU, E., *Histoire du patriarche copte Isaac*, Bulletin du Correspondance Africaine, Paris 1890, and Bulletin de l'Institute Égyptien, 2e série, no. 6, 1885.

ANFRAY, F., *Chronique archéologique (1960-1964)*, AE VI, 1965, pp. 3-26.

——, *La poterie de Matara*, RSE XXII, 1966, pp. 5-74.

——, *Deux villes Axoumites, Adoulis et Matara*, in: VI Congresso Internazionale di Studi Etiopici, Rome 1972, Rome 1974, pp. 745-65.

——, *Les anciens Ethiopiens: Siècles d'histoire*, Paris 1990, p. 185.

ANFRAY, F., CAQUOT, A., and NAUTIN, P., *Une nouvelle inscription grecque d'Ezana, roi d'Axoum*, Journal des Savants 70, 1970, pp. 260ff.

ASSEMANI, J.S., Bibliotheca Orientalis, Rome 1725.

ATIYA, Aziz S., *et al.*, eds., Sawirus ibn al-Mukaffa, "History of the Patriarchs of the Egyptian Church", Vol. II; Parts I-III, Cairo 1943, 1948, 1959.

Athanasius, "Apologia ad Constantium Imperatorem", PG XXV; also trans. J.M. SZYMUSIAK, Paris 1958.

AYELE TEKLAHAYMANOT, Abba, *The Egyptian Metropolitans of the Ethiopian Church*, a paper read to the Eighth International Conference of Ethiopian Studies, Addis Ababa University, Nov. 1984. Also Orientalia Christiana Periodica 54, 1988, pp. 175-222.

BAIRU TAFLA, *The Establishment of the Ethiopian Church*, Tarikh 2, no. 1.

BAYAN, G., ed., Le Synaxaire Armenien de Ter Israel, PO XV.

BARNES, J. W. B., *Christian Monuments from Nubia*, KUSH II, 1954, pp. 26-32.

BASSET, R., ed., "Le Synaxaire Arabe Jacobite" (Rédaction Copte), PO III, fasc.3.

BECKINGHAM, C. F., and HUNTINGFORD, G. W. B., eds., The Prester John of the Indies, Cambridge 1961, Hakluyt Society.

BERG, B., *The Letter of Palladius on India*, Byzantion 44, 1947, pp. 5-16.
BEVERIDGE, W., II, Oxford 1672.
BEZOLD, C., *Kebra Nagast; Die Herrlichkeit der Könige*, Abhandlungen der Wissenschaften XXIII, Munich 1905.
BONJOUR, Monumenta coptica seu Aegyptiaca bibliothecae vaticanae brevis exercitatio, Rome 1699.
BROOKS, E.W., ed., see John of Ephesus.
BROWN, C.F., The Conversion Experience in Axum during the fourth and fifth centuries, Howard Univ. Washington 1973.
BUDGE, E. A. W., The Queen of Sheba and her only son Menyelek..., a complete translation of the Kebra Nagast with introduction, London 1922.
——, The Book of the Saints of the Ethiopian Church; A translation of the Ethiopic Synaxarium, London 1928.
——, *A History of Ethiopia, Nubia and Abyssinia*, London 1928.
BURCKHARDT, J. L., Travels in Nubia, London 1822.
BUTCHER, E.L., The Story of the Church of Egypt, London 1897.
BUTLER, A. J., *On the Identity of 'Al Mukaukis' of Egypt*, Proceedings of the Society for Biblical Archaeology 23, 1901, pp. 275-90,
——, The Arab Conquest of Egypt, Oxford 1902; reprinted, FRASER, P. E., ed., 1978.
BUXTON, D., The Abyssinians, London 1970.
CABRAL, F., and LECLERCQ, H., Dictionnaire d'Archéologie chrétienne et de Liturgie, Paris 1922.
CAQUOT, A., *Apercue préliminaire sur le Mashafa Tefut de Gechen Amba*, AE I, pp. 89ff.
CARAMAN, P., The Lost Empire. The Story of the Jesuits in Ethiopia, London 1985.
CARPENTIER, E., ed., Commentarium preavis ad Martyrium Arethae, Acta Sanctorum, Oct. 24, tomus X, 1891, pp. 721-759.
Cedrenus, "Historium Compendium", PG CXXI.
CERULLI, E., *Il sultanato dello Scioa nel secolo XIII*, RSE I, 1941, pp. 5-14.
——, Etiopi in Palestina; Storia della communità etiopica in Gerusalemme, Rome 1943-7.
CHABOT, J. B., see Michael the Syrian: Pseudo-Dionysios.
CHAÎNE, M., La chronologie des temps chrétiens de l'Égypte et de l'Éthiopie, Paris 1925.
CHEIKHO, L., see Ibn Rahib.
EL-CHENNAFI, M., *Mention nouvelle d'une 'reine Ethiopienne' au IVe s. de l'Hegire / Xe s. ap J-C.*, AE X, 1976, pp. 119-121.
CHRISTIDES, V., *The Himyarite-Ethiopian war and the Ethiopian occupation of South Arabia in the Acts of Gregentius (ca. 530 A.D.)*, AE IX, pp. 115-46.

CONTENSON, H. de, *Les fouilles à Axoum en 1957, Rapport préliminaire*, AE III, 1959, pp. 25-42.
—, *Les fouilles à Haoulti-Melazo en 1958*, AE IV, 1961, pp. 39-60.
—, *Principales étapes de l'Ethiopie antique*, Cahiers d'Études Africaines 2, 1961.
—, *Les fouilles à Ouchatei Golo près d'Axoum en 1958*, AE IV, 1961, pp. 3-16.
—, *Les fouilles à Axoum en 1958, Rapport préliminaire*, AE V, 1963, pp. 1-40;
CONTI ROSSINI, C., *Appunti ed osservazioni sui re Zague e Takla Haymanot*, RRAL, ser. 5, Vol. IV, 1895, pp. 444-468.
—, *Note Etiopiche I, Una guerra fra la Nubia e l'etiopia nel secolo VII*, Giornale della Societa Asiatica Italiana X, 1897, pp. 141-3.
—, *L'evangelo d'oro di Dabra Libanos*, RRAL, Ser. 5, Vol. 10, 1901, pp. 177-219.
—, *Il Gadla Libanos*, Ricordi di un soggiorno in Eritrea, Asmara 1903, III.
—, ed., "Acta Yared et Pantelewon", CSCO, Scriptores Aethiopici, Series altera, T. XVII, Vitae Sanctorum Antiquorum, I, 1904.
—, ed., "Gadla Marqorewos seu Acta Sancti Mercuri", CSCO, Scriptores Aethiopici, Ser II T. XXII, versio, Vitae Sanctorum Indigenorum, I, 1904.
—, ed. and trans., "Acta S. Basalota Mika'el et S. Anorewos", CSCO, Scriptores Aethiopici , T. XX, 1905, pp. 22-3.
—, *Les listes des rois d'Aksum*, JA, 1909, pp. 265-320
—, "Liber Axumae", CSCO, Script. Aeth., series altera, T. VIII, 1909.
—, *Studi su Popolazione dell'Etiopia. IV, Antichi Popolazioni Nuba-Etiopiche*, RSO VI, 1913.
—, *Notice sur les manuscrits Éthiopiens de la collection d'Abbadie*, JA, Ser. II, T.6, 1915, pp. 195-6.
—, *Il libro delle leggende, e tradizione abissine dell'Eccaghie Filpos*, RRAL, Ser.5, vol. XXVI, 1917.
—, *Un documento sul cristianesmo nello Iemen ai tempi del Re Sarahbil Yakkuf*, RRAL, Ser.V, Vol. IX, 1920, pp. 705-750.
—, *A propos des textes éthiopiens concernant Salama (Frumentius)*, Aethiops I, 1922, pp. 2-4, 17-18.
—, *Egitto ed Etiopia nei tempi antichi e nell'eta di mezzo*, Aegyptus III, 1922.
—, *La caduta della dinastia Zague e la versione amarica del Be'ela Nagast*, RRAL, Vol. 31, Ser. IV, 1923, pp. 279-314.
—, *Storia d'Etiopia*, Bergamo 1928.
—, *Pubblicazione etiopistiche dal 1936-1945*, RSE IV, 1944-5, p. 36.
Cosmas Indicopleustes: "Cosmae Indicopleustae Topographiae Christia-

nae", Lib. III, PG LXXXVIII; see also WOLSKA-CONUS, ed.

COULBEAUX, J. B., Histoire Politique et religieuse d'Abyssinie, depuis les temps les plus reculés jusqu'à l'avènement de Ménélick II, Paris n.d (preface dated 1928).

CRUM, W. E., Coptic Dictionary, Oxford 1939.

CUOQ, J., Islamisation de la Nubie chrétienne VIIe- XVIe siècles, Paris 1986.

DESANGES, J., *Une mention alterée d'Axoum dans l'Expositio totius mundi et gentium,* AE VII, 1967, pp. 141-58.

DERRETT, J. D. M., *The History of Palladius on the Races of India and the Brahmanes,* Classica et Medievalia XXI, 1960, pp. 64-135.

DEWING, H. B., see Procopius.

The Dictionary of Ethiopian Biography, eds., BELAYNESH MICHAEL, S.CHOJNACKI, R.K.P. PANKHURST, Addis Ababa 1975.

DIHLE, A., Umstrittene Daten, Köln und Opladen 1965.

DILLMANN, C. F. A., *Zur Geschichte des Axumitischen Reichs im vierten bis sechsten Jahrhundert,* Abhandlungen der K. Preussische Akademie der Wissenschaften zu Berlin, Berlin 1880.

——, Chrestomathia Aethiopica, Leipzig 1866, (reprinted Berlin) 1950.

DORESSE, J., Histoire Sommaire de la Corne Orientale de l'Afrique, Paris 1971.

——, Ethiopia, London 1959, first published as Au Pays de la Reine de Saba, L'Éthiopie Antique et Moderne, Paris 1956.

ERPENIUS, T., ed., see el-Makin.

Eutychius: "Eutychii Patriarchae Alexandrini Annales", PG CXI.

EVETTS, B.T.A., ed., `History of the Patriarchs of the Coptic Church of Alexandria' by Sawirus ibn al-Mukaffa, bishop of al-Ashmunin. Vol. I; I. St. Mark to Theonas, PO I, fasc. 2, 1904, pp. 99-214. II. Peter I to Benjamin, PO I, fasc. 4, 1904, pp. 381-518. III. Agathon to Michael I, PO V, fasc. 1, 1909, pp. 1-215. IV. Menas I to Joseph, PO X, fasc. 5, 1914, pp. 357-551.

EVETTS, B.T.A., and BUTLER A.J., eds., The Churches and Monasteries of Egypt and some Neighbouring Countries, attributed to Abû Sâlih, the Armenian, Oxford 1895.

FIACCADORI, G., *Per una nova inscrizione Etiopica da Aksum,* Egitto e Vicino Oriente IV, 1981, pp. 357-367.

——, *Teofilo Indiano,* (Parts I and II) in: Studi Classici e Orientali 33 and 34, 1983 and 1984, pp. 295-331 and 271-308 respectively.

GADALLAH, F. F., *The Egyptian Contribution to Nubian Christianity,* SNR XL, 1959.

GARITTE, G., *La version georgienne de la vie de S. Cyriaque par Cyrille de Scythopolis,* Le Muséon 75, 1962, pp. 399-440.

GAUDEFROY-DEMOMBYNES, M., see al-Qalqashandi, al-'Umari.

GEDDES, M., The Church-History of Ethiopia, London 1646.

Gelasius, "Kirchengeschichte", Die Griechischen Christlichen Schriftsteller der ersten drei Jahrhunderte, Band 28, Leipzig 1918.

GELZER, H., *Ungedruckte und wenig bekannte Bistümerverzeichnisse der orientalischen Kirche*, BZ II, 1893.

GETATCHEW HAILE, *A New Look at some Dates of Early Ethiopian History,* Le Muséon 1982, T. 95, pp. 311-322.

GIBBON, E. The History of the Decline and Fall of the Roman Empire, London 1788.

GLUBB, J.B., The Life and Times of Muhammad, London 1970.

Gregory of Nyssa, "Contra Eunomium", PG XLV.

GRIFFITH, F.Ll., *Christian Documents from Nubia*, Proceedings of the British Academy XIV, London 1928.

——, *Oxford Excavations in Nubia,* LAAA XIV, 1927.

GUIDI, I., Catalogue of the Ethiopian Manuscripts in the British Museum, London 1871.

——, *La Chiesa Abissina,* Oriente Moderno II, 1922.

——., *Il Gadla Aragawi*, RRAL, Atti...2, 1896.

GUILLAUME, A., The Life of Muhammad, a translation of Ibn Ishaq's Sirat Rasul Allah, OUP (Pakistan) 1955.

HARRIS, W. C., The Highlands of Ethiopia, London 1844.

HASAN, Y. F., The Arabs and the Sudan, Khartoum 1973.

HENNIG, R., *Frumentius und Aedesius im Reiche Axum,* Terrae Incognitae I, 1944, pp. 5-17.

HEYER, F., Die Kirche Äthiopiens, Berlin and New York, 1971.

HONIGMANN, E., *Un évêque d'Adulis au Concile de Chalcédoine,* Byzantion 20, 1950, pp. 295-301.

HUNTINGFORD, G. W. B., The Land Charters of Northern Ethiopia, Addis Ababa 1965.

——, *The Lives of Saint Takla Haymanot,* JES IV, 1966, pp. 35ff.

Ibn Khaldun, "The Muqaddimah, An Introduction to History", trans. F. ROSENTHAL, New York 1965.

Ibn Rahib: Butrus ibn Muhaddib (Abu Shakir) called Petrus Ibn Rahib, "Chronicon Orientale", ed. CHEIKHO, P. L., CSCO, Scriptores Arabici, versio, ser. III, T. I, Paris 1903.

Ioannes Psaltes, "Hymn on the Himyarite Martyrs", ed. Scroter, R., ZDMG 31, 1877, pp. 400-405.

ISAAC, E., *An Obscure Component in Ethiopian Church History,* Le Muséon 85, 1972, pp. 225-258.

JAKOBIELSKI, S., *La liste des évêques de Pakhoras,* ET I, 1966, pp. 151-170.

——, *Nouvelle lecture d'un nom de la liste des évêques*, ET V, 1970, pp. 193-199.

——, Faras III, A History of the Bishopric of Pachoras, Warsaw 1972.

JARRY, J., *Hérésies et factions dans l'Empire Byzantin du IVe au VIIe siècle*, Le Caire 1968.

JEFFERY, A., *The Acts of Azqir*, Moslem World 37, 1946, pp. 200ff.

John of Ephesus: "Iohannis Ephesini Historiae Ecclesiasticae Pars Tertia", ed., E. W. BROOKS, versio, CSCO 106, Scriptores Syri 55, Louvain 1952.

John of Nikiu, "The Chronicle of John of Nikiu", trans. R.H. CHARLES, London 1916.

JONES, A. H. M., and MONROE, E., A History of Abyssinia, Oxford 1935

JUNKER, H., *Die Christliche Grabsteine Nubiens*, ZÄS 60, 1925, pp. 11-148.

KAMAL, Prince Youssef, ed. Monumenta Cartographica Africae et Aegypti, Le Caire 1928-39.

AL-KHOWAYTER, A., A Critical Edition of an Unknown Source of the Life of ...Baibars, Ph.D thesis, London Univ, 1960.

KIRWAN, L. P., *Christianity and the Kura'an*, JEA XX, 1934.

——, *Studies in the later History of Nubia*, LAAA XXIV, 1936, pp. 67-105.

——, *A Contemporary Account of the Conversion of the Sudan to Christianity*, SNR XX, 1937.

——, *The Oxford University Excavations at Firka*, Oxford 1939.

——, *Notes on the Topography of the Christian Nubian Kingdoms*, JEA 21, 1935.

KOBISHCHANOV, Y. M., Axum, Pennsylvania and London 1979.

Kosmas Indikopleustes: see Cosmas.

KRALL, J., *Beiträge zur Geschichte der Blemyer und Nubier*, Denkschriften der Kaiserlichen Akademie der Wissenschaften, (Phil-Hist. Classe), Band 46, Vienna 1900, IV, pp. 1-26.

KRAMERS J. H. and WIET, G., ed., La configuration du terre, Beyrouth and Paris 1964.

KUR, S., ed., "Actes de Iyasus Mo'a, abbé du couvent de St. Etienne de Hayq", CSCO, 259, Scriptores Aethiopici, T. 49, Louvain 1965.

——, trans., "Actes de Samuel de Dabra Wagag", CSCO, Scriptores Aethiopici, T.50, Louvain 1968, p. VII.

LABIB, S.Y., Handelsgeschichte Ägyptens im Spätmittelalter (1171-1517), Wiesbaden 1965.

LANE-POOLE, S., A History of Egypt in the Middle Ages, 4th Ed., London 1968.

LATOURETTE, K.S., A History of the Expansion of Christianity, London 1953, Vol. I,

LATRIE, L. DE MAS., Trésor de Chronologie et de Geographie pour l'étude et l'emploi des documents du Moyen Age, Paris 1889.

LEPAGE, C., *Bilan des Recherches sur l'Art Médiéval d'Ethiopie; Quelques Résultats Historiques*, Proceedings of the Eighth International Conference of

Ethiopian Studies, Addis Ababa 1984, Addis Ababa 1989, Vol. 2, p. 55.
LEPSIUS, C. R., Denkmäler aus Ägypten und Äthiopen, Berlin 1849-53.
LE QUIEN, M., Oriens Christianus, II, Paris 1740.
LITTMANN, E., *et al.*, Deutsche Aksum-Expedition, 4 vols, Berlin 1913.
LOBO, J., trans. by LE GRAND, Voyage Historique d'Abyssinie, Paris 1728; trans. by Dr. Samuel JOHNSON, A Voyage to Abyssinia, London 1789.
LUDOLPH, I, History of Ethiopia, London 1684, (trans. anon.).
MACMICHAEL, H. A., A History of the Arabs in the Sudan, Cambridge 1922, Vol. I.
El-Makin, Historia Saracenica, ed. T. ERPENIUS, Leyden 1625.
Malalas: Ioannes Malalas "Chronographia", ed. L. DINDORF, CSHB, Bonn 1831, pp. 433-434; see also PG XCVII, 433, col. 639/640. For a translation from the Church Slavonic, SPINKA and DOWNEY, Bk. 18,111.
MALAN, S.C., trans., A Short History of the Copts and of their Churches, trans. from the Arabic of Taqi ed-Din El-Maqrizi, London 1873.
Maqrizi, "Kitab al-Suluk", ed. M. ZIADA, Cairo 1934-9; see also MALAN, S. C.
MASPERO, G., Histoire des patriarches d'Alexandrie depuis la morte de l'empereur Anastase jusqu'à la reconciliation des églises jacobites (518-616), Paris 1923.
MASPERO, G., *Le roi Mercure à Tafah*, ASAE X, 1909, p. 17.
MATHEW, D., Ethiopia. The Study of a Polity, 1540-1935, London 1947.
MEINARDUS, O. F. A., *A Brief History of the Abunate of Ethiopia*, Wiener Zeitschrift für die Kunde des Morgenländes, 58, 1962, pp. 39-65.
——, Ethiopian Monks in Egypt, Alexandria 1962.
——, *Ecclesiastica Aethiopica in Aegypto*, JES III, 1, 1965, pp. 30ff.
——, *The Ethiopians in Jerusalem*, Zeitschrift für Kirchengeschichte, Vierte Folge 14, 1965, p.117-147, 217-232.
——, *The Christian kingdom of Nubia*, Cahiers d'Histoire Égyptienne X, Le Caire 1967.
Michael the Syrian: "Chronique de Michel le Syrien", ed. J.B. CHABOT, J. B., Paris 1905.
MOBERG, A., The Book of the Himyarites, Lund 1924.
MOMMSEN, Th., ed., "Chronica Joannis abbatis monasterii Biclarensis", Monumenta Germaniae Historica, Leipzig 1894.
MONNERET DE VILLARD, U., Aksum, Rome 1938.
——, *Note Nubiane*, Aegyptus XII, fasc. IV.
——, Storia della Nubia Cristiana, Rome 1938.
——, *Mose, Vescovo di Adulis*, Orientalia Christiana Periodica 13, 1947, pp. 613-23.
MORDINI, A., *Informazioni preliminari sui resultati delle mie recherche..*, RSE IV, 1944, pp. 145-150.

Mufaddal: Mufazzal Ibn Abil-Fazail, "Histoire des sultans mamluks", ed. and trad., E. Blochet, PO XIV, 1919-20.

Munro-Hay, S. C. H., *Ezana (Ezana/Ezanas): Some Numismatic Comments*, Azania XV, 1980, pp. 109-120.

—, *Kings and Kingdoms of Ancient Nubia*, RSE XXIX, 1982-3, pp. 87-137.

—, The Chronology of Aksum, unpublished doctoral thesis, SOAS, Univ. of London, 1978.

—, The Coinage of Aksum, New Delhi 1984.

—, Aksum: An African Civilisation of Late Antiquity , EUP 1991.

—, *The British Museum Excavations at Adulis, 1868*, The Antiquaries Journal 69i, 1989, pp. 43-52.

—, Excavations at Aksum 1972-4, London 1989.

Neale, J. M., A History of the Holy Eastern Church; The Patriarchate of Alexandria, London 1842.

Niccolo of Poggibonsi, "A Voyage beyond the Seas (1346-1350)", trans., by T. Bellorini and E. Hoade, Jerusalem 1945.

Nicephorus Callistus, "Historia Ecclesiastica", PG CXLVI.

Oates, J., *A Christian Inscription in Greek from Arminna in Nubia*, JEA 49, 1963, pp. 161-71.

O'Leary, de L., The Ethiopian Church: Historical Notes on the Church in Abyssinia, London 1936.

Papadopoullos, T. C., Africanobyzantina; Byzantine influence on Negro-Sudanese Cultures, tomos 27, Pragmateiai tes Akademias Athenon, Athens 1966.

Paribeni, R., *Ricerche nel luogo dell'antica Adulis*, Monumenti antichi, pubblicati per cura della Reale Accademia dei Lincei, Vol. XVIII, Roma 1907.

Parthey, M., and Pinder, G., Ravennatis Anonymi Geographia et Guidenis Geographica, (reprint of 1860 ed.) Aalem 1962.

Payne-Smith, R., trans., The Third Part of the Ecclesiastical History of John, Bishop of Ephesus, Oxford 1860.

Pereira, F. M. E., ed., Historia dos Martyres de Najran; Lisbon 1899.

Perruchon, J., *Notes pour l'histoire d'Ethiopie; Extrait de la vie d'Abba Jean, 74e patriarche d'Alexandrie, relatif à l'Abyssinie*, VI, 1898, pp. 267-71, Arabic text pp. 366-72.

—, *Note pour l'histoire d'Ethiopie; Vie de Cosmas, patriarche d'Alexandrie, de 923 à 934*, RS 1894.

Pétridès, S. P., *Essai sur l'évangelisation de l'Éthiopie, sa date et son protagoniste*, Abba Salama, III, 1972, pp. 208-232.

PHILBY, H. St. J., *Note on the last Kings of Saba*, Le Muséon 63, 1950.

Philostorgius; "The Ecclesiastical History of Philostorgius, as epitomised by Photius, trans. E. WALFORD, London 1855.

PIRENNE, J., *Le cadre chronologique de l'histoire ethiopienne du IV au VI siècle*, Etudes Sémitiques, Actes du XXIXe Congrès internationale des Orientalistes, Paris 1975.

——, *L'imbroglio de trois siècles de chronologie aksumite, IVe à VIe s.*, DSHCE, fasc. 6, 1975, pp. 49-58.

PLUMLEY, J. M., *An Eighth Century Letter to the King of Nubia*, JEA 61, 1975, pp. 241 ff, and 60, 1974, pp. 237-238.

——, *Qasr Ibrim 1966*, JEA 52, 1966, pp. 3 ff.

——, *Qasr Ibrim 1974*, JEA 61, 1975, pp. 5-27.

——, The Scrolls of Bishop Timotheos: Two Documents from Medieval Nubia, London 1975.

POCOCKE, R., Description of the East, I, London 1743.

POLLERA, A., Lo Stato Etiopico e la sua Chiesa, Rome and Milan 1926.

POLOTSKY, I., ed., Mani, "Kephalaia", Stuttgart 1940.

PORCHER, E., ed. and trans., "Vie d'Isaac, Patriarche d'Alexandrie de 686 à 689", PO IX.

Procopius: Procopius Caesariensis, ed. and trans., H.B. DEWING, "History of the Wars", I, Loeb ed., London 1961,

——, ed. and trans., H.B. DEWING, "De Bello Persico", Loeb ed., London 1914.

Pseudo-Dionysios Telmahrensis; ed. I.B. CHABOT, "Incerti auctoris Chronicon anonymum pseudo-Dionysianum vulgo dictum", II. Accedunt Iohannis Ephesini fragmenta, curante E.W. BROOKS, CSCO 104 (1933) .

Ptolemy, "The Geography of Claudius Ptolemy", ed. E.L. STEVENSON, New York 1932.

al-Qalqashandi, "La Syrie sous les Mamlouks", ed. M. GAUDEFROY-DEMOMBYNES, Paris 1923, t. VIII, p. 119.

QUATREMÈRE, E., Histoire des sultans mamlouks de l'Egypte, I, Pt. II, Paris 1840,

——, Mémoires géographiques et historiques sur l'Égypte et sur les contrées voisines, Paris 1811.

RENAUDOT, E., Historia Patriarcharum Alexandrinorum Jacobitarum a D. Marco usque ad finem saeculi XIII, Paris 1713.

REY, C.F., The Romance of the Portuguese in Abyssinia, London 1929.

RICCI, L., *Communication*, AE X, 1976, pp. 327-8;

Rufinus, "Historia Ecclesiastica", PL XXI.

RYCKMANS, G., *Une inscription chrétienne sabéenne aux Musées d'Antiquities d'Istanbul*, Le Muséon 59, 1946, pp. 171-2.

RYCKMANS, J., *Le Christianisme en Arabie du Sud pre-islamique*, Atti del convegno internazionale sul tema, "L'Oriente cristiano nella storia della civiltà", Accademia nazionale dei Lincei, 361, 1964, pp. 422-32.

SALT, H., Voyage to Abyssinia, London 1814.

SCHER, A., ed., "Histoire nestorienne (Chronique de Séert)", PO VII, 2, 1911.

SCHNEIDER, R., *Trois nouvelles inscriptions royales d'Axoum*, IV Congresso Internazionale di Studi Etiopici, T. I., Accademia dei Lincei, Quaderno 191, Roma 1974.

—, A *propos de l'imbroglio de trois siècles de chronologie aksumite*, DSHCE, fasc. 7, 1976, pp. 41ff.

SCHWARZ, E., *Ein Bischof der römischen Reichskirche in Abessinien*, Philologus 91, 1936, pp. 356-7.

SCROTER, R. ed., *Ioannes Psaltes Hymn on the Himyarite Martyrs*, ZDMG 31, 1877, pp. 400-405.

SERGEW HABLE SELLASSIE, *Die Aethiopische Kirche im 4 bis 6 Jahrhundert*, Abba Salama, II, 1971, pp. 43-75.

—, *The Problem of Gudit*, JES 10, I, 1972, pp. 113-124.

—, Ancient and Mediaeval Ethiopian History to 1270, Addis Ababa 1972,

— *et al.*, The Church of Ethiopia, Addis Ababa 1971.

Severus: "The Hymns of Severus and others in the Syriac version of Paul of Edessa as revised by James of Edessa", PO VII, 5, 1911.

SHAHID, I., The Martyrs of Najran, New Documents, Subsidia Hagiographica no. 49, Bruxelles 1971.

—, *Byzantium in South Arabia*, Dumbarton Oaks Papers, 33, 1979.

—, *The Book of the Himyarites, Authorship and Authenticity*, *Le Muséon* 76, 1963, pp. 349-362.

SILVESTRE DE SACY, A. I., tr., Abd al-Latif, Relation de l'Egypte, Paris 1810.

Simon Metaphrastes; BHG 167; PG CXV/2.

SKALIERES, G., To Patriakheion Alexandreias: To klima kai i dikaiodosia autou, Athens 1927.

SMITH, S., *Events in Arabia in the 6th century*, BSOAS 16, 1954.

Socrates, "Historia Ecclesiastica", PG LXVII.

Sozomen, "Historia Ecclesiastica", PG LXVII.

STEIN, E. E. A., Histoire du Bas Empire, Paris-Bruxelles-Amsterdam 1949.

STROTHMANN, R., Die Koptische Kirche in der Neuzeit, Tubingen 1932.

TADDESSE TAMRAT, *The Abbots of Däbrä Hayq 1248-1535*, JES VIII, 1970, pp. 104-5.

——, Church and State in Ethiopia 1270-1527, Oxford 1972.

TEDESCHI, S., *L'Etiopia nella Storia dei Patriarchi Alessandrini,* RSE XXIII, 1967-8, pp. 232-271.

TEKLE SADIK MEKURIA, Ya Ityopya Tarik; Nubia, Aksum, Zagwiye, Addis Ababa 1951 EC.

TELLES (Tellez), B., Historia geral de Ethiopia a alta, composta ... pelo Padre M. d'Almeyda ... abreviada pelo Padre B. Tellez, Coimbra 1660.

——, The Travels of the Jesuits in Ethiopia, trans. into English, London 1710.

Theodoret, "Historia Ecclesiastica", PG LXXXII.

Theophanes "Chronographia", PG CVIII.

TRIMINGHAM, J. S., Islam in the Sudan, London 1952.

TURLA, A., *La religione in Ethiopia,* Rassegna Sociale dell'Africa Italiana II, 9, 1939, pp. 1068-73.

ULLENDORFF, E., *Note on the Introduction of Christianity into Ethiopia,* Africa 19, 1949, pp. 61-62.

——, The Ethiopians, OUP, 1937.

al-'Umari, "Ta'rif", Cairo 1312: GAUDEFROY-DEMOMBYNES, M., de, Ibn Fadl Allah al-'Omari,"Masalik el Absar fi Mamalik el Amsar", Paris 1927.

VANTINI, G., The Excavations at Faras, A contribution to the History of Christian Nubia, Bologna 1970.

——, Oriental Sources Concerning Nubia, Heidelberg and Warsaw 1975.

VERGHESE, P., *The Ethiopian Orthodox Church...* in: ARBERRY, A. J., ed., Religion in the Middle East, CUP 1969, pp. 454ff.

——, Koptisches Christentum, "Kirchen der Welt" series, Stuttgart 1973.

VASILIEV, A., *The Life of St. Gregentius,* Vizantiyskiy Vremennik XIV, pp. 23-67, in Greek and Russian.

——, Justin the First, Harvard 1950.

——, History of the Byzantine Empire, Madison 1952.

——, *Justin I (518-527) and Abyssinia,* BZ 33, 1933, pp. 67ff.

WANSLEBEN, J. M., L'Histoire de l'église d'Alexandrie, Paris 1677.

——, Nouvelle relation d'un voyage fait en Egypte, Paris 1677.

——, English translation in: The Present State of Egypt, or, A new Relation of a late Voyage into that Kingdom performed in the Years 1672 and 1673, by F. Wansleb, R.D., London 1678.

WHITE, J., Abdollatiphi *Historiae Aegypti Compendium,* arabicè ei latinè, Oxford 1800.

WHITEWAY, R. S., The Portuguese Expedition to Abyssinia, 1541-3, London, Hakluyt Soc., 1902.

WILDING, R. in: MUNRO-HAY, S. C. H., Excavations at Aksum, 1972-4, BIEA Memoir no. 10, London 1989.

WINCKLER, H., *Zur Geschichte des Judentums in Jemen*, Altorientalische Forschungen I, III, 1897.

WOLSKA-CONUS, W., La topographie chrétienne de Cosmas Indicopleustes, Sources chrétiennes, no 141, 159, & 197, Paris 1968 etc.

WÜSTENFELD, H. F., Macrizi's Geschichte der Kopten, Gottingen 1845.

ZOTENBERG, H., ed., Chronique de Jean, évêque de Nikiu, Paris 1883.

—, Catalogue des manuscrits éthiopiens de la Bibliothèque Nationale, Paris 1877, p. 263

—, trans., "Chronique de Tabari", version Persane de... Belami, Paris 1869, T. II, pp. 174ff.

ZYHLARZ, E., *I reami della Nubia prima dell'Islam*, RSE III, 1943.

IX Index

K

N

O

P

Q

R

S